access to history

I0809816

Cambridge International AS Level

The History of the USA 1820–1941

Alan Farmer

HODDER EDUCATION
AN HACHETTE UK COMPANY

> Note: this book contains historical sources which may use words that were widely used at the time of the source, but are derogatory, offensive and are not used today. These words may include 'coloured' (person or people), 'Negro', and 'non-white', as well as racist words such as 'n______', which we do not print in full.

Exam-style questions and sample answers have been written by the authors. References to assessment and/or assessment preparation are the publisher's interpretation of the syllabus requirements and may not fully reflect the approach of Cambridge Assessment International Education. Cambridge International recommends that teachers consider using a range of teaching and learning resources in preparing learners for assessment, based on their own professional judgement of their students' needs.

The Publishers would like to thank the following for permission to reproduce copyright material.

Photo credits

p.8 © Fotosearch/Getty Images; **p.19** Library of Congress Prints and Photographs Division , LC-DIG-ppmsca-26791; **p.28** © Science History Images/Alamy Stock Photo; **p.34** Library of Congress Prints and Photographs Division Washington, LC-USZ61-1938; **p.45** Library of Congress Prints and Photographs Division Washington, LC-DIG-ppmsca-26716; **p.51** Library of Congress Prints and Photographs Division, LC-DIG-ppmsca-32284; **p.62** © CORBIS/Corbis via Getty Images; **p.65** Library of Congress Prints and Photographs Division Washington, LC-DIG-cwpb-04402; **p.66** © CORBIS/Corbis via Getty Images; **p.67** Library of Congress Prints and Photographs, LC-DIG-ppmsca-39802; **p.92** © Granger Historical Picture Archive/Alamy Stock Photo; **p.100** Library of Congress Prints and Photographs, LC-DIG-ppmsca-05704; **p.109** Library of Congress Prints and Photographs Division Washington, LC-USZ62-128619; **p.128** Library of Congress Prints and Photographs Division Washington, LC-USZ62-123825; **p.130** Library of Congress Prints and Photographs Division , LC-USZC4-494; **p.143** Creative Commons, 5389939434, https://commons.wikimedia.org/wiki/File:Bandit%27s_Roost_by_Jacob_Riis.jpeg; **p.166** Library of Congress Prints and Photographs, LC-DIG-ppmsca-36694; **p.169** Library of Congress Prints and Photographs Division Washington, LC-DIG-ppmsca-35663; **p.172** Library of Congress Prints and Photographs Division Washington, D.C. LC-USZ62-101977; **p.174** Library of Congress Prints and Photographs Division Washington, LC-USZ62-13028; **p.204** © Bettman/Getty Images; **p.207** Library of Congress Prints & Photographs/LC-DIG-ggbain-25292; **p.213** © Bettman/Getty Images; **p.217** Library of Congress Prints and Photographs Division Washington, LC-USZ62-117121; **p.222** © Granger Historical Picture Archive/Alamy Stock Photo; **p.232** Library of Congress Prints & Photographs, LC-USZ62-22375; **p.237** © Fotosearch/Getty Images; **p.239** *b* © Library of Congress/Corbis/VCG via Getty Images, *t* © Bettmann/Getty Images; **p.245** © Granger Historical Picture Archive/Alamy Stock Photo; **p.246** © Punch Limited/TopFoto.

Every effort has been made to trace all copyright holders, but if any have been inadvertently overlooked, the Publishers will be pleased to make the necessary arrangements at the first opportunity.

Orders: please contact Hachette UK Distribution, Hely Hutchinson Centre, Milton Road, Didcot, Oxfordshire, OX11 7HH. Telephone: +44 (0)1235 827827. Email education@hachette.co.uk. Lines are open from 9 a.m. to 5 p.m., Monday to Friday. You can also order through our website: www.hoddereducation.com

ISBN: 978 1 5104 4868 1

First published in 2019 by
Hodder Education,
An Hachette UK Company
Carmelite House
50 Victoria Embankment
London EC4Y 0DZ
www.hoddereducation.com

Impression number 10 9 8 7 6 5

Year 2024

Cover photo © Archive Image/Alamy Stock Photo

Illustrations by Integra Software Services Ltd.

Typeset in Palatino LT Std Light 10/13 by Integra Software Services Pvt. Ltd., Pondicherry, India

Printed and bound by CPI Group (UK) Ltd, Croydon CR0 4YY

A catalogue record for this title is available from the British Library.

FSC www.fsc.org MIX Paper | Supporting responsible forestry FSC™ C104740

Contents

Introduction

This book has been written to support your study of the American Option: The History of the USA 1820–1941 for Cambridge International AS Level History (syllabus code 9489). The book has been endorsed by Cambridge Assessment International Education and is listed as an endorsed textbook for students studying the syllabus.

This introduction gives you an overview of:

- the content you will study for the American Option: The History of the USA 1820–1941
- structure of the syllabus
- the different features of this book and how these will aid your learning.

1 What you will study

In the period 1820–1941 the USA underwent a series of massive transformations. Its economy went from being agricultural to industrial, with the country becoming the world's greatest economic power. This development, which was accompanied by rapid immigration and urbanization, was due to a variety of factors including natural resources, railroad-building, technological innovations, the growth of corporations and US trade policies. By the early twentieth century, Americans were the world's most prosperous people. However, this prosperity was to be affected by the Wall Street Crash of 1929 and the Great Depression which followed. Millions of Americans were unemployed throughout the 1930s.

Politically, the USA also experienced a number of dramatic developments. Perhaps the most important of these was the American Civil War, fought between the Union and Confederate states (1861–65). Had the Confederacy won the Civil War, the USA would no longer have been united. Nor would slavery in the southern states have been so quickly abolished. The process of Reconstruction, which both accompanied and followed the end of the Civil War, was an issue of considerable controversy at the time and remains a subject of huge historical debate to this day. Another crucial political debate was the extent to which the federal government should involve itself in economic and social matters. For much of the period 1820–1941 most Americans believed the best form of government was the least form of government. Nevertheless, in the early twentieth century many Americans thought that the federal (and state) governments should tackle the economic, social and political problems arising from industrialization and urbanization. After the onset of the Great Depression, most Americans supported the interventionist New Deal policies of President Franklin Roosevelt. By the 1920s American women as well as men could vote but many southern states prevented black Americans – male and female – from taking part in the political process. How and why these great economic, social and political developments took place is very much the focus of this book.

The book covers the following topics:

- Chapter 1 examines the causes of the American Civil War, not least the importance of the issue of slavery, and the reasons why fighting broke out between the Confederacy and the Union in April 1861.
- Chapter 2 considers why the Civil War lasted for four years and its immediate impact, particularly in the southern states. It then focuses on the process of Reconstruction and explores the extent to which Reconstruction succeeded/failed.
- Chapter 3 traces the USA's rapid industrialization in the late nineteenth century and the social and economic consequences arising from industrialization and urbanization. It then examines the aims and successes of the so-called Progressive Movement which was influential in the first two decades of the twentieth century.
- Chapter 4 explores the causes and impact of the Great Crash of 1929 and the Great Depression which followed. It then examines the effectiveness and popularity of President Roosevelt's New Deal policies in the period 1933–41.

2 Structure of the syllabus

The Cambridge International AS Level History will be assessed through two papers, a Document paper and an Outline study.

Paper 1: For Paper 1 you need to answer one two-part document question on one of the options given. You will need to answer both parts of the option you choose. This counts for 40 per cent of the AS Level.

Paper 2: For Paper 2 you need to answer two two-part questions from three on one of the options given. You must answer both parts of the question you choose. This counts for 60 per cent of the AS Level.

AS Level topics rotate between papers 1 and 2 year-on-year – the prescribed topic for Paper 1 in the June and November series of any given year is not used for Paper 2.

Examination questions

For Paper 1 there will be two parts to each question. For part (a) you will be expected to consider two sources on one aspect of the material. For part (b) you will be expected to use all the sources and your knowledge of the period to address how far the sources support a given statement.

For Paper 2 you will select two questions from the option on USA 1820–1941. There will be two parts to each question. Part (a) requires a causal explanation and Part (b) requires you to consider and weigh up the relative importance of a range of factors. You will need to answer both parts of the question you choose.

Command words

When choosing the two essay questions, keep in mind that it is vital to answer the actual question that has been asked, not the one that you might have hoped for. A key to doing well is understanding the demands of the question. Cambridge International AS Level History use key terms and phrases known as command words. The command words are listed in the table below, with a brief explanation of each.

Command word	What it means
Assess	Make an informed judgement
Compare	Identify/comment on similarities and/or differences
Contrast	Identify/comment on differences
Discuss	Write about issue(s) or topic(s) in depth in a structured way
Evaluate	Judge or calculate the quality, importance, amount or value of something
Explain	Set out purposes or reasons/make the relationships between things evident/provide why and/or how things happen and support with relevant evidence

Questions may also use phrases such as:

- How far do/does … support … ?
- To what extent … ?
- Account for … ?

Key concepts

The syllabus also focuses on developing your understanding of a number of key concepts and these are also reflected in the nature of the questions set in the examination. The key concepts for AS History are:

Cause and consequence

The events, circumstances, actions and beliefs that have a direct causal connection to consequential events and developments, circumstances, actions or beliefs. Causes can be both human and non-human.

Change and continuity

The patterns, processes and interplay of change and continuity within a given time frame.

Similarity and difference

The patterns of similarity and difference that exist between people, lived experiences, events and situations in the past. Historical significance is a constructed label that is dependent upon the perspective (context, values, interests and concerns) of the person ascribing significance and is therefore changeable.

Significance

The importance attached to an event, individual or entity in the past, whether at the time or subsequent to it.

The icons above appear next to questions to show where key concepts are being tested and what they are.

Answering the questions

With Paper 1, the Document Paper, you have 1 hour 15 minutes to answer the two parts to the question. On Paper 2, the Outline Study, you have 1 hour 45 minutes to answer two two-part questions. It is important that you organize your time well. In other words do not spend 70 minutes on one question on Paper 2 and leave yourself just 35 minutes to do the second question. Before you begin each question, take a few minutes to draw up a brief plan of the major points you want to make and your argument. You can then tick them off as you make them. This is not a waste of time as it will help you produce a coherent and well-argued answer. Well-organized responses with well-supported arguments and a conclusion will score more highly than responses which lack coherence and jump from point to point.

The answers that you write for both Papers will be read by trained examiners. The examiners will read your answers and check what you write against the mark scheme. The mark scheme offers guidance to the examiner but is not comprehensive. You may write an answer that includes analysis and evidence that is not included in the mark scheme and that is fine. It is also worth remembering that the examiner who marks your answers is looking to reward arguments that are well supported, not to deduct for errors or mistakes.

On Paper 1, Question (a) will be marked out of 15 and Question (b) out of 25. The total mark will be weighted at 40 per cent of your final grade. On Paper 2, Question (a) will be marked out of 10 and Question (b) out of 20. The total will be weighted at 60 per cent of your final grade.

Answering source questions

For the Comparison Question (a) you should be able to:

- Make a developed comparison of the two sources.
- Explain why points of similarity and difference exist.
- Use contextual knowledge or source evaluation to explain the similarities and differences.

For Question (b) you should be able to:

- Evaluate the sources to reach a supported judgement as to how far the sources support the statement.

Answering essay questions

Both the short and long answer questions should:

- Be well focused.
- Be well supported by precise and accurate evidence.
- Reach a relevant and supported conclusion or judgement.
- Demonstrate knowledge and understanding of historical processes.
- Demonstrate a clear understanding of connections between causes.

Your essay should include an introduction which sets out your main points. Do not waste time copying out the question but do define any key terms that are in the question. The strongest essays will show awareness of different possible approaches to the question. You will need to write an in-depth analysis of your main points in several paragraphs, providing detailed and accurate information to support them. Each paragraph will focus on one of your main points and be directly related to the question. Finally, you should write a concluding paragraph. All of these skills are developed throughout the book in the Study skills section at the end of each chapter.

What will the examination paper look like?

Cover

The cover of the examination paper states the date of the examination and the length of time you have to complete it. Instructions on the front are limited, but it does remind you that you should answer questions from only ONE section, Section B, the American Option. The cover will also tell you the total number of marks for the Paper, 40 for Paper 1 and 60 for Paper 2 and will also tell you the number of marks for each question or part question.

Questions

Read through Section B, the American Option. With Paper 1 you will have no choice but to answer the Document Question from that section, but for Paper 2 choose which two out of three questions you can answer most fully.

With Paper 1 you might find it helpful to:

- Spend ten minutes reading the sources carefully.
- Identify the key terms and phrases in the question so that you remain focused on the actual question.
- Underline any quotations you will use to support your arguments.

If you spend about ten minutes carefully reading the sources you will have about 1 hour left to answer the two questions. It is advisable to spend around 20–25 minutes answering (a) and 35–40 minutes answering (b).

With Paper 2 you might find it helpful to:

- Circle the two questions you intend to answer.
- Identify the command terms and key words and phrases so that you remain focused on them.

Then spend time drawing up plans. If, for Paper 2, you allow 5 minutes to decide which questions to answer you will have 50 minutes for each question, 5 minutes to plan and 45 minutes to write answers to part (a) and (b). It is advisable to spend around 15–20 minutes answering (a) and 30–35 minutes on (b).

3 About this book

Coverage of the course content

This book addresses the key areas listed in the Cambridge International syllabus. The content follows closely the layout and sequence of the Cambridge syllabus with each chapter representing each topic. Chapters start with an introduction outlining key questions they address. Each key question is accompanied by content that you are expected to understand and deploy when addressing the key question. Throughout the chapters you will find the following features to aid your study of the course content.

Key terms

Key terms are the important terms you need to know to gain an understanding of the period. These are emboldened in the text the first time they appear in the book and are defined in the margin. They also appear in the glossary at the end of the book.

Key figures and profiles

Key figures highlight important individuals and can be found in the margin. Some chapters contain profiles that offer more information about the importance and impact of the individual. This information can be very useful in understanding certain events and providing supporting evidence to your arguments.

Sources

Throughout the book you will encounter both written and visual sources. Historical sources are important components in understanding more fully why specific decisions were taken or on what contemporary writers and politicians based their actions. The sources are accompanied by questions to help you dig deeper into the History of the USA 1820–1941. To help with analysing the sources think about the message of the source, their purpose, and their usefulness for a particular line of enquiry. The questions that accompany the source will help you with this.

Extension box

Sometimes it is useful to go beyond the syllabus to help further your understanding of the topic. The extension boxes will include a variety of additional information such as useful debates and historians' views.

Summary diagrams

At the end of each section is a summary diagram which gives a visual summary of the content of the section. It is intended as an aid for revision. Try copying the diagram into your own set of notes and using information from the chapter to provide precise examples to develop each point. This will help build your knowledge of the issues that relate to the key question.

Chapter summary

At the end of each chapter is a short summary of the content of that chapter. This is intended to help you consolidate your knowledge and understanding of the content.

Refresher questions

Questions at the end of each chapter will serve as a useful tool to test your knowledge of what you have read. These are not exam-style questions, but will serve as prompts and show where you have gaps in your knowledge and understanding.

Study skills

At the end of each chapter you will find guidance on how to approach both writing a successful essay and how to evaluate sources. These pages take you step-by-step through the examination requirements and show you the kinds of questions you might be asked. We also analyse and comment on some sample answers. These are not answers by past candidates. We have written them to help you to see what part of a good answer might look like.

End of the book

The book concludes with the following sections.

Glossary

All key terms in the book are defined in the glossary.

Further reading

This contains a list of books and websites which may help you with further independent research. At this level of study, it is important to read around the subject and not just solely rely on the content of this textbook. The further reading section will help you with this. You may wish to share the contents of this area with your school or local librarian.

Online Teacher Support

In an addition to this book there is an online teacher resource* for sale that will provide support for all three AS Level Paper 1 and Paper 2 options:

- The History of the USA, 1820–1941
- Modern Europe, 1750–1921
- International History, 1870–1945

The online material can be found here: **www.hoddereducation.com**

It includes:

- Simple factual knowledge recall tests.
- Quizzes to test understanding of definitions and key terms to help improve historical understanding and language.
- Schemes of work.
- Worksheets to be used in the classroom or study at home.
- Sample exam-style questions and answers.
- Links to websites and additional online resources.

*The online teacher support component is not endorsed by Cambridge Assessment International Education.

CHAPTER 1

The origins of the Civil War, 1820–61

In the early nineteenth century most Americans were proud of the achievements of their country and optimistic about its future. There seemed good cause for optimism. The USA had the most democratic system of government in the world; it was also one of the world's most prosperous nations. However, the USA did face a serious problem. This was to do with the fact that northern and southern states were growing apart, economically, socially, culturally and politically. Most of the North–South differences and disagreements were concerned with the issue of slavery. The problems arising from slavery eventually resulted in the outbreak of Civil War in April 1861. This chapter will consider the reasons for the war by examining the following questions:

★ How was the issue of slavery addressed between 1820 and 1850?

★ How and why did sectional divisions widen between 1850 and 1856?

★ Why did the Republicans win the 1860 presidential election?

★ Why did the Civil War begin in April 1861?

KEY DATES

1820		Missouri Compromise
1846	**May**	Start of Mexican War
	August	Wilmot Proviso
1848		Treaty of Guadalupe Hidalgo
1850		1850 Compromise
1856		Buchanan won presidential election
1857		Dred Scott decision
1858		Mid-term elections: Lincoln–Douglas debates
1859		John Brown's raid
1860	**November**	Lincoln elected president
	December	South Carolina seceded
1861	**January–February**	Mississippi, Florida, Alabama, Georgia, Louisiana and Texas seceded
	February	Confederacy established
	March	Lincoln inaugurated president
	April	Confederate forces opened fire on Fort Sumter
	April–June	Virginia, Arkansas, North Carolina and Tennessee seceded

1 How was the issue of slavery addressed between 1820 and 1850?

KEY TERMS

Peculiar institution Southerners referred to slavery as their 'peculiar institution'.

Federal A government in which several states, while largely independent in home affairs, combine for national purposes.

Platform The publicly declared principles and intentions of a political party.

Tariff Customs duty on imported goods.

By the mid-nineteenth century, there was one main issue which divided Americans more than any other. This was the issue of slavery. Most southerners supported their **peculiar institution**. Most northerners opposed it. The problem of slavery was made worse by the USA's political system and the impact of westward expansion. Between 1820 and 1850 politicians struggled to find compromises which would ensure that the United States remained united.

The US political system and the balance of sectional interests

The 1787 Constitution created a system whereby power would be divided between the central (or **federal**) government in Washington and the individual states. The federal government had well-defined executive, legislative and judicial branches, each of which was able to check the actions of the others (see Figure 1.1). State governments tended to replicate the federal government: each state had its governor, its own legislative body and its own Supreme Court. In the late eighteenth century the USA had devised a system for admitting new states. New areas first assumed territorial status, electing a territorial government. Once the population of a territory had reached 60,000, it could submit its proposed constitution to Congress and apply to become a state. In 1820 there were 23 states. By 1850 the USA comprised 30 states.

The Constitution implicitly accepted slavery because, for the purposes of counting population (to work out each state's representation in the House of Representatives), each enslaved person was considered to be three-fifths of a free person.

American democracy

By the 1820s, the USA was far more democratic than the rest of the world. Although women and most black Americans could not vote, almost all white males could do so. By the 1830s the USA had two major political parties: the Democrats and the Whigs. The parties, although operating nationally, were not particularly united. They were really an assortment of state parties that only came together every four years to nominate a presidential candidate and devise a national **platform**.

- Democrats believed that most issues should be decided at state, not federal, level. They opposed government intervention in economic matters and supported the lowering of **tariffs**.
- Whigs were more likely to favour government intervention in economic and social matters and supported higher tariffs.

THE AMERICAN PEOPLE

ELECT

CONGRESS (The Legislative)

Congress makes laws, has the power of the purse, declares war and checks the work of the President.

Senate

- Two Senators represent each state (no matter how large or small the state).
- Senators sit for six years – one-third come up for re-election every two years.

House of Representatives

- Members of the House represent constituencies based on population.
- The House is elected en masse every two years.

- Both houses of Congress need to agree before a law can be carried out.
- Congress may override a presidential veto.
- Congress may impeach and remove the President from office.

THE PRESIDENT
(The Executive)

- Elected every four years by the Electoral College (Electoral College representatives are selected by the party with the most votes in each state).
- If the President resigns or dies, the Vice-President takes over.
- The President is head of state but also has some real powers. He may call special sessions of Congress, may recommend legislation and may veto bills.
- Presidents appoint their own ministers, or secretaries, who sit in the cabinet but who are forbidden to sit in Congress.
- The President is the Commander-in-Chief of the armed forces.

THE SUPREME COURT (The Judiciary)

- This is the highest court. It approves the laws and decides whether they are Constitutional.
- The (usually nine) Supreme Court Judges are appointed by the President, but only when one dies or retires.
- The Senate ratifies the President's appointments.

Figure 1.1 The American Constitution

Limited government

Given that it was unusual for one party to control the presidency, both houses of Congress and the Supreme Court at the same time, it was often difficult for the federal government to bring about much change. The fact that many matters were seen as state (not federal) concerns was another limiting factor. Presidents were more figureheads and distributors of **patronage** than active policy-makers. Congress, only in session from December to March, rarely passed major legislation. State legislatures had more influence on Americans' day-to-day lives than the federal government.

KEY TERM

Patronage The giving of jobs or privileges to supporters.

Sectional interests

The United States had never been particularly united. For much of the early nineteenth century there were rivalries between the newer western states and the established eastern states. Far more important, however, were the differences between North and South. Some historians have underplayed the differences, stressing instead the similarities between the two sections: the common language, the shared religion, the same legal, political and racial assumptions, and the celebration of the same history. Other historians, however, believe that there were deep divisions – divisions that helped to bring about the Civil War.

Economic differences

There were economic differences between North and South. The North developed more industry and relied more on mixed farming and free labour. The South was characterized by large-scale cultivation of crops like cotton and tobacco which relied on slave labour. However, it is important not to generalize. Historians once claimed that the Civil War was a conflict between a backward, **agrarian**, **planter**-dominated South and a modern, industrialized and **egalitarian** North. This view is far too sweeping. In reality, there was not one but many 'Souths' encompassing several distinct geographical regions. Eastern states such as Virginia were very different from newer western states (like Mississippi). The **lower South** was different from the upper South. Accordingly, it is difficult to generalize about the 'Old' South.

KEY TERMS

Agrarian Relating to land and farming.

Egalitarian A society in which people are equal.

Lower South This area comprised Alabama, Louisiana, Georgia, Texas, Florida, South Carolina and Mississippi.

Planters Men who owned plantations with 20 or more enslaved workers.

There were also many 'Norths'. Moreover, in many respects, these 'Norths' were not dissimilar economically to the 'Souths'. The North was industrializing, not industrialized. In 1820, fewer than one in ten Americans lived in towns (defined as settlements with more than 2500 people): one in five did so by 1860. Nor was the South economically backward. By the mid-nineteenth century southern cotton sales made up at least half of the USA's total exports.

Slavery apart, the North was not more egalitarian than the South. In 1820 the typical northerner was a self-sufficient farmer, owning 50–500 acres of land. The same was true of southerners. In 1820, two-thirds of southern families were not slave owners.

Planters, who comprised less than five per cent of the white population, owned the South's best farmland and the major portion of its wealth, including most of its enslaved people. The historian Eugene Genovese believed that the planters led southern politics and set the tone of social life. However, in the North a minority of wealthy men wielded similar influence.

North–South differences

- The North was more industrial. The southern states, with about 35 per cent of the USA's population, produced only 10 per cent of the nation's manufactured output by 1850.

- The North was more urban. In 1850 only six of the USA's largest thirty cities were southern.
- Between 1820 and 1860 most of the five million immigrants to the USA settled in the North. Thus, one in six northerners in 1860 was born overseas compared with one in 30 southerners.

Southern economic grievances

The two sections had different economic interests. The tariff was a source of constant grievance to most southerners, who argued that it benefited northern industrialists at the expense of southern farmers. The South also felt exploited in other ways. Southerners depended upon northern credit to finance the growing of cotton, tobacco, sugar and rice: they relied upon northerners to market these goods; and they were reliant on northern ships to transport them. Inevitably much of the profits from '**King Cotton**' ended up in pockets of northern businessmen.

Values

There was a general southern belief that old agrarian ways and values were better than those of the **Yankees**. The historian Wyatt-Brown (1982) claimed that southerners were more concerned about their personal honour than northerners. In Brown's view, southern males were highly sensitive to personal insult, reacting violently to even trivial incidents, including resorting to duelling. There were other perceived differences. Northerners were believed to be more responsive to new ideas. Southerners, by contrast, tended to oppose radical 'isms', viewing them as a threat to old values and institutions.

Slavery

The main difference between the sections, and the main reason for the growth of sectionalism, was slavery. In 1776 slavery existed in what was then all the 13 colonies of British America. However, it was of major importance only in the South, largely because the northern climate was not suited to **plantation agriculture**. In the late eighteenth century, radical Protestants condemned slavery as a moral evil. Other Americans thought it inconsistent with enlightened ideas that stressed liberty, equality and free enterprise. After independence from Britain, northern states abolished slavery, some at a stroke, others gradually. In 1787 Congress passed an ordinance that kept slavery out of the North West Territory. In 1808 the USA banned the slave trade with Africa.

Cotton ensured that slavery survived and thrived. In 1790 only 9000 bales of cotton were produced in the USA. But Eli Whitney's invention of a cotton engine (or 'gin') in 1793 enabled southern short-fibre cotton to be quickly separated from its seed. Suddenly it became highly profitable to grow cotton. By the 1830s the South was producing two million bales per year. Cotton outstripped all other plantation crops in economic importance. Such was the demand (mainly from Britain), and such were the profits, that the cotton belt

KEY TERMS

King Cotton Cotton was so important to the US economy that many Americans claimed that 'cotton was king'.

Yankees Americans who live in the northern, as opposed to the southern, states.

Plantation agriculture Sugar, rice, tobacco and cotton woro grown on southern plantations.

spread westwards. Cotton production needed a large quantity of unskilled labour to pick the cotton. Slave labour was seen as ideal.

Abolitionists

KEY TERMS

Abolitionist Someone who wanted to end slavery.

Evangelical A passionate belief in Christianity and a desire to share that belief with others.

Most **abolitionists** in the early nineteenth century supported gradual emancipation – freeing the enslaved people over a period of time with the slave owners receiving some financial compensation. Abolitionists also believed that formerly enslaved people who had been freed should be encouraged to return to Africa. In 1822 the USA purchased Liberia, on the west coast of Africa, as a base for returning formerly enslaved people. However, only 10,000 black people had returned to Africa by 1860; in the same period the USA's enslaved population increased by two million. There were never enough funds to free and then transport more than a fraction of the enslaved people. Moreover, most formerly enslaved people had no wish to move to Liberia.

Militant abolitionism

In the early 1830s, a new and far more forceful abolitionist movement developed. This was associated with William Lloyd Garrison who, in 1831, launched a new abolitionist journal, *The Liberator.* Convinced that slavery was a sin, Garrison demanded immediate abolition (though he did not actually mention how it should be done). In 1833 a militant National Anti-Slavery Society was established. By 1838 it had 250,000 members. Most of its leaders were well-educated and fairly wealthy. Women and free black people played crucial roles. Helped by the new steam-driven printing press, abolitionists churned out a mass of anti-slavery literature. They also organized massive petitions to Congress. To prevent North–South division, Congress introduced the 'gag rule' in 1836, which ensured that abolitionist petitions were not discussed.

Some historians stress that militant abolitionism was part of a world-wide phenomenon, in which Britain in particular played an important role. Others stress American roots. Mid-nineteenth century America was a religious society and the Church had a powerful effect on most people's lives. Most Americans were Protestants: Baptists, Methodists, Unitarians, Presbyterians and Episcopalians. In the early nineteenth century, there was an upsurge in **evangelical** Protestantism known as the Second Great Awakening. Evangelical preachers fired up Americans to do battle against the sins of the world – including slavery.

Abolitionist problems in the North

The abolitionist movement had only limited appeal in the North. Many northerners, fearing an exodus of liberated formerly enslaved people to their states, hated the abolitionists. Anti-slavery meetings were broken up by angry mobs. In 1837 Elijah Lovejoy became the first abolitionist martyr when he was murdered in Illinois. Failing to win the support of either the Whig or Democrat Party, abolitionists set up the Liberty Party. In 1840 its presidential candidate won only 7000 votes. Abolitionists were unable to agree on their general strategy. This resulted in a major division in the Anti-Slavery Society in 1840. Nevertheless, despite their problems, the abolitionists did stir the consciences of a growing number of northerners and kept slavery at the forefront of public attention.

Abolitionist problems in the South

The abolitionists had no success whatsoever in winning support from white southerners. They were not helped by the fact that in 1831 Nat Turner, an enslaved man in Virginia, led a slave revolt in which 55 white people were killed. The revolt was quickly crushed, and Turner and the other enslaved rebels killed or executed. Nevertheless, the revolt appalled southerners who blamed abolitionists for inciting trouble among enslaved people.

Abolitionist attacks provoked southerners to praise the virtues of their peculiar institution. Southern writers now argued that slavery was a positive good rather than a necessary evil. History, religion, anthropology and economics were all used to defend slavery. As well as vigorously defending slavery in print and in words, southern authorities also took action against abolitionists. In some southern states the penalty for circulating 'incendiary' literature among black people was death. Southerners suspected of having abolitionist sympathies were driven out.

The nature of slavery

- In 1860 there were nearly four million enslaved people (compared to eight million white people) in the 15 southern states. They were concentrated mainly in the lower South.
- In 1850 one in three white southern families were slave owners. By 1860, this figure was one family in four.
- In 1860 50 per cent of slave owners owned fewer than five enslaved people. Over 50 per cent of enslaved people lived on plantations with over 20 enslaved workers. Thus the 'typical' slaveholder did not own the 'typical' enslaved person.
- Most enslaved people were held by about 10,000 families.
- Of all enslaved people, 55 per cent worked in cotton production, 10 per cent in tobacco, 10 per cent in sugar, rice and hemp, while 15 per cent were domestic servants and 10 per cent lived in towns or worked in industry.

Free black people

By 1860 there were about 250,000 free black people in the South. Most of these were of mixed heritage and had been given their freedom by their white fathers. Southern free black people had to carry documentation proving their freedom at all times or risk the danger of being enslaved. They had no political rights and their legal status was precarious. Some 200,000 black people lived in the North. Many northern white people were as racially prejudiced as southerners. Northern black people usually had the worst jobs and **segregation** was the norm in most aspects of life. Only three states allowed black people to vote on equal terms with white people in 1860. Some northern states tried to exclude black people from voting altogether.

KEY TERM

Segregation The system whereby black and white people are separated from each other on grounds of race.

SOURCE A

Administrator's Sale, by Order of the Ordinary.

A PRIME AND ORDERLY GANG OF

68 Long Cotton Field Negroes,

Belonging to the Estate of the late Christopher J. Whaley.

WILBUR & SON

Will sell at PUBLIC AUCTION in Charleston,

At the Mart in Chalmers Street,

On Thursday, Feb. 2d, 1860,

COMMENCING AT ELEVEN O'CLOCK,

THE FOLLOWING GANG OF LONG COTTON NEGROES,

Who are said to be remarkably prime, and will be sold as per Catalogue.

NAMES.		AGES.	NAMES.		AGES.
Jimmy,	driver,	30	Carter,		36
Flora,	seamstress,	24	Taffy,		13
James,		5	Rachel,	($ 720,)	8
Charles,	($ 125,)	1	Jannett,		18
August,		52	Phebe,	($ 860,)	40
Mathias,	($ 1,220,)	18	Judy,		8
Sandy,		16	Major,		40
John,		13	Lavinia,		30
Tom,		70	Billy,	($ 550,)	10
Jack,		38	Tamor,		6
James,		6	Jimmy,		52
Leah,		5	Kate,		46
Flora,		2	Susan,		25
Andrew,		42	Thomas,	($ 380,)	6
Binah,		40	Kate,		1
Phillis,		20	Edward,	coachman,	49
Mary,		15	Amey,		22
Lymus,		10	Teneb,	washer,	30
Abram,	($ 275,)	2	Josephine,		9
Binah,		2 mos.	Sam,		11
Andrew,		29	Isaac,		5
Hagar,		25	William,		1
Dayman,		4	Amey,		27
Cuffy,		21	Louisa,	($ 750,)	8
Hagar,	($ 1,320,)	20	Joe,		3
Margaret,		85	Sam,	ruptured,	65
Lucy,	cripple,	60	Andrew,	dropsical,	61
John,		22	Daniel,		70
Ellick,	($ 1,160,)	18	Lymus,		30
Libby,		19	Lucy,	nurse,	58

TERMS.

One-third Cash; balance in one and two years, secured by bond, and mortgage of the negroes, with approved personal security. Purchasers to pay us for papers.

29

Notice of slave sale, 1860

How useful is Source A for historians studying slavery?

The future of slavery

Some historians have argued that once cotton prices fell, then slavery would have eventually died of its own accord. If this is correct, the blood-letting of the Civil War was unnecessary. However, in 1860 there was still a worldwide demand for cotton and thus no economic reason for believing slavery was about to die out. Moreover, slavery was not simply an economic institution. It was also a system of social control. It kept black people 'in their place' and ensured white supremacy. Southerners feared that an end to slavery would result in economic collapse, social disintegration and race war. Thus slaveholders and non-slaveholders alike were committed to the peculiar institution: so committed that (ultimately) they were prepared to secede (withdraw formally) from the Union and wage a terrible war in an effort to maintain it. Given this commitment, it is difficult to see how slavery would have ended without the Civil War.

Conclusion

By the mid-nineteenth century there were significant differences between North and South – differences that were growing as the North's industrial development outstripped that of the South. The North was changing: the South resisted change. By 1850 southerners were conscious of their distinct 'southern-ness'. North and South might speak the same language – but by the mid-nineteenth century (as the historian James McPherson (1988) has pointed out) they were increasingly using this language to attack each other. Even the shared commitment to Protestantism had become a divisive rather than a unifying factor, with most of the major denominations splitting into hostile southern and northern branches over the question of slavery.

The impact of territorial expansion: westward expansion and the absorption of Texas

In the early nineteenth century, Americans moved west and filled the area between the Appalachian Mountains and the Mississippi River. By 1819 the original 13 states had grown to 22. Of these, 11 states were free; 11 were slave. Further westward expansion threatened to tilt the sectional balance in favour of the North or South. Northern states wanted new western states to be free states. Southern states, by contrast, wanted them to be slave states. This caused political problems throughout the period 1820–50.

The Missouri Compromise

In 1819 Missouri applied to join the Union as a slave state. Given that this would tilt the balance against them, northern states opposed Missouri's admittance. The result was a series of furious debates, with southern and northern Congressmen lined up against each other. In 1820 a compromise was worked out. To balance the admittance of Missouri, a new free state of Maine was created. It was also agreed that henceforward there should be no slavery in the **Louisiana Purchase Territory**, north of latitude 36°30′ (see Figure 1.3). South of that line, slavery could exist.

KEY TERM

Louisiana Purchase Territory The huge area bought from France in 1803.

Texan independence

Americans had settled in Texas, then part of Mexico, from the 1820s. Most were southerners and many had taken enslaved people with them. In 1829 Mexico passed a law to free its enslaved people and in 1830 prohibited further American immigration into Texas. American Texans defied both laws, and for some years the Mexican government was too weak to enforce its authority. By 1835 there were about 30,000 American immigrants in Texas (and 5000 enslaved people) and only about 5000 Mexicans.

The efforts of the Mexican President Santa Anna to enforce Mexican authority were resented by the American Texans and over the winter of 1835–36 they declared independence. Santa Anna marched north with a large army. A force of 187 Texans put up a spirited defence at the Alamo, a fortified mission near San Antonio, but this fell in March 1836. All the Texan defenders were killed. Although US President Andrew Jackson (1929–37) sympathized with the Texans, he sent no official help. However, hundreds of Americans from the South and West rushed to the Texans' aid. In April 1836 an American-Texan army, led by Sam Houston, defeated Mexican forces at the battle of San Jacinto. Santa Anna was captured and forced to recognize Texan independence.

Texas and the USA

Although the Mexican government did not ratify Santa Anna's action, Texas was now effectively independent. Most Texans, with southern support, hoped to join the USA. However, many northerners opposed the move, fearing that it would lead to the expansion of slavery. Texas was so large that it could feasibly be divided into five new states, which would tilt the balance between free and slave states heavily in the South's favour. Given that Texas was a major political problem, President Andrew Jackson shelved the issue. So too did his successor Martin Van Buren, Democratic president from 1837 to 1841. The result was that for a few years Texas was an independent republic, unrecognized by Mexico and rejected by the USA.

Texas became a major issue in the 1844 presidential election, fought between the Whig Henry Clay and the Democrat James Polk. Polk, a slaveholder from Tennessee, was elected president on a platform that promised the annexation

Figure 1.2 The impact of westward expansion 1783–1840

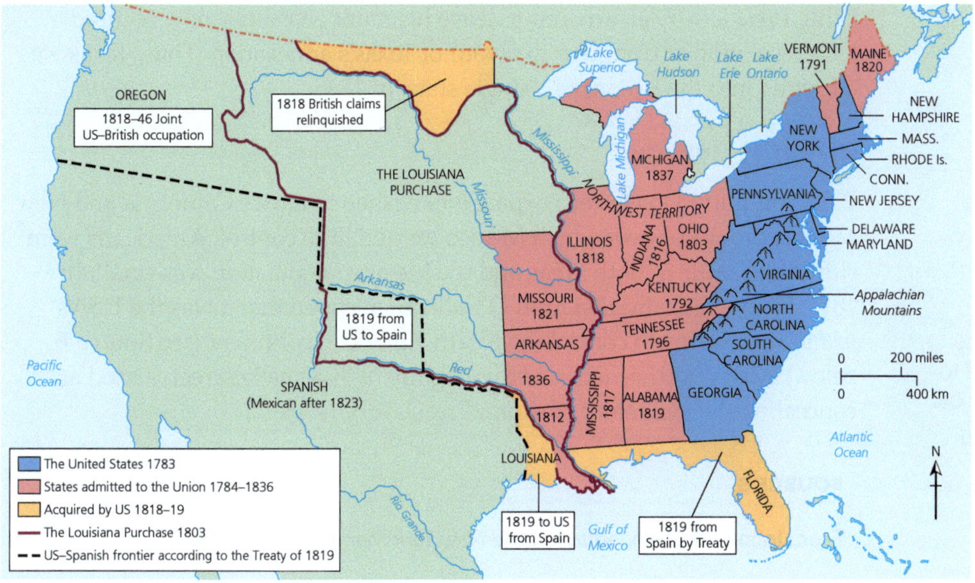

Figure 1.3 The Missouri Compromise

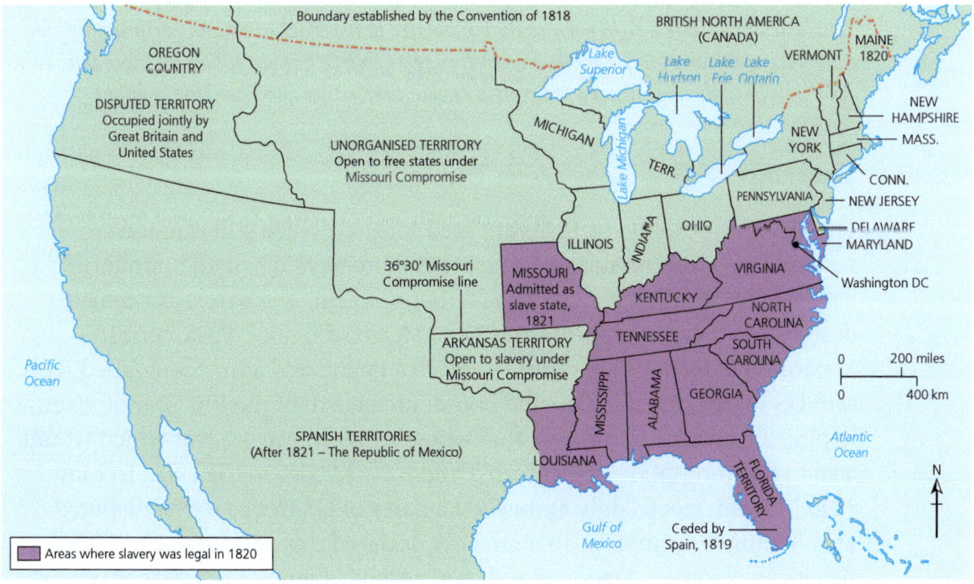

(take-over) of both Texas and Oregon – an area claimed by Britain. Outgoing Whig President Tyler, anxious to leave his mark on events, now secured a joint resolution of Congress in favour of Texas's annexation. Thus, Texas was admitted into the Union, as a single state, in 1845.

Manifest destiny

Polk, committed to western expansion, wished to annex California and New Mexico, provinces over which Mexico exerted little control. Americans were starting to settle in both areas and the Mexican population was small. In 1845, Democrat journalist John O'Sullivan declared that it was the USA's **manifest destiny** to control the North American continent (see Source B below). Many northerners saw this argument as a smokescreen aimed at concealing the evil intent of expanding slavery.

KEY TERMS

Manifest destiny The USA's god-given right to take over North America.

Sovereignty Ultimate power.

SOURCE B

From John O'Sullivan, editor of the *New York Morning News*, 1845

Away, away with all these cobweb tissues of rights of discovery, exploration, settlement, contiguity [nearness] etc ... The American claim is by the right of our manifest destiny to overspread and to possess the whole of the continent which Providence has given us for the development of the great experiment of liberty and federated self-government entrusted to us. It is a right such as that of the tree to the space of air and earth suitable for the full expansion of its principle and destiny of growth ... It is our future far more than in our past or in the past history of Spanish exploration ... that our True Title is found.

What arguments does O'Sullivan use in Source B to justify manifest destiny?

The outbreak of war with Mexico

The USA's annexation of Texas angered Mexico, which still claimed **sovereignty** over the state. The fact that there were disputed boundaries between Texas and Mexico was a further problem. The barely-concealed designs of Polk on California and New Mexico did not help American–Mexican relations. When efforts to reach a negotiated agreement failed, Polk sent US troops into the disputed border area north of the Rio Grande river, hoping to provoke an incident that would result in war – a war which would lead to the annexation of California and New Mexico to the USA. In May 1846 Mexican troops duly ambushed a party of US troops in the disputed area, killing or wounding 16 men. Polk declared that Mexicans had 'shed American blood on American soil' and asked Congress to declare war. Congress obliged. While most southerners and westerners supported the war, many northerners saw it as a southern war of aggression.

The Mexican War

Although the USA had a smaller army, it had twice as many people and a much stronger industrial base than Mexico and thus far greater military potential. Mexican forces were poorly led and equipped. The USA had several further advantages:

- superior artillery
- a pool of junior officers, most of whom had been well trained at West Point military academy
- enthusiastic (mainly southern and western) volunteers
- naval supremacy.

In the summer of 1846 US troops, led by Colonel Kearney, annexed New Mexico. They then marched to California. By the time they arrived the province was largely under US control. American colonists had proclaimed independence from Mexico. They were helped by Colonel John C. Frémont, in the region on an exploratory expedition, and by a US naval squadron, conveniently stationed off the Californian coast. Kearney's arrival in December 1846 ended what little Mexican resistance remained.

Polk hoped that Mexico would accept defeat and the loss of New Mexico and California. But Santa Anna, once again in control of Mexico, refused to surrender.

The USA's war heroes were General Zachary Taylor and General Winfield Scott.

- In February 1847 General Zachary Taylor defeated the Mexican military at Buena Vista.
- Scott, with only 11,000 men, marched 260 miles (420 km) inland over difficult terrain, storming several fortresses before capturing Mexico City in September 1847.

By the autumn of 1847 the Mexican War was essentially over. It had cost the USA $100 million and the death of 13,000 soldiers. The USA was now in a position to enforce peace. Some southerners called for the annexation of the whole of Mexico. However, many northerners wanted to annex no territory whatsoever.

The Treaty of Guadalupe Hidalgo

By the Treaty of Guadalupe Hidalgo (February 1848), California and New Mexico (including present-day Nevada, Utah, most of Arizona, and parts of Colorado and Wyoming) were ceded to the USA. This makes up two-fifths of the USA's present territory. President Polk was unhappy with the treaty. Despite the fact that the USA had gained everything it had gone to war for, he thought that even more territory could have been gained. Spurred on by southerners, who saw the dizzying prospect of dozens of new slave states, Polk considered rejecting the treaty. However, given northern opinion and the fact that some southerners had no wish to rule Mexico's mixed Spanish and Native American population, he reluctantly accepted the treaty, which was ratified by the Senate in May 1848.

Figure 1.4 The USA in the 1850s

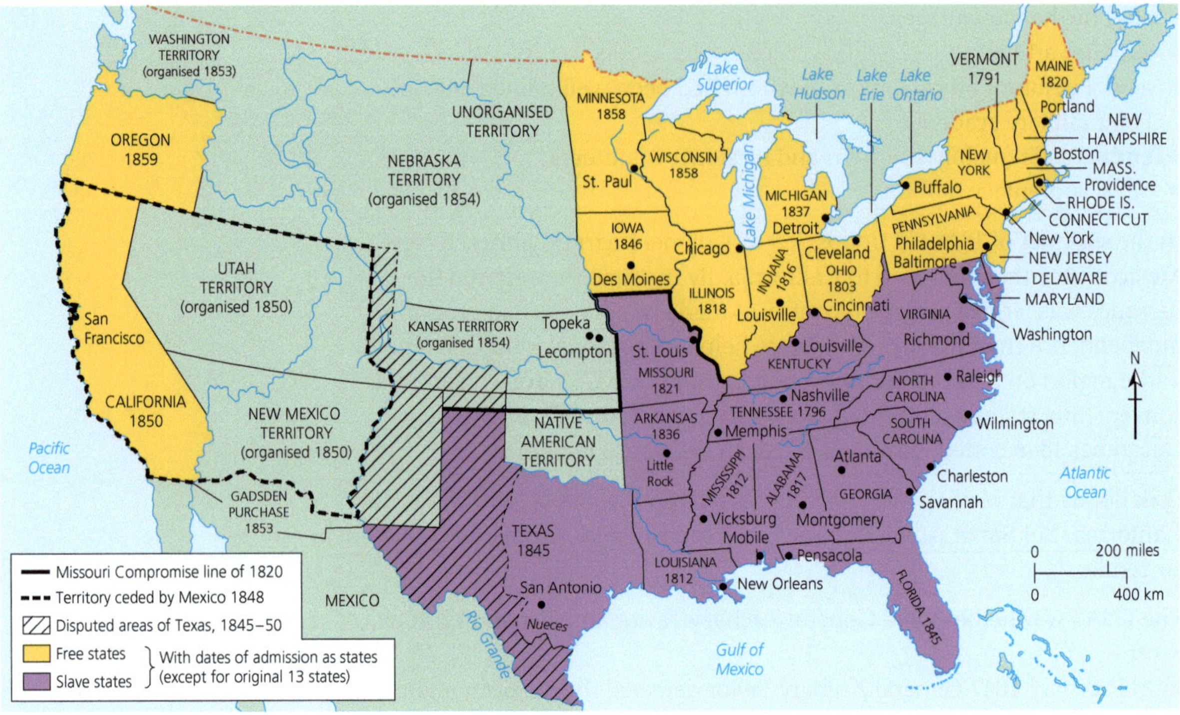

The impact of population growth and movement

> **KEY TERM**
>
> **GNP (Gross National Product)** The total value of all goods and services produced within a country.

The USA had enormous reserves of almost every commodity – land, timber and minerals. Between 1800 and 1850 the USA's **GNP** increased seven-fold and the average American's income doubled. This encouraged population growth – as did western expansion and immigration.

The USA's population grew rapidly in the early nineteenth century. In 1820 it had been just over 9.5 million. By 1840 it stood at 17 million; by 1850 it had reached 23 million. By then, more than one in two Americans lived west of the Appalachians – largely due to the opening up of vast new tracts of land. Most of the population growth came from natural increase: the average woman had five children. Population growth was also the result of immigration, especially from Britain, Ireland and Germany.

Southern fears

In 1820 there had been a similar number of southerners to northerners. But by 1850 northerners outnumbered southerners by more than three to two. (This was largely because most immigrants settled in northern states.) The fact that there was a widening disparity in numbers between North and South concerned southerners. Given that northern states had more seats in the House of Representatives, southerners were determined to maintain a position of equality in the Senate. This meant that westward expansion was a crucial issue because each new state resulted in two more senators in Congress.

ACTIVITY

Group work:
'Westward expansion was a greater problem for American politicians than slavery abolition in the period 1820–50.' In pairs look through this section and find four points that might support this view. Discuss which point is the most important, then try and put the the other points in order of importance. If you disagree, try and work out why.

Attempts at compromise

In 1819–20 US politicians had been able to resolve the problem of Missouri – a problem that had threatened to tear the Union apart (see page 11). However, politicians found it more difficult to deal with the problems which arose (ironically) from American success in the Mexican War.

The impact of the Mexican War 1846–50

Northerners and southerners were divided over the Mexican War before it began. They remained divided during it and were even more divided by the end of it. Anticipating winning territory from Mexico at the start of the war, American politicians could not agree whether states created from Mexican land should become slave or free.

The Wilmot Proviso

In 1846 David Wilmot, a northern Democrat, proposed in the House of Representatives that slavery should be excluded from any territory gained from Mexico. Wilmot was not an abolitionist. Like many northern Democrats, Wilmot resented the fact that Polk seemed to be pursuing a pro-southern policy. While happy to fight the Mexican War, Polk went back on his promise to take the whole of Oregon. Instead, an agreement had been reached whereby Britain took the area north of the 49th parallel and the USA took southern Oregon. This made sense: the USA did well out of the deal and it would have been foolish to have fought both Mexico and Britain. Nevertheless, northern Democrats disliked Polk's seeming pro-southern bias.

In supporting the **Proviso**, northern Democrats hoped to keep black Americans out of the new territories and ensure that white colonists would not face competition from slave planters. Concerned at the coming **mid-term elections**, northern Democrats were warning Polk of their unease with the direction of his policies.

After a bitter debate, the Proviso narrowly passed the House of Representatives by 83 votes to 64. The voting was sectional: every southern Democrat and all but two southern Whigs voted against it. Most northerners voted for it. Senator Toombs of Georgia warned that if the Proviso became law, he would favour disunion rather than 'degradation'. However, the Proviso did not become law as it failed to pass the Senate. Nevertheless, for anti-slavery forces, the Proviso became a rallying cry. Many northern state legislatures endorsed it. Most southern states denounced it.

KEY TERMS

Proviso A provision or condition.

Mid-term elections The whole of the House of Representatives and a third of the Senate are re-elected every two years. This means that there are major elections half way through a president's term of office.

The Calhoun Doctrine

Northerners believed that Congress had the power to exclude slavery from the territories and should exercise that power. Southerners responded aggressively to this threat, not least **John C Calhoun** from South Carolina who had been largely responsible for the Nullification Crisis (see textbox). In 1847 he issued a series of resolutions in which he claimed that citizens from every state had the right to take their 'property' to any territory. Congress, he asserted, had no authority to place restrictions on slavery in the **territories**. If the northern majority continued to disregard the rights of the southern minority, southern states would have little option but to secede.

KEY FIGURE

John C Calhoun (1782–1850) dominated politics in South Carolina and indeed the South generally in the early nineteenth century. Elected to Congress in 1810, he served as vice-president under both John Quincy Adams and Andrew Jackson. By the late 1820s Calhoun was a major defender of states' rights. He supported the theory of nullification and helped secure the annexation of Texas as a slave state.

Nullification Crisis

In the late 1820s Calhoun had proclaimed the right of any state to over-rule or nullify any federal law deemed unconstitutional. When South Carolina disallowed two tariff acts in 1832, President Jackson threatened to use force. Unable to muster support from other southern states, South Carolina pulled back from declaring secession.

The search for compromise

Moderate politicians, fearful that the issue could destroy the Union, tried to find a compromise. The most successful idea was the notion of **popular sovereignty**, associated with two mid-western Democrats, Senator Lewis Cass and Senator Stephen Douglas. They argued that it was not Congress which should decide on whether a territory should allow slavery. That decision should be made instead by the people in that territory. Consistent with democracy and self-government, popular sovereignty seemed to offer something to both sections.

- It met the South's wish for federal non-intervention and held out the prospect that slavery might be extended to some of the former Mexican territories.
- It could be presented to the North as an exclusion scheme because it was unlikely that colonists in the new territories would vote for slavery's introduction.

KEY TERMS

Territories Areas in the USA that had not yet become states and which were still under federal government control.

Popular sovereignty The notion that colonists, not Congress, should decide whether a territory should or should not allow slavery.

There were problems with popular sovereignty. Firstly, it went against previous practice. In the past, Congress had decided on what should happen in the territories. Did popular sovereignty mean that it no longer had that power? Then there were practical difficulties, not least when exactly a territory should decide on the slavery question. Nevertheless, popular sovereignty was supported by many Democrats. It was opposed by those southerners who thought they had the right to take their 'property' anywhere, and by those northerners who believed that slavery should not be allowed to expand under any circumstances.

The 1848 election

Worn out by constant opposition, Polk did not seek a second term. The Democrats, rallying round the concept of popular sovereignty, chose Lewis Cass as their presidential candidate. The Whigs nominated Mexican war hero Zachary Taylor. The fact that he was a slave owner from Louisiana did not endear him to abolitionists. Nevertheless, many northern Whigs were prepared to endorse Taylor if only because he seemed a likely winner. A new party, the Free Soil Party, which supported the Wilmot Proviso, was formed to fight the election. It included a number of northern Democrats, who disliked Cass, 'Conscience' Whigs, who disliked Taylor, and Liberty Party supporters. Former president Martin Van Buren was nominated as its presidential candidate. The election was a triumph for Taylor, who won 1,360,000 votes and 163 electoral college votes. Cass won 1,220,000 votes and 127 electoral votes. Van Buren won 291,000 votes but no electoral votes. Taylor's victory was not sectional. He carried 8 of the 15 slave states and 7 of the 15 free states.

California and New Mexico

Few Americans had thought that California or New Mexico would speedily apply for statehood because both areas seemed to have little to offer colonists. But the discovery of gold in California led to the 1848–49 Gold Rush. Within months, there were 100,000 people in California, more than enough to enable the area to apply for statehood. New Mexico had fewer people. However, thousands of **Mormons** had settled around Salt Lake City in 1846–47. As a result of the Mexican War, they found themselves under US jurisdiction.

President Taylor determined to act decisively. Hoping that a quick solution to the California–New Mexico problem might reduce the potential for sectional strife, he encouraged colonists in the areas to frame constitutions and apply immediately for admission to the Union without first going through the process of establishing territorial governments.

In 1849 California duly ratified a proposed state constitution prohibiting slavery and applied for admission to the Union. Taylor was also prepared to admit New Mexico, even though it did not have enough people to apply for statehood. There was a further problem with New Mexico: it had a boundary dispute with Texas. Southerners supported Texas's claim; northerners supported New Mexico. A clash between Texan state forces and the US army suddenly seemed imminent.

Southern resentment

Taylor's actions enraged southerners, Democrats and Whigs alike. Having won the war against Mexico, most believed they were now being excluded from the territory gained. In October 1849 Mississippi issued a call to all slave states to send representatives to a convention to meet at Nashville in June 1850 to devise and adopt 'some mode of resistance to northern aggression'. Bitter sectional divisions were reflected in Congress, which met in December 1849. As well as

KEY TERM

Mormons Members of a religious sect, founded in the 1820s by Joseph Smith, a visionary who claimed that an angel had appeared to him.

The 1793 Fugitive Slave Act

This guarded the rights of slaveholders to recover enslaved people who had escaped. However, many Northern states passed legislation to protect enslaved people who had run away. These laws, known as personal liberty laws, required slave owners to produce evidence that their captives were truly enslaved people who had escaped.

fierce debates over slavery expansion, southerners also raised the issues of fugitive slaves, claiming that many northern states were breaking the 1793 Fugitive Slave Act (see textbox) and frustrating slaveholders' efforts to catch enslaved people who had run away and return them to the South. Northerners, by contrast, objected to the fact that slavery was allowed in Washington.

The 1850 Compromise

President Taylor determined to make no concessions to the South. If necessary, he was ready to lead an army into the South to prevent secession. However, many politicians from mid-western states, including Whig elder statesman **Henry Clay**, were worried by events and felt that something had to be done to calm the anger of southerners. In January 1850 Clay, who had been instrumental in the 1820 Missouri Compromise (see page 11) offered the Senate a set of resolutions as a basis for a compromise.

- California was to be admitted as a free state.
- Utah and New Mexico were to be organized as territories without any mention of, or restriction on, slavery.
- Slave-trading but not slavery should end in Washington.
- A more stringent Fugitive Slave Act should be passed to placate the South.
- In order to resolve the Texas–New Mexico dispute, Texas should surrender the disputed land to New Mexico. In return, Congress would assume the $10 million public debt that Texas still owed.

KEY FIGURES

Henry Clay (1777–1852) A slaveholding Whig Senator from Kentucky, Clay had the reputation of being a master legislator and for being able to find compromise solutions between northerners and southerners.

Daniel Webster (1782–1852) A famous northern lawyer, Whig politician and orator. An opponent of slavery, he had been secretary of state from 1841 to 1843.

The next few months were marked by a series of epic speeches as Clay's proposals, rolled into a single 'omnibus' bill, were debated in Congress. The more moderate and conciliatory politicians such as Clay and **Daniel Webster** gained little support. With every call for compromise, some northern or southern speaker would inflame passions.

SOURCE C

John C Calhoun, in a speech to the Senate, March 1850

How can the Union be saved? There is but one way by which it can be, and that is by adopting such measures as will satisfy the states belonging to the southern section, that they can remain in the Union consistently with their honour and their safety. But can this be done? Yes, easily; not by the weaker party, for it can of itself do nothing – not even protect itself – but by the stronger. The North has only to will it to accomplish it – to do justice by conceding to the South an equal right in the acquired territory, and to do her duty by causing the stipulations relative to fugitive slaves to be faithfully fulfilled – to cease the agitation of the slave question.

What is the message of Source C? What additional knowledge could you use to decide whether the view of Calhoun was justified?

The end of the crisis

In June 1850 delegates from nine slave states met at Nashville. The fact that six slave states did not send delegates was disconcerting to those '**fire-eaters**' who supported secession. Moreover, the convention displayed little enthusiasm for secession. The Nashville convention, therefore, had little impact.

KEY TERM

Fire-eaters People who look for quarrels.

Taylor's death in July had a greater impact. Vice-President Millard Fillmore, a Northerner who was sympathetic to the South, now became President. Unlike Taylor, he supported Clay's bill. But he could not prevent it being defeated. **Senator Douglas** now demonstrated his political skill. Instead of reintroducing Clay's bill in its entirety, he submitted each of its parts separately. This strategy was successful. Southerners and northerners voted for those proposals they liked. Moderates, like Douglas himself, swung the balance. By September 1850, all the parts (see page 18) had passed through Congress. Douglas and other leaders hailed the compromise as a settlement of the issues that threatened to divide the nation.

KEY FIGURE

Stephen Douglas (1813–61) Douglas, Democrat Senator for Illinois from 1847, played a major role in American politics throughout the 1850s. Known as the 'Little Giant', he stood against Abraham Lincoln in 1858 and 1860.

Many northerners believed that Congress had surrendered to southern threats. However, the North probably gained more than the South from the compromise. The entry of California into the Union gave the free states a majority in the Senate. The resolutions on New Mexico and Utah were hollow victories for the South. The odds were that both areas would enter the Union as free states at some time in the future. The Fugitive Slave Act was the North's only major concession.

ACTIVITY

What were the reasons why the 1850 Compromise was perceived as necessary? Which do you think was the most important reason?

Summary

Slavery was the crucial issue dividing northerners from southerners in the early nineteenth century. By 1850 northerners outnumbered southerners by a ratio of more than three to two. This meant that free states had more seats in the House of Representatives. Accordingly, southerners were determined to maintain a position of equality in the Senate. Westward expansion thus became a crucial issue because each new state sent two Senators to Congress. Southerners feared that slavery would be declared illegal by a northern-dominated Congress. Although relatively few northerners were abolitionists, most were determined to prevent slavery's expansion. A series of sectional confrontations arose between 1820 and 1850 but politicians eventually agreed to compromises, for example, the 1820 Missouri Compromise and the 1850 Compromise.

Stephen Douglas

SUMMARY DIAGRAM

How was the issue of slavery addressed between 1820 and 1850?

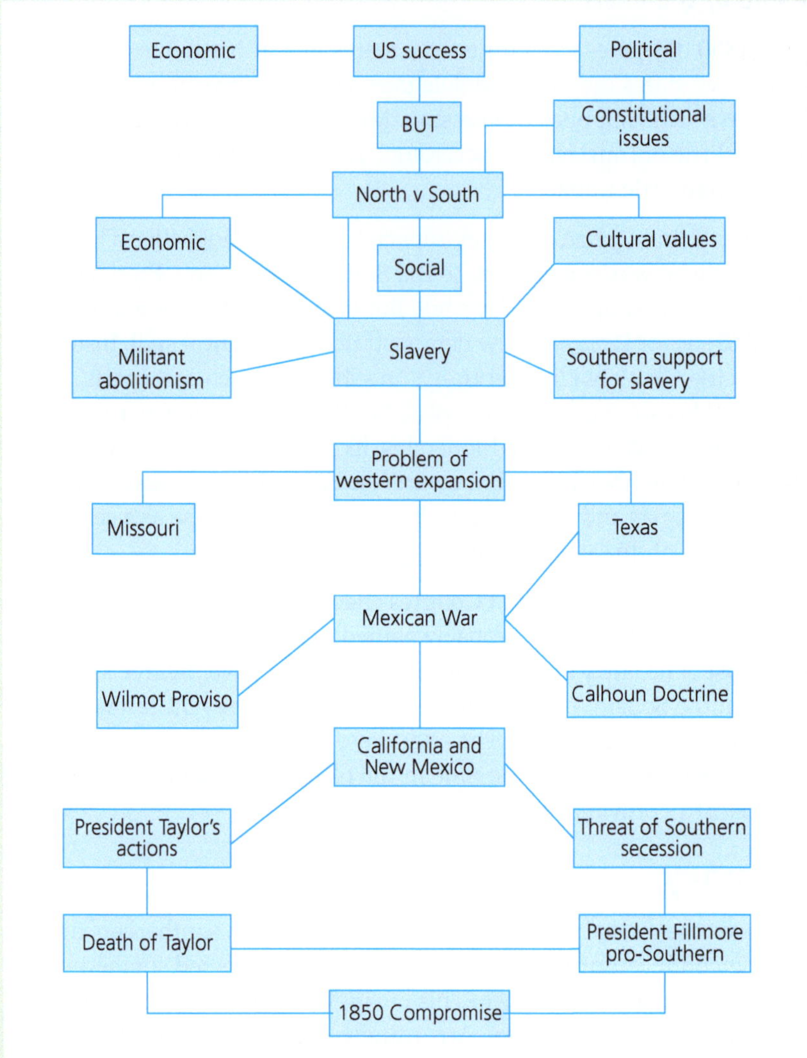

2 How and why did sectional divisions widen between 1850 and 1856?

Most Americans seemed prepared to accept the 1850 Compromise. Across the USA, there were mass meetings to celebrate its passage. In the southern state elections of 1851–52, unionist candidates defeated secessionists. Nevertheless, northern–southern tensions continued to simmer and problems were to arise from the implementation of the 1850 Compromise, not least the application of the Fugitive Slave Act.

Problems arising from the implementation of the 1850 Compromise and the application of the Fugitive Slave Act

Some northerners accepted the Fugitive Slave Act as the price the North had to pay to save the Union. However, it contained a number of features that were outrageous to abolitionists. For example, it authorized federal marshals to raise **posses** to pursue fugitives on northern soil. Those who refused to join risked a $1000 fine. In addition, the law targeted not only enslaved people who had recently run away but also those who had fled the South decades earlier. Efforts to catch and return fugitive enslaved people inflamed feelings. During the 1850s, nine northern states passed new personal liberty laws (see page 18). By such provisions as forbidding the use of state jails to imprison alleged fugitives, the liberty laws made it difficult to enforce federal law. Such actions caused huge resentment in the South.

KEY TERM

Posse A group of men called out by a sheriff or marshal to aid in enforcing the law.

The impact of *Uncle Tom's Cabin*

In 1851 Harriet Beecher Stowe began publishing *Uncle Tom's Cabin*, in weekly instalments in an anti-slavery newspaper. The complete novel, which presented a fierce attack on slavery, sold 300,000 copies when it was published in 1852 and a further two million copies in America over the next ten years. Even those northerners who did not read it were familiar with its theme because it was turned into songs and plays. Stowe, who had little first-hand knowledge of slavery, drew heavily on abolitionist literature when describing its brutalities. The book undoubtedly helped arouse northern sympathy for enslaved people.

The 1852 presidential election

The Democrats were confident of victory in 1852. They expected the large numbers of Irish and German immigrants to support them. The Democrats chose Franklin Pierce as their presidential candidate. Although he was a northerner, he was sympathetic to the South. The Democrats campaigned on a platform supporting the 1850 Compromise and popular sovereignty.

The Whig Party was divided North against South. While most northerners supported Mexican War hero General Winfield Scott (a southerner), most southern Whigs hoped to retain Millard Fillmore (a northerner). Scott was finally nominated on the 53rd ballot. Although they managed to agree on a leader, the Whigs could not agree on policies. Thus their platform said virtually nothing. The election was a triumph for Pierce who won 1,601,274 votes and carried 27 states (254 electoral college votes). Scott won 1,386,580 votes but carried only 4 states (42 electoral college votes). John Hale, the Free Soil Party (see page 17) candidate, won 156,000 votes, carrying not a single state.

President Pierce (1853–57)

President Pierce seemed to be in a strong position in 1853 despite the problems arising from the implementation of the 1850 Compromise.

- The Democrats had large majorities in both houses of Congress.
- The economy continued to boom.
- The Whig Party, seriously divided, was unable to mount much of a challenge and two of its best known leaders, Webster and Clay, died in 1852.

Pierce intended to maintain the unity of his party by supporting expansionist policies. Southerners hoped that US expansion into Central America and/or Cuba would lead to the expansion of slavery.

The Gadsden Purchase

In 1853 Pierce gave James Gadsden, a diplomat and railway entrepreneur, the authority to negotiate the purchase of 250,000 square miles (650,000 km^2) of Mexican territory. Gadsden eventually agreed to purchase 54,000 square miles (140,000 km^2). This proved controversial. Southerners supported the acquisition of this territory, not because of its slavery potential, but because it would assist in the building of a southern railroad to the Pacific. Gadsden's treaty gained Senate approval only after a northern amendment slashed 9000 square miles (23,000 km^2) from the proposed purchase.

Cuba

Pierce was keen to acquire Cuba, still ruled by Spain. Initially he supported a major southern military expedition to the island. However, northerners viewed this suggestion as another example of southern efforts to expand slavery. Alarmed by Northern opposition, Pierce abandoned his support for the expedition.

Still hoping to obtain Cuba, Pierce authorized Pierre Soule, the US minister in Spain, to offer up to $130 million for the island. Events, however, soon slipped out of Pierce's control. In October 1854 the US ministers to Britain, France and Spain met in Belgium and issued the Ostend Manifesto. This stated that if Spain refused to sell the island, the USA would be justified in taking it. Details of the Ostend Manifesto were leaked and immediately denounced by northerners. Pierce said that he did not support the Manifesto, and Soule resigned. The unsuccessful expansionist efforts angered northerners who believed that the South aspired to establish a Latin American slave empire.

The problem of Kansas–Nebraska

Nebraska, part of the Louisiana Purchase, was still unsettled in the early 1850s. Until Congress organized the area into a territory, land could not be surveyed and put up for sale. While northerners were keen to see Nebraska developed, southerners were less enthusiastic. Nebraska lay north of latitude 36°30′ and, by the terms of the Missouri Compromise, new states in the area would enter the Union as free states.

Douglas' motives

In January 1854 Senator Douglas introduced the Kansas–Nebraska bill into Congress. Douglas, a man of energy and (presidential) ambition, had pushed – unsuccessfully – for Nebraska to become a territory since 1844. In order to get a Nebraska bill enacted he knew he needed the support of some southern senators. A number, including Senator Atchison of Missouri, agreed to support Douglas if his bill:

- specifically repealed the Missouri Compromise
- divided the Nebraska territory into two: Kansas in the south and Nebraska in the north. There was little chance of slavery taking hold in Nebraska: the climate was too cold for plantation agriculture. But it was possible that it might spread to Kansas.

Douglas, a supporter of popular sovereignty, accepted the southern demands. He was confident that the people of Kansas and Nebraska would not vote for slavery. He believed that the Kansas–Nebraska measure would enhance his reputation nationally and also in Illinois, where many people (not least himself) stood to benefit financially from a trans-continental railway running west from Chicago.

A 'hell of a storm'

Douglas's bill created, in his own words, a 'hell of a storm'. It was proof to many northerners that the **Slave Power conspiracy** was still at work. The ferocity of northern criticisms of Douglas' measure led to a southern counter-attack. Passage of the bill suddenly became a symbol of southern honour. The result was a great Congressional struggle. Northern Democrats and Whigs joined forces in opposing the measure: Southern Whigs and Democrats united in supporting it. After months of bitter debate, the bill passed both houses of Congress, becoming law in May 1854. While 90 per cent of southerners voted for it, 64 per cent of northerners voted against it. By failing to predict the extent of northern outrage, Douglas had weakened his party, damaged his own presidential ambitions and helped to revive North–South rivalry.

KEY TERMS

Slave Power conspiracy A northern notion that southerners were plotting to expand slavery.

Second party system The period from the mid-1830s to the mid-1850s when the Democrats and Whigs were the two main parties.

Changes in the party-political system: the decline of the Whigs and the rise of the Republican Party

From the 1830s to the early 1850s the Democrats and Whigs drew upon national, not sectional, support. As long as voters placed loyalty to party ahead of sectional loyalty neither North nor South could easily be united one against the other. But in the early 1850s the **second party system** collapsed.

The 1854 mid-term elections

In the 1854 mid-term elections, the Democrats, apparently blamed for sponsoring the Kansas–Nebraska Act, lost all but 23 of their (previously 91) free state seats in Congress. Before 1854 the Whigs would have benefited. By 1854, however, the Whig Party was no longer a major force in many free states. The Whig collapse had little to do with the Kansas–Nebraska Act. It had far more to do with another issue – immigration.

Catholic immigrants

Between 1845 and 1854 some three million immigrants entered the USA. Over one million of these were Irish Catholics. German Catholics also made up a considerable number of the immigrants. Fear of a plot by the Catholic Church to subvert the USA was deep-rooted among native-born Americans, most of whom were strongly Protestant. Many were horrified by the growth of Catholicism: between 1850 and 1854 the number of Catholic bishops, priests and churches almost doubled. Native-born Americans resented the growing political power of Catholic voters, claiming that the Irish voted as their political bosses, or their priests, told them. This was seen as a threat to democracy. Mass immigration also had serious social and economic consequences. Irish immigrants provided a source of cheap labour, pulling down wage levels. Native-born Americans also associated them with increased crime and welfare costs.

KEY TERM

Nativism Suspicion of immigrants.

Given that most Irish and German people voted Democrat, that party was unlikely to support anti-immigrant measures. The Whigs also failed to respond to **nativist** concerns. Indeed, in the 1852 election some Whig leaders made efforts to win the immigrant vote. Frustrated northerners began to look to new parties to represent their views.

The Know Nothings

As concern about immigration and Catholicism grew, the Know Nothing movement increased in strength. Know Nothings pledged to vote for no one except native-born Protestants. When asked questions, they were supposed to have replied, 'I know nothing', thereby giving the movement its name. The Know Nothing order (movement) first entered politics by throwing its support behind suitable candidates from the existing parties. It had so much success that it soon became a political party in its own right. Most Know Nothings wanted checks on immigration and a 21-year probationary period before immigrants could become full American citizens. But northerners joined the movement for a variety of other reasons.

- Most supported its anti-Catholic stance.
- Some approved of the fact that it promised to return power to the people.
- The unpopularity of the Kansas–Nebraska Act, associated with the Democrats, helped the Know Nothings.

So many Whigs joined the Know Nothing order that leading Democrats initially thought it was an arm of the Whig Party. They soon discovered that their own supporters were also streaming into the movement. In 1854–55 it won control of several northern states. It also won large-scale support, mainly from ex-Whigs, in the South. By 1855 the order called itself the American Party.

The Republican Party

Northerners were not just concerned with anti-immigrant issues. The Kansas–Nebraska Act awakened the threat of the Slave Power and many northerners were keen to give support to parties opposed to slavery's expansion. In 1854 several anti-slavery coalitions were formed under various names. The Republican name finally caught on.

By 1854–55 it was not clear whether the Know Nothings or Republicans would replace the Whigs as the Democrats' main rival in the North. In most free states the two parties were not necessarily in competition; indeed they often tried to avoid a contest in order to defeat the Democrats. Many northerners hated both Catholicism and the Slave Power. Given the Democrat reverses in the North in 1854, it was clear that there would be an anti-Democrat majority in the 1855–56 Congress. Whether the anti-Democrat Congressmen were more concerned with limiting immigration or preventing the expansion of slavery remained to be seen. At this stage, many Republicans were Know Nothings and vice versa. For those 'pure' Republicans who were opposed to nativism, the 1854 elections were a major setback. Indeed, most political observers expected the Know Nothings to be the main opponents of the Democrats in 1856. The Republican Party could never be more than a northern party. In contrast, the Know Nothings drew support from both North and South.

The issue of Kansas 1854–56

After 1854 colonists began to move into Kansas. Their main concern was land and water rights. However, for politicians far more was at stake. Northerners thought that if slavery expanded into Kansas it might expand anywhere. Southerners feared that a free Kansas would be another nail in the slavery coffin. Senator Seward of New York declared: 'We will engage in competition for the virgin soil of Kansas and God give the victory to the side which is stronger in numbers as it is in right'. Senator Atchison of Missouri took up the challenge. 'We are playing for a mighty stake; if we win we carry slavery to the Pacific Ocean; if we fail, we lose Missouri, Arkansas and Texas and all the territories; the game must be played boldly.' Northerners and southerners tried to influence events in Kansas.

- The Massachusetts Emigrant Aid Company sponsored over 1500 northerners to settle in Kansas in 1854–55.
- Atchison formed the Platte County Defensive Association which was pledged to ensure that Kansas became a slave state.

ACTIVITY

Construct a spider diagram to show the impact of the 1854 Kansas–Nebraska Act in the period 1854–56.

Elections in Kansas

In March 1855 Kansas elected its first territorial legislature. Hundreds of pro-slavery Missourians crossed into Kansas to vote and then returned home. This ensured that the legislature which met at Lecompton was dominated by pro-slavers. It proceeded to pass a series of pro-slavery laws. 'Free-state' or 'free-soil' colonists in Kansas denied the validity of the pro-slavery legislature and set up their own government at Topeka. The free-staters were divided, especially between 'moderates' and 'fanatics'. While the 'fanatics' held abolitionist views, the 'moderates' were not dissimilar to the pro-slavers. Most were openly racist: one of the main reasons they opposed slavery was that it would result in an influx of black people. The Topeka government, dominated by moderates, banned black people, enslaved or free, from Kansas.

'Bleeding Kansas'

KEY FIGURE

John Brown (1800–59), a northern businessman, committed himself to the abolitionist cause in the 1830s. He was prepared to die for that cause and did so: he was executed after leading the Raid on Harper's Ferry in 1859.

In May 1856 a pro-slavery posse, trying to arrest free-state leaders, 'sacked' and burned some buildings in Lawrence, a free-state centre. This event, blown up out of all proportion by northern journalists, sparked off more serious violence. At Pottawatomie Creek, **John Brown**, a fervent abolitionist, and several of his sons murdered five pro-slavery colonists. Northern newspapers, suppressing the facts, claimed that Brown had acted in self-defence. Overnight, he became a northern hero. In Kansas, his actions led to a series of tit-for-tat killings. The northern press again exaggerated the situation, describing it as 'civil war'. With events seemingly drifting out of control, Pierce appointed a new governor, John Geary, who managed to patch up a truce between the warring factions. Nevertheless, events in Kansas, and the distorted reporting of them, helped to boost Republican fortunes. 'Bleeding Kansas' became a rallying cry for northerners opposed to what they perceived to be the Slave Power at work.

American Party problems

The American Party (the Know Nothings' party) had success in both northern and southern states in 1855. Ironically, success in the South was to be a major reason for the American Party's undoing. The Know Nothings had won massive northern support in 1854–55 because they had been able to exploit anti-slavery and nativist issues. However, the American Party, to retain southern support, had to drop its anti-Kansas–Nebraska position. By so doing, it lost northern support. Other factors also damaged the Party.

- The decline of immigration in the mid-1850s resulted in a decline of nativism.
- The failure of legislatures dominated by Know Nothings to make good their campaign promises enabled critics to claim that the movement did nothing.

Events in Congress, which met in December 1855, also weakened the American Party. Nativists split North and South. After a great struggle, Nathanial Banks, an ex-Know Nothing who was now a Republican, eventually became speaker of the House. The speakership contest helped to weld the Republicans into a more coherent party.

ACTIVITY

In pairs, list five reasons for the rise of the Republican Party in the period 1852–56. Then choose the reason you think is the most important and debate your choice with a partner.

Republican policies

The Republican Party included abolitionists and those who had previously been Whigs, Democrats or Know Nothings. Unsurprisingly historians have different opinions about what the Party stood for and why northerners supported it. It is easier to say what Republicans were against than what they were for. Obviously they were against the Democrat Party. They were also opposed to the Slave Power which was seen as conspiring against northern interests. However, Republican leaders were not consistent in defining who was conspiring. Was it all or just some planters? All slaveholders or all southerners? Republicans also had different views about the nature of the conspiracy. Many were convinced it sought to re-establish slavery in the North. Such fears were grossly exaggerated. Nevertheless, the idea of a Slave Power conspiracy was an **article of faith** for virtually all Republicans. However, while almost all Republicans were opposed to slavery expansion, few supported immediate abolition or believed in equality for black people. Many viewed with horror the prospect of thousands of former enslaved people, now freed, pouring northwards.

KEY TERM

Article of faith A main belief.

'Bleeding Sumner'

An event in Congress in May 1856 possibly helped Republican fortunes more than the situation in Kansas. Following a speech in which Senator Sumner attacked southern Senator Butler, Congressman Preston Brooks entered the Senate, found Sumner at his desk and proceeded to beat him, shattering his cane in the process. 'Bleeding Sumner' outraged northerners as much as 'bleeding Kansas'. Here was more evidence of the Slave Power at work, using brute force to silence free speech. While Sumner became a northern martyr, Brooks became a southern hero. Resigning from Congress, Brooks stood for re-election and won easily. Southerners sent him new canes to replace the one he had broken.

The 1856 presidential election

The American Party held its national convention in February 1856. After a call to repeal the Kansas–Nebraska Act was defeated, many northern delegates left the organization. The American Party went on to select ex-President Fillmore as its presidential candidate. Fillmore, more an old-fashioned Whig than a Know Nothing, had pro-southern sympathies. He thus had limited appeal in the North.

SOURCE D

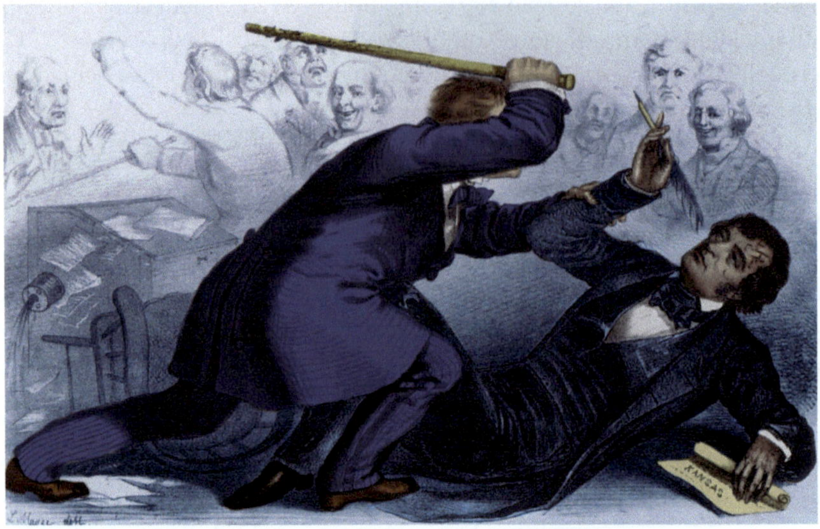

A northern cartoon condemning Preston Brooks for his caning of Sumner. The cartoon shows southern Senators enjoying the sight and preventing the intervention of Sumner's friends.

What do you think was the cartoonist's purpose in creating the cartoon in Source D?

Republican leaders decided that 43-year old John C Frémont would be the Party's best presidential candidate. Born in the South, Frémont had had a colourful career as a western colonist. Many saw him (wrongly) as the 'Conqueror of California' in 1846 (see page 13). An ex-Know Nothing, he had been a (Democrat) Senator for California for just 17 days. He was thus a strange choice for Republican candidate. But the romance surrounding Frémont's career was likely to make him popular. The Republican platform was radical. Congress, it declared, had 'both the right and the imperative duty … to prohibit in the Territories those twin relics of barbarism – **Polygamy** and Slavery'. (The polygamy reference was a popular attack on Mormon practices in Utah.) The Republican slogan was clear: 'Free Soil, Free Labour, Free Men, Frémont'.

KEY TERM

Polygamy The practice of having more than one wife.

KEY FIGURE

James Buchanan (1791–1868) Born in Pennsylvania, Buchanan was a successful lawyer who soon turned to politics. A Democrat, he served successively as a state legislator, Congressman, minister to Russia, US Senator, secretary of state under President Polk and ambassador to Britain. He was elected president in 1856.

The Democrats nominated **James Buchanan**. He had spent four decades in public service. A northerner, he was nevertheless acceptable to the South. Given that he came from Pennsylvania, regarded as a crucial state to win, he was probably the Democrats' strongest candidate. The Democrat platform endorsed popular sovereignty. In the North, the contest was essentially between Buchanan and Frémont. In the South, it was between Buchanan and Fillmore. For the first time since 1849–50 there was widespread fear for the Union's safety. If Frémont won, it was conceivable that many southern states would secede.

In November Fillmore obtained 21.6 per cent of the popular vote and 8 electoral college votes. Frémont won 33.1 per cent of the total vote: 45 per cent of the northern vote, but virtually no southern votes. He won 114 electoral votes. Buchanan, with 45.3 per cent of the popular vote and 174 electoral votes, became president. He won all but one southern state plus Pennsylvania, New Jersey,

Indiana, Illinois and California. The Democrats had cause for celebration. They had seen off the Fillmore challenge in the South and retained their traditional supporters in the North. The Republicans, however, also had cause for optimism. If the Republican Party had carried Pennsylvania and Illinois, Frémont would have become president. Republican leaders, confident that they could win over the remaining anti-Democrat groups in the North, were soon predicting victory in 1860. Nevertheless, there was no guarantee that northerners would continue to vote Republican. The Party might collapse as quickly as it had risen.

ACTIVITY

Draw up a table with two columns. In the first column, list the reasons why the Republican Party did so well in the 1856 presidential election. In the second column, list the reasons why the Republican Party did not win the 1856 presidential election.

The significance of states' rights

'States' rights' refers to the struggle between the federal government and individual states over political power. By the 1850s most southerners supported the principle of states' rights – the view that most issues should be decided at state rather than federal level. They could claim that the Tenth Amendment to the Constitution stated that any rights not explicitly granted to the federal government in the Constitution should be given to the states. Some southerners accepted Calhoun's view that individual states had the right to nullify any federal law with which they disagreed (see page 16).

In reality, however, there was only one state right that really concerned southerners: this was the right to maintain the institution of slavery. By the 1850s most southerners believed that the North, with its much larger population, was set on the abolition of slavery. The rise of the Republican Party seemed evidence of northerners' intent. Southerners feared that a Republican-dominated federal government would infringe their state's rights, particularly with regard to slavery.

In some respects, southerners were correct in their assumptions. Some radical abolitionists in the North were determined to abolish slavery, even if this meant abolishing the Constitution at the same time. But radical abolitionists were a small minority in the North. The Republican Party was committed to stopping the expansion of slavery: it was not committed to abolishing slavery or tearing up the Constitution.

The Constitution clearly allowed individual states the right to maintain slavery. It was, of course, possible to amend the Constitution. To do so, both houses of Congress have to support the proposed amendment with a two-thirds majority. Three-quarters of the individual states then have to back the proposed amendment. In short, it is difficult to see how a proposal to add a constitutional amendment abolishing slavery could have been passed. There were 15 slave states. If they continued to support slavery, 45 free states would have been required to change the Constitution – that is, 60 states in total. Even today, there are only 50 states in the USA.

Slavery in the southern states was thus under no immediate threat. But this was not how southerners saw things. Many viewed the prospect of Republican success in 1860 with alarm. If that were to happen, there were some southerners who believed that individual states had the right to secede from the Union.

Summary

Slavery, especially the issue of its expansion, continued to divide southerners from northerners in the period 1850 to 1856. The most serious crisis came in the territories of Kansas and Nebraska. The Democrat Party – and most southerners – were committed to popular sovereignty – the notion that people in territories should be able to decide whether their new states were slave or free. Pro-slavery supporters and free-staters fought for control of Kansas. Convinced that a Slave Power conspiracy was at work, many northerners came to support the Republican Party which was pledged to stop slavery expanding. The 1856 presidential election was won by the Democrat candidate James Buchanan. His victory prevented a crisis that would undoubtedly have occurred if the Republican Frémont had been elected.

SUMMARY DIAGRAM

How and why did sectional divisions widen between 1850 and 1856?

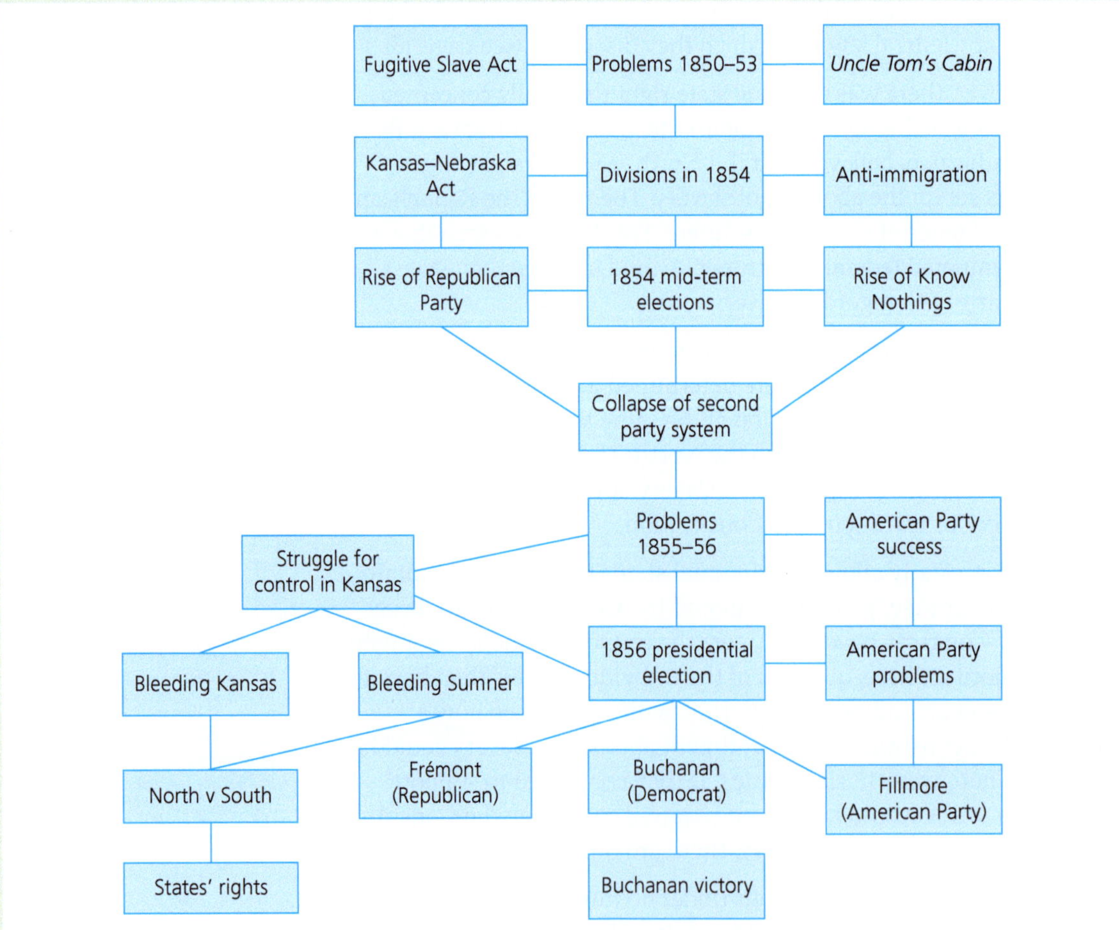

3 Why did the Republicans win the 1860 presidential election?

At the start of 1857 many Americans were optimistic about the future. Buchanan's victory had prevented a major schism (division). If the problem of Kansas could be solved, then sectional tension was likely to ease. No other territory was likely to be so contentious.

The emerging notion of 'slave power'

Buchanan's position seemed strong in 1857. Both houses of Congress and the Supreme Court were dominated by Democrats. However, by the end of 1857, the historian Kenneth Stampp (1990) claimed that North and South had reached 'the political point of no return'. According to Stampp, the events of 1857 prevented a peaceful resolution to sectional strife. Buchanan, in Stampp's view, must shoulder much of the blame, pursuing policies which pushed most northerners into the Republican camp. Ideologically attached to the South and aware that he needed southern support to ensure a majority in Congress, Buchanan chose a pro-southern cabinet. From the start, many northerners feared that he was a tool of the Slave Power. His actions soon confirmed this fear.

The Dred Scott case

Dred Scott was an enslaved man who had accompanied his master (an army surgeon) first to Illinois, then to the Wisconsin territory, before returning to Missouri. In the 1840s, with the help of anti-slavery lawyers, Scott went before the Missouri courts claiming he was free on the grounds that he had resided in a free state and in a free territory. The Scott case, long and drawn out, eventually reached the Supreme Court. By March 1857, the court – composed of five southerners and four northerners – was ready to pass judgement.

Buchanan referred to the case in his **inaugural address**. Claiming (not quite truthfully) that he knew nothing of the Court's decision, he said he was ready to 'cheerfully submit' to its verdict and urged all good citizens to do likewise. Two days later the Supreme Court's decision was made public. Led by pro-southern Chief Justice Roger Taney, the Court decided that:

- Scott could not sue for his freedom. Black Americans, whether slave or free, did not have the same rights as white citizens.
- Scott's stay in Illinois did not make him free.
- Scott's stay in Wisconsin made no difference. The 1820 Missouri Compromise ban on slavery in territories north of 36°30′ was illegal. All US citizens had the right to take their 'property' into the territories.

KEY TERM

Inaugural address A president's speech, made immediately after he has been sworn in as president.

Northern reaction

To northerners the Dred Scott decision seemed further proof of the Slave Power at work. Republicans claimed that the whispered conversations between Taney and Buchanan on inauguration day proved that the President had been aware of the Court's decision when he asked Americans to accept it. Northern papers launched a fierce onslaught on the Supreme Court and some editors talked of defying the law. However, the judgement was easier to denounce than defy. In part, it simply annulled a law which had already been repealed by the Kansas–Nebraska Act. The Court's decision even had little effect on Scott as thanks to northern sympathisers, he soon purchased his freedom. Nevertheless, the verdict was important. Rather than settling the uncertainty about slavery in the territories, the decision provoked further sectional antagonism. It was seen by some northerners as an attempt to outlaw the Republican Party, which was committed to slavery's exclusion from the territories.

The Panic of 1857

In 1857 US industry was hit by depression, resulting in mass unemployment. Buchanan, believing the government should not involve itself in economic matters, did nothing. He and his party were blamed by northerners for their seeming indifference. Republican economic proposals – internal improvement measures and higher tariffs – were blocked in Congress. The short-lived depression (it was over by 1859) helped the Republicans in the 1858 mid-term elections.

Increasing confrontation within and between the North and South

The Dred Scott case and the 1857 economic depression angered northerners. Many regarded Buchanan as a southern puppet. Events in Kansas in 1857–58 confirmed their fears.

Problems in Kansas

In Kansas, Buchanan faced a situation which offered some hope. Although there were still two governments, the official pro-slave one at Lecompton and the unofficial free state one at Topeka, Governor Geary had restored order in the territory. It was obvious to Geary, and to other observers, that free-staters now had a majority in Kansas. Given his declared commitment to popular sovereignty, all that Buchanan needed to do was ensure that the majority's will prevailed. A fair solution of the Kansas problem would deprive the Republicans of one of their most effective issues.

In March 1857 Buchanan appointed Robert Walker, an experienced southern politician, as governor of Kansas. Walker was committed to fair elections in Kansas. His first task was to convince free-staters to take part in the June election for a convention to draw up a constitution that would set the territory on the road to statehood. Suspecting that any election organized by the pro-slavers would be rigged, free-staters refused to get involved. Pro-slavers thus won all the convention seats.

The pro-slavers' success, while making a mockery of popular sovereignty, raised the expectations of southerners who realized that the creation of a new slave state was now a real possibility. Meanwhile, the election for a new territorial legislature in Kansas was held in October. Walker convinced free-staters that they should participate, assuring them that he would do all he could to see that the election was fairly conducted. Attempts by the pro-slavers to fix the election failed. Walker overturned enough fraudulent results to give the free-staters a majority in the legislature.

The Lecompton constitution

The Lecompton constitutional convention now drafted a pro-slavery constitution. While agreeing to allow a **referendum** on its proposals, it offered voters something of a spurious choice:

- They had to accept the pro-slavery constitution as it was.
- They could accept another constitution which banned the future importation of enslaved people but guaranteed the rights of slaveholders already in Kansas.

KEY TERM

Referendum A vote on a specific issue.

Walker denounced the convention's actions as a 'vile fraud'. But Buchanan supported the Lecompton convention rather than Walker. In December, Walker resigned. That same month Kansas voted on the Lecompton constitution. In fact, most free-staters abstained in protest. The pro-slave returns showed a large majority for the constitution. Buchanan endorsed the actions of the Lecompton convention, claiming that the question of slavery had been 'fairly and explicitly referred to the people'.

Buchanan versus Douglas

By accepting the Lecompton constitution, Buchanan gave Republicans massive political ammunition. More importantly, he enraged northern Democrats, like Douglas, who were committed to popular sovereignty. In an impassioned speech in the Senate, Douglas attacked both Buchanan and the Lecompton constitution. Southern Democrats immediately denounced Douglas. The Democrat Party, like almost every other American institution, was now split on North/South lines. A major Congressional contest followed with Douglas siding with the Republicans. Using all the powers of patronage at his disposal, Buchanan tried to ensure that northern Democrats voted for the Lecompton constitution. The Senate passed the measure but enough northern Democrats in the House of Representatives opposed the president, ensuring that the Lecompton constitution was defeated. Buchanan accepted that Kansas should vote again on the issue. The vote in August 1858 resulted in a free-state victory: 11,300 voted against the Lecompton constitution: only 1788 voted for it. Kansas now set about drawing up a new constitution. It finally joined the Union in 1861 as a free state.

ACTIVITY

Using information in this chapter, find information to support the view that events in Kansas determined the outcome of the 1860 presidential election.

The 1858 Congressional elections

The 1858 mid-term elections came at a bad time for northern Democrats, with the party split between those who supported Buchanan and those who supported Douglas. Given that Douglas had to stand for re-election, national attention focused on the Illinois campaign. The fourth largest state, its voters might determine the outcome of the 1860 presidential election. The Republicans chose Abraham Lincoln to run against Douglas.

Abraham Lincoln

Born in a log cabin, Lincoln had little formal schooling. A loyal Whig, he was elected to the House of Representatives in 1846. Defeated in 1848, he returned to Illinois, and resumed his successful law practice. The Kansas–Nebraska Act brought him back into politics. Previously, his main concern had been economic matters. Now his speeches became more anti-Slave Power. Although he had not much of a national reputation in 1858, he was well known in Illinois. Douglas commented: 'He is the strong man of the party – full of wit, facts, dates – and the best stump speaker with his droll ways and dry jokes, in the West. He is as honest as he is shrewd.'

Abraham Lincoln

1809	Born in Kentucky
1831	Moved to Illinois. Experienced a host of jobs: store clerk, postmaster and surveyor
1832	Volunteered to fight in the Black Hawk War
1834	Elected as a Whig state legislator
1837	Moved to Springfield, Illinois' state capital, and became a lawyer
1842	Married Mary Todd, daughter of a Kentucky slaveholder
1846	Elected to the House of Representatives
1856	Joined the Republican Party
1858	Challenged Douglas for election as Senator for Illinois
1860	Elected president
1862	Issued the Emancipation Proclamation (see page 86)
1864	Re-elected president
1865	Assassinated

Lincoln was a complex character. On the one hand he was a calculating politician, often non-committal and seemingly devious. On the other, he was a humane, witty man who never seemed to worry much about his own bruised ego. Historians continue to debate whether he was moderate, radical or conservative. He was certainly cautious, preferring to think over problems slowly before reaching a decision. This was true on the slavery issue. He had always been opposed to slavery, believing it to be immoral. But realizing that it was a divisive issue, he had kept quiet on the subject for much of his early political career.

SOURCE E

Part of Lincoln's acceptance speech as Republican candidate in June 1858

A House divided against itself cannot stand. I believe this government cannot endure permanently half slave and half free. I do not expect the Union to be dissolved – I do not expect the house to fall – but I do expect it will cease to be divided. It will become all one thing or all the other. Either the opponents of slavery will arrest the further spread of it, and place it where the public mind shall rest in the belief that it is on the course of ultimate extinction; or its advocates will push it forward till it shall become alike lawful in all the states, old as well as new – North as well as South.

Assess the value of Source E to a historian studying the views of Lincoln and the Republican Party in the late 1850s.

The Lincoln–Douglas debates

Douglas agreed to meet Lincoln for seven open-air debates. These debates, from August to October 1858, drew vast crowds. Both men were gifted speakers. The debates were confined almost exclusively to three topics – race, slavery and slavery expansion. By today's standards, Lincoln and Douglas do not seem far apart. This is perhaps not surprising: both men were moderates as far as their parties were concerned and both were fighting for the middle ground. Both considered black people to be inferior to white. Lincoln declared: 'I am not, nor ever have been in favour of bringing about in any way the social and political equality of the white and black races'. However, the two did differ in one key respect. Douglas never once said in public that slavery was a moral evil. Lincoln may not have believed in racial equality but he did believe that black and white people shared a common humanity: 'If slavery is not wrong', he said, 'then nothing is wrong'.

SOURCE F

From Senator Douglas' opening speech in his first debate with Lincoln, 21 August 1858

Mr Lincoln here says that our government cannot endure permanently in the same condition in which it was made by its framers. It was made divided into free states and slave states. Mr Lincoln says it has existed for near eighty years thus divided; but he tells you that it cannot endure permanently on the same principle and in the same conditions relatively in which your fathers made it ... Why can't it exist upon the same principles upon which our fathers made it? Our fathers knew when they made this government that in a country as wide and broad as this – with such a variety of climate, of interests, of productions as this – that the people necessarily required different local laws and local institutions in certain localities from those in other localities. Hence they provided that each state should retain its own legislature and its own sovereignty, with the full and complete power to do as it pleased within its own limits in all that was local and not national. One of the reserved rights of the states was that of regulating the relations between master and slave.

Compare the views in Sources E and F with regard to the issue of slavery.

The Illinois result

Lincoln won some 125,000 popular votes to Douglas' 121,000. However, Douglas' supporters kept control of the Illinois legislature which re-elected Douglas as Senator. This was a significant triumph for Douglas, solidifying his leadership of the northern Democrats. However, during the debates with Lincoln, Douglas had said much that angered southerners, not least his stressing of the **Freeport Doctrine**. Although Lincoln had lost, at least he had emerged from the election with his reputation boosted.

KEY TERMS

Freeport Doctrine A view that voters in a territory could exclude slavery by refusing to enact laws that gave legal protection to owning enslaved people.

Arsenal A place where military supplies are stored or made.

State militia All able-bodied men of military age (in most states) could be called up to fight in an emergency.

Generally, the 1858 elections were a disaster for the northern Democrats. The Republicans won control of the House of Representatives, their share of the vote in the crucial states of Pennsylvania, Indiana, Illinois and New Jersey rising from 35 per cent in 1856 to 52 per cent. If the voting pattern was repeated in 1860, the Republicans would win the presidency.

The growing strength of abolitionism

Most southerners regarded the Republican Party as an abolitionist party. Republican success in the mid-term elections in 1858 seemed proof that the abolitionists were growing in power in the North. Other events in 1859 strengthened this fear.

John Brown's raid

John Brown had become famous – or infamous – for his violent acts in Kansas (see page 26). Now in his late fifties, Brown wished to do something decisive for the anti-slavery cause. The fact that he was able to win financial support from hard-headed northern businessmen is testimony to both his forceful personality and the intensity of abolitionist sentiment. In 1859 Brown determined to raid the federal **arsenal** at Harper's Ferry in Virginia, seize weapons, retreat to the Appalachian mountains and spark a slave revolt. On 16 October 1859, Brown and 18 men succeeded in capturing the arsenal and a number of hostages. But rather than escape, Brown remained in Harper's Ferry. Virginia and Maryland **state militia** units and a detachment of troops, led by Colonel Robert E Lee, converged on the town. A 36-hour siege of the fire-engine house in which Brown had taken refuge, followed. On 18 October, Lee ordered the fire-engine house to be stormed. In the ensuing struggle Brown was captured along with six of his men. Ten of his 'army' were killed. Seven other people also died.

The results of Brown's raid

Brown, found guilty of treason, was executed in December 1859. Most southerners were appalled at what had happened. Their worst fears had been realized. An abolitionist had tried to stir up a slave revolt. They suspected that most northerners sympathized with his action. While some northerners did see Brown as a hero, many did not approve of his actions and leading Republicans criticized the raid. Few southerners were reassured. Most saw Republicans and abolitionists (like Brown) as one and the same.

Sectional tension 1859–60

Over the winter of 1859–60 there were rumours of slave insurrection in many southern states. Local vigilante committees were set up and **slave patrols** strengthened. Southern state governments purchased additional weapons and southern militia units drilled rather more than previously. When Congress met in December 1859, both houses divided along sectional lines. Southerners opposed all Republican measures: **free homesteads**, higher tariffs and a Pacific railroad. Northerners blocked all pro-southern proposals. By 1860 northern and southern politicians attacked each other in passionate speeches. Northerners feared a conspiracy by the Slave Power. Southerners feared the growing strength of the '**Black Republicans**'. Far from easing tension, Buchanan's policies had helped to widen the sectional rift. His presidency must thus be regarded as one of the great failures of leadership in US history.

KEY TERMS

Slave patrol Armed men who rode round slave areas, especially at night, to ensure that there was no disorder.

Free homesteads The Republicans hoped to provide 160 acres of land to farmers who settled in the West.

Black Republicans A term used by southerners to describe Republicans who were seen as being sympathetic to enslaved people.

The election campaign of 1860 and the divisions of the Democratic Party

The prospect of a Republican electoral triumph in 1860 filled southerners with outrage. It was not merely that a Republican victory might threaten slavery. More fundamentally, southerners believed that the North was treating the South as its inferior. Submission to the Republicans, declared Mississippi Senator Jefferson Davis, 'would be intolerable to a proud people'. The stakes in the 1860 election, therefore, were alarmingly high.

Democrat Party divisions

In 1858 the Democrat Party had split over the issue of Kansas (see page 33). Many northern Democrats had supported Senator Douglas' stand against President Buchanan. Southern Democrats, who had remained loyal to Buchanan, were highly critical of Douglas. Douglas, determined to run for president in 1860, tried to build bridges to the South in 1859–60. Rationally he was the South's best hope: he was the only Democrat who was likely to carry some free states. But Douglas' stand against the Lecompton constitution (page 33) alienated him from many southerners.

The Democratic convention

Events at the Democrat convention, which met in April 1860 at Charleston, showed that the Party, never mind the country, was a house divided against itself. Although Douglas had the support of most of the delegates, he failed to win the two-thirds majority which Democrat candidates were expected to achieve. After 57 ballots, the Democrat convention agreed to reconvene at Baltimore in June. When some southern delegates who had left the Charleston convention tried to take their seats at Baltimore, the convention, dominated by Douglas' supporters, preferred to take pro-Douglas delegates. This led to a mass southern walk-out. With so many southern delegates gone, Douglas easily won the convention's nomination.

Douglas v Breckinridge

Southern delegates now set up their own convention and nominated current Vice-President John Breckinridge on a platform that called for the federal government to protect slavery in the territories. Although Breckinridge was supported by Cass, Pierce and Buchanan (the last three Democratic presidential candidates who were all northerners), it was clear that the Democrat Party had split along sectional lines between North and South. The split is often seen as ensuring Republican success. However, the fact that Douglas could now campaign in the North without having to try to maintain a united Democrat Party, probably helped his cause.

The Republican convention

The Republican convention met in May at Chicago. Its platform called for:

- higher protective tariffs
- free 160-acre homesteads (plots of land) for western colonists
- a northern trans-continental railway.

While opposed to any extension of slavery, the platform specifically promised that the party had no intention of interfering with slavery where it already existed and it condemned John Brown's raid as 'the gravest of crimes'.

KEY FIGURE

William Seward (1801–72) A New York lawyer, Seward was a major Whig – and then Republican – politician. He was the favourite to win the Republican nomination in 1860, but was defeated by Lincoln. Lincoln then appointed him as secretary of state, a position he held from 1861 to 1869.

Lincoln becomes the Republican candidate

William Seward, Governor of New York, was favourite to win the Republican presidential nomination. But the fact that he had been a major figure in public life for so long meant that he had many enemies. Although there were a number of other potential candidates, Seward's main opponent turned out to be Lincoln. Lincoln had several things in his favour.

- He came from the key state of Illinois.
- He had gained a national reputation as a result of his debates with Douglas in 1858.
- He had made dozens of speeches across the North in 1859–60, making himself known.
- Given that it was difficult to attach an ideological label to him, he was able to appear to be all things to all men.
- His lack of administrative experience helped his reputation for honesty and integrity.
- Lincoln's ambitions were helped by the convention being held at Chicago in his home state of Illinois. His campaign managers were able to pack the convention hall with his supporters.

On the first ballot, Seward won most votes but not enough for victory. As other candidates dropped out, most of their votes went to Lincoln. By the third ballot there was an irresistible momentum in Lincoln's favour. Lincoln's campaign managers almost certainly made secret deals with delegates from Pennsylvania and Indiana, probably to the effect that Lincoln would appoint Simon Cameron (from Pennsylvania) and Caleb Smith (from Indiana) to his cabinet. These deals helped Lincoln win the Republican nomination.

The Constitutional Unionist Party

A new party, the Constitutional Unionists, composed mainly of ex-southern Whigs, nominated John Bell of Tennessee as presidential candidate. Its platform was the shortest in US political history: 'The Constitution of the Country, the Union of the States and the Enforcement of the Laws of the United States'. The Party essentially wanted to maintain the Union and was opposed to extreme views both in North and South. It denounced the Republicans as abolitionist fanatics and Breckinridge's Democrats as wanting to break the Union.

ACTIVITY

Produce a presentation to show the reasons why Abraham Lincoln won the 1860 presidential election.

The campaign

In the North the main fight was between Lincoln and Douglas. Bell and Breckinridge fought it out in the South. Douglas was the only candidate who actively involved himself in the campaign. At some personal risk, he campaigned in the South, warning southerners of the dangerous consequences of secession.

Throughout the campaign, Lincoln remained in Springfield, conferring with Republican chiefs, but saying nothing. Perhaps he should have made some effort to reassure southerners that he was not a major threat to their section. However, he could hardly go out of his way to appease the South: this would have harmed his cause in the North. Moreover, it is difficult to see what he could have said to allay southern fears, given that the very existence of his Party was offensive to southerners.

Although Lincoln, Bell and Breckinridge kept silent this did not prevent their supporters campaigning for them. Republican propaganda concentrated on the Slave Power conspiracy. Southern Democrats stereotyped all northerners as abolitionists. In some states the three anti-Republican parties tried to unite but these efforts were too little and too late. The bitter feuds that existed between the supporters of Breckinridge, Douglas and Bell prevented compromise.

The election results

In November, Bell won 593,000 votes carrying the states of Virginia, Kentucky and Tennessee. Breckinridge, with 843,000 votes won 11 of the 15 slave states. Douglas obtained 1,383,000 votes but won only 2 states, Missouri and New Jersey. Lincoln won 1,866,000 votes – 40 per cent of the total vote. Although he got no votes at all in 10 southern states, he won 54 per cent of the northern vote and, except for New Jersey, carried all the free states. With a majority of 180 to 123 in the electoral college, he became president. Even if the opposition had combined against him in every free state, Lincoln would still have triumphed because he won a majority of votes in virtually every northern state.

Why did northerners vote Republican?

Northerners voted for Lincoln because he seemed to represent their section. A vote for Lincoln was a vote against the Slave Power. While not wishing to get rid of slavery immediately, most northerners had no wish to see it expand. Slavery and the Slave Power, however, were not northerners' only concerns. Nativism had not disappeared with the demise of the Know Nothings. Although the Republicans took an ambiguous stand on nativist issues, anti-Catholic northerners had little option but to vote Republican, if only because the Democrat Party remained the home of Irish and German Catholics. Many northerners approved of Republican economic proposals. The corruption issue was also important. In 1860 a House investigative committee, dominated by Republicans, had found corruption at every level of Buchanan's government. This had tarnished the Democrat Party.

Summary

Relations between northerners and southerners worsened between 1857 and 1860. Southerners feared what they perceived to be the growing strength of abolitionism, represented by the Republican Party. Northerners continued to see the Slave Power conspiracy at work and believed President Buchanan was a puppet of the South. The situation in Kansas and John Brown's Raid served to increase tensions. By 1860 the Democrat Party, like most other organizations, had split: northerners supported Douglas while southerners supported Breckinridge. Abraham Lincoln, who had built up his reputation following his debates with Douglas in the mid-term elections in Illinois in 1858, won the Republican nomination. Winning the support of virtually all the free states, he was elected president in 1860.

SUMMARY DIAGRAM

Why did the Republicans win the 1860 presidential election?

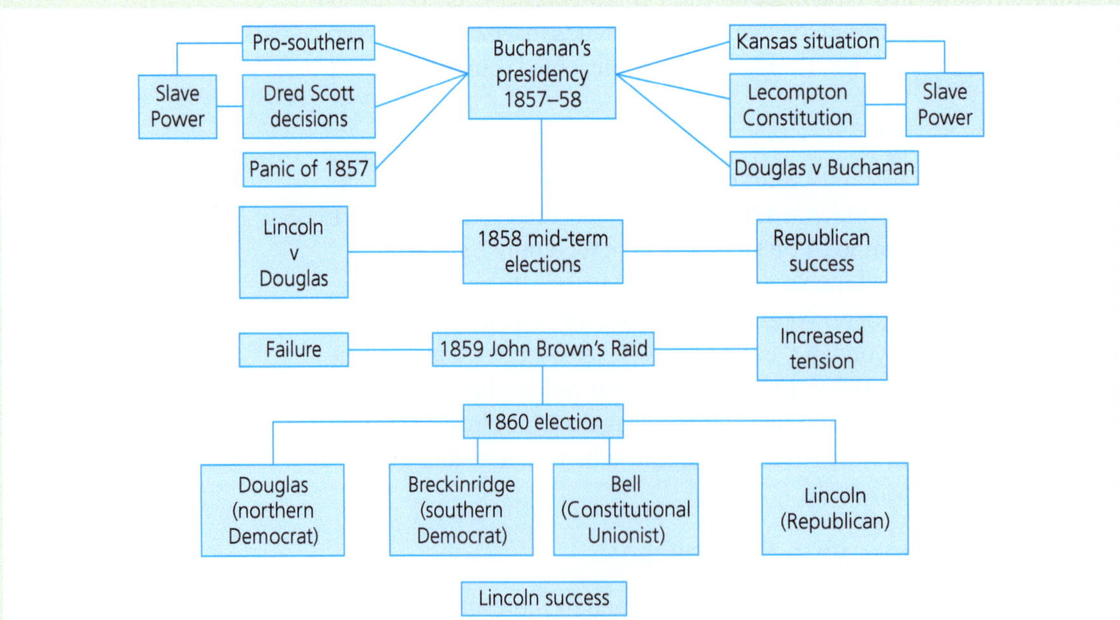

4 Why did the Civil War begin in April 1861?

Few Americans expected war in the days following Lincoln's presidential election triumph. It was evident that most southerners were outraged that a northern anti-slavery party had captured the presidency. But this, in itself, did not necessarily mean war. Yet it soon became evident that the USA faced a terrible crisis – a crisis which ultimately led to Civil War.

The results of the 1860 presidential election

Rationally, there were excellent reasons why the southern states should not secede from the Union.

- Lincoln had promised he would not interfere with slavery in those states where it existed.
- Even if Lincoln harboured secret ambitions to abolish slavery, there was little he could do: his party did not control Congress or the Supreme Court, and presidential power was strictly limited by the Constitution.
- Secession would mean abandoning an enforceable Fugitive Slave Act.
- Secession might lead to civil war, which would threaten slavery far more than Lincoln's election.

Southern fears

Few southerners regarded things so calmly. A northern anti-slavery party, with no pretence of support in the South, had captured the presidency. Lincoln was depicted as an abolitionist who would encourage slave insurrections. He would certainly stop slavery's expansion. Southerners feared they would be encircled by a swelling majority of free states and that, ultimately, slavery would be voted out of existence. Southerners saw themselves as aggrieved innocents in an unequal struggle that unleashed more and more northern aggression on southern rights. Honour demanded that a stand be taken against the latest outrage, the election of Lincoln. Across the South there was a strange mixture of moods – hysteria, despair and elation. Fire-eaters, who had agitated for years for southern independence, capitalized on the mood. Long on the fringe of southern politics, they now found themselves supported by 'mainstream' politicians.

Problems for the secessionists

Southerners were far from united. There was still much Unionist sympathy in the South. Nor was there agreement on the best political strategy to adopt. While some believed that Lincoln's election was grounds enough for secession, others thought it best to wait until he took hostile action against the South. 'Immediate' secessionists knew that if they forced the issue, they might destroy the unity they were seeking to create; but if they waited for unity, they might never act. How to force the issue was another problem. If individual states acted alone, there was the danger that they would receive no support from other states, as South Carolina had found in the 1832 Nullification Crisis. Yet trying to organize a mass move for secession might ensure nothing happened – as in 1849–50.

Secession of the seven Deep South states

Events moved quicker than most people expected.

South Carolina secedes

On 10 November 1860 South Carolina's state legislature called for elections to a special convention to meet on 17 December to decide whether the state would secede. This move created a chain reaction. Alabama, Mississippi, Georgia, Louisiana and Florida all put similar convention procedures underway. In Texas, Governor Sam Houston, who opposed disunion, delayed proceedings but only by a few weeks.

Individual states committed themselves, initially, to individual action. However, it was clear that many southerners were equally committed to joint action. When Congress met in early December, 30 representatives from nine southern states declared: 'We are satisfied the honour, safety and independence of the southern people are to be found only in a Southern Confederacy – a result to be obtained only by separate state secession'. Separate state secession was not long in coming. On 20 December the South Carolina convention voted 169 to 0 for secession. South Carolina sent commissioners to other southern states to propose a meeting, in Montgomery, Alabama on 4 February 1861, to create a new southern government.

Summarise in your own words the message in Source G.

SOURCE G

South Carolina's Declaration of Causes of Secession

And now the state of South Carolina, having resumed her separate and equal place among nations deems it due to herself, to the remaining United States of America, and to the nations of the world, that she should declare the immediate causes which have led to this act ... We affirm that these ends for which this Government was instituted have been defeated, and the Government itself has been destructive of them by the action of the non-slaveholding states. Those states have assumed the right of deciding upon the propriety of our domestic institutions; and have denied the rights of property established in fifteen of the states and recognized by the Constitution; they have denounced as sinful the institution of slavery; they have permitted the open establishment among them of societies whose avowed object is to disturb the peace and eloign [remove] the property of the citizens of other states.

Secession spreads

Over the winter of 1860–61 the election of delegates for conventions that would decide on secession took place in six other lower South states. Voters generally had a choice between 'immediate secessionists' and 'co-operationists'. While the standpoint of the immediate secessionists was clear, the co-operationists represented a wide spectrum of opinion. Some were secessionists but believed the time was not yet right to secede; others were unionists, opposed to secession.

- In Mississippi there were 12,000 votes for candidates whose views remain unknown. 12,218 voted for co-operationist candidates. 16,800 voted for immediate secession. On 9 January 1861 the Mississippi convention supported secession by 85 votes to 15.
- On 10 January a Florida convention voted 62 to 7 for secession but co-operationists won over 35 per cent of the vote.
- Alabama voted to secede by 61 votes to 39 on 11 January. The secessionists won 35,600 votes, co-operationists 28,100.
- Secessionist candidates in Georgia won 44,152 votes, co-operationists 41,632. The Georgia convention voted to secede on 19 January by 208 votes to 89.
- In Louisiana secessionists won 20,214 votes, the co-operationists 18,451. On 26 January the Louisiana convention voted to secede by 113 votes to 17.
- On 1 February a Texas convention voted for secession by 166 votes to 8. Texas then had a referendum to ratify the convention's action. Secession was approved by 44,317 votes to 13,020.

A Slave Power conspiracy?

Republicans, including Lincoln, saw events in the South as a continuation of the Slave Power conspiracy. They claimed that a few planters had conned the electorate into voting for secession, to which most southerners were not really committed. The debate about whether secession was led by a small aristocratic clique or was a genuinely democratic act has continued. Slaveholders certainly dominated politics in many lower South states. Secession sentiment was strongest wherever the percentage of enslaved people was highest. Areas with few enslaved people, by contrast, tended to vote against disunion. According to historian David Potter (1976), 'To a much greater degree than the slaveholders desired, secession had become a slave owners' movement'. Potter believed that a secessionist minority, with a clear purpose and at a time of intense excitement, were able to win mass support.

However, Potter conceded that the secessionists acted democratically and in an 'open and straightforward' manner. By no means all secessionists were great planters. Nor did all great planters support secession. Many non-slaveholders supported secession. While secessionists opposed efforts by co-operationists to submit the secession ordinances to a popular referendum, this would probably have been superfluous. The southern electorate had made its position clear. There was no conspiracy to thwart the will of the majority.

Figure 1.5 The Confederate and Union states

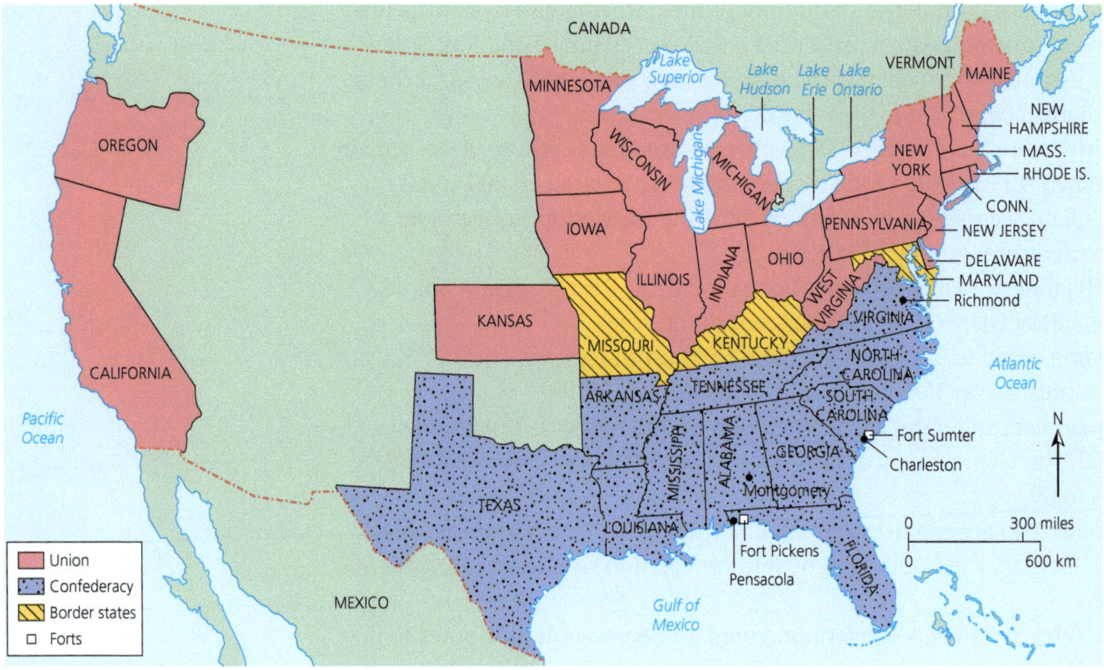

The aims of Lincoln and Davis

Few Americans expected war in early 1861. Most northerners believed that the seceded states were bluffing or thought that an extremist minority had seized power against the wishes of the majority. Either way, the seceded states would soon be back in the Union: the southern bluff would be called or the unionist majority would assert itself. In contrast, most southerners thought that the North would not fight to preserve the Union. **Border state** Americans were confident that a compromise could be arranged which would bring the seceded states back into the Union. These hopes and expectations were not to be realized. Was this the fault of blundering politicians, not least Abraham Lincoln and Jefferson Davis?

KEY TERM

Border states The slave states between the North and the Confederacy – Virginia, Kentucky, Maryland, Delaware, Tennessee, Arkansas and Missouri.

The Confederacy

On 4 February 1861, 50 delegates of the seceded states met at Montgomery to launch the Confederate government. Chosen by the secession conventions:

- most of the delegates were lawyers or planters
- 49 were slave owners and 21 owned at least 20 enslaved people
- 60 per cent were former Democrats: 40 per cent were former Whigs.

All-in-all they comprised a broad cross-section of the South's traditional political leadership. Almost half the delegates were co-operationists. The convention, desperate to win the support of the upper South, tried to project a moderate, united image. On 9 February it set up a committee to draft a permanent constitution. This was approved in March and quickly ratified. Closely modelled on the US Constitution, the main differences were features that more closely protected slavery and guaranteed states' rights.

Jefferson Davis

1808	Born in Kentucky
1825	Graduated from West Point
1835	Resigned from the army after marrying General Zachary Taylor's daughter Sarah against her father's wishes. Sarah died three months after their marriage
1835–45	Planter at Brierfield, Mississippi
1845	Married Varina Howell and elected to Congress
1846	Fought in the Mexican War
1847	Elected to the US Senate
1853–57	Secretary of war
1861	Became Confederate president
1865	Captured by Union troops and imprisoned
1867	Released from prison
1889	Died

Historians differ sharply in their evaluations of Jefferson Davis. Most agree that he was inferior to Abraham Lincoln as a war president. Yet in 1861 he seemed to many a far better choice of leader. He had useful experience in government and military matters, looked every inch the southern aristocrat, over six feet tall, erect in bearing and with the habit of command. But in contrast to Lincoln, he was sensitive to criticism and lacked the safety valve of a keen sense of humour. Nor was he able to bolster the morale of southerners by writing or delivering great speeches. He also suffered from poor health. James Seddon, his secretary of war, declared that Davis 'was the most difficult man to get along with'. However, historians David Donald, Jean Baxter and Michael Holt (2001) are more positive. They argue that no other southern political leader approached Davis in reputation and ability.

Jefferson Davis

On 9 February 1861 the convention elected Senator Jefferson Davis of Mississippi as provisional president. He seemed a good appointment. Educated at West Point, he had served with distinction in the Mexican War and had been a successful secretary of war. Although a champion of southern rights, he had worked hard to maintain national unity. Alexander Stephens, from Georgia, became vice-president. As a leading anti-secessionist, he seemed the logical choice to attract co-operationists to the new government. Davis' cabinet was made up of men from each Confederate state. In his inaugural speech Davis asked only that the Confederacy be left alone. His aim was simply to create a viable new nation.

SOURCE H

Part of Davis' inauguration speech, 18 February 1861

We have entered upon the career of independence, and it must be inflexibly pursued. Through many years of controversy with our late associates of the northern states, we have vainly endeavoured to secure tranquillity and obtain respect for the rights to which we were entitled. As a necessity, not a choice, we have resorted to the remedy of separation, and henceforth our energies must be directed to the conduct of our own affairs and the perpetuity of the Confederacy which we have formed. If a just perception of mutual interest shall permit us peaceably to pursue our separate political career, my most earnest desire will have been fulfilled. But if this be denied to us and the integrity of our territory and jurisdiction be assailed, it will but remain for us with firm resolve to appeal to arms and invoke the blessing of Providence on a just cause.

How convincing is Davis's explanation for secession in Source H?

The upper South

In January 1861 the state legislatures of Arkansas, Virginia, Missouri, Tennessee and North Carolina called elections for conventions to decide on secession. The results of these elections proved that the upper South was far less secessionist-inclined than the lower South. In Virginia only 32 immediate secessionists won seats in a convention with 152 members. Tennessee and North Carolina had referendums which opposed conventions being held. Arkansas voted for a convention but the delegates voted to reject secession. Secessionists made no headway in Maryland, Delaware, Missouri or Kentucky. The upper South states did not vote immediately for secession for a number of reasons.

- These states had a smaller stake in slavery than the lower South. Less than a third of the upper South's population was black.
- Many non-slaveholders questioned how well their interests would be served in a planter-dominated Confederacy.
- The upper South had close ties with the North and thus more reason to fear the economic consequences of secession.

In many respects the results of the upper South's voting came as no surprise: the majority of its voters had supported Bell and Douglas in 1860, not Breckinridge. Nevertheless, if they were forced to choose between the Union and the Confederacy, many in the upper South would put loyalty to their state before their loyalty to the Union.

The search for compromise

Lincoln did not take over until March 1861. In the meantime, Buchanan continued as president. Blaming the Republicans for the crisis, he did little to stem the secessionist tide. His main concern was not to provoke war. He thus took no action as federal institutions across the South – forts, custom houses and post offices – were taken over by the Confederate states. Buchanan has been criticized for not doing more to seek a compromise. But it is difficult to see what he could have done, given that Republicans did not trust him and the lower South was set upon leaving the Union.

Congressional efforts

Congress met in December. Most Congressmen from the Confederate states did not attend and those who did soon left. However, northern Democrats and representatives from the upper South hoped to work out a compromise. The House Committee, with 33 members, proved to be too cumbersome. The Senate Committee of 13, on which Kentucky unionist John Crittenden played a significant role, was more effective. It recommended a package of compromise proposals.

- The main idea was to extend the Missouri Compromise line to the Pacific, giving the South some hope of slavery expansion. Slavery would be recognized south of 36°30′ in all present territories, as well as those 'hereafter acquired'.
- A constitutional amendment would guarantee that there would be no interference with slavery in those states where it already existed.
- Congress would not be allowed to abolish slavery in Washington.

Republicans, whose strength in Congress had grown significantly with the withdrawal of southern delegates, rejected the proposals, which seemed to be more like a surrender than a compromise.

The Virginia Peace Convention

In February 1861 a Peace Convention met in Washington, at the request of Virginia, to see if it could find measures that would bring the seceded states back into the Union. It was attended by 133 delegates, including some of the most famous names in US politics. After three weeks, the Convention supported proposals similar to those of Crittenden. These proposals were ignored by Congress.

Lincoln's position

Up to 1860 slavery had been the main issue dividing North from South. That had now been replaced by secession. While there were some northerners who thought that the 'erring' Confederate states should be allowed to 'go in peace', most were unwilling to accept the dismemberment of the USA or allow the great experiment in self-government to collapse. 'The doctrine of secession is anarchy', declared a Cincinnati newspaper. 'If the minority have the right to break up the Government at pleasure, because they have not had their way, there is an end of all government.' Few Republicans, however, demanded the swift despatch of troops to suppress the 'rebellion'. There was an appreciation that precipitous action might have a disastrous impact on the upper South. The best bet seemed to be to avoid provocation, hoping that the lower South would see sense and return to the Union.

Lincoln thought it best to maintain a strict silence until his inauguration. While he was ready to make some concessions to the South, he refused to budge on the territorial question. He believed that he had won the 1860 election on principles fairly stated and was determined not to concede too much. 'If we surrender it is the end of us', he said. Like many Republicans, he exaggerated the strength of union feeling in the South; he thought that secession was a plot by a small group of planters. His hope that inactivity might allow southern unionists a chance to rally and overthrow the extremists was naive. But this probably made little difference. Even with hindsight, it is difficult to see what Lincoln could have said or done before he became president that would have changed matters.

SOURCE I

From a letter sent by Lincoln to Seward, 1 February 1861

I say now ... as I have all the while said, that on the territorial question – that is the question of extending slavery under the national auspices – I am inflexible. I am for no compromise which assists or permits the extension of the institution on soil owned by the nation. And any trick by which the nation is to acquire territory, and then allow some local authority to spread slavery over it, is as obnoxious as any other ... As to fugitive slaves, District of Columbia, slave trade among the slave states and whatever springs of necessity from the fact that the institution is amongst us, I care but little, save that what is done be comely and not altogether outrageous. Nor do I care much about New Mexico, if further extension were hedged against.

How far does Source I explain why there was no compromise in 1861?

Lincoln's inauguration

On 4 March 1861 Lincoln became president. His inaugural speech was conciliatory but firm. He said that he would not interfere with slavery where it already existed. Nor would he take immediate action to reclaim federal property or appoint federal officials in the South. However, he made it clear that, in his view, the Union was unbreakable and that secession was illegal. He thus intended to 'hold, occupy and possess' federal property within the seceded states. He ended with the words below.

SOURCE J

The end of Lincoln's inauguration speech

In your hands, my dis-satisfied fellow countrymen, and not in mine, is the momentous issue of civil war. The government will not assail you. You can have no conflict without being yourselves the aggressors. You have no oath registered in heaven to destroy the government, while I shall have the most solemn one to 'preserve, protect, and defend' it ... We are not enemies, but friends. We must not be enemies. Though passion may have strained, it must not break, our bonds of affection.

How far does Source J show Lincoln's skill as a leader?

Most Republicans liked Lincoln's firm tone. Border state unionists and many northern Democrats approved of his attempts at conciliation. Unfortunately, the speech had no impact whatsoever in the Confederate states.

Fort Sumter and its impact

Over the winter the Confederacy had taken over most of the (virtually unmanned) forts and arsenals in the South. There were two exceptions: Fort Pickens and Fort Sumter. Both forts were on islands. Pickens, off Pensacola, Florida, was out of range of shore batteries and could easily be reinforced by the federal navy. Sumter, in the middle of Charleston harbour, was a more serious problem. Union troops in Sumter, led by Major Robert Anderson, an ex-Kentucky slaveholder, numbered less than 100. By March 1861 Fort Sumter had become the symbol of national sovereignty for both sides. If the Confederacy was to lay claim to the full rights of a sovereign nation it could hardly allow a 'foreign' fort in the middle of one of its main harbours. Lincoln had made it clear in his inaugural speech that he intended to hold on to what remained of federal property in the South. Retention of Sumter was thus a test of his credibility.

Lincoln's position in March 1861

Lincoln had spoken as he did at his inauguration, believing that time was on his side. But within hours of his speech, he learned that the Sumter garrison would run out of food in under six weeks. Lincoln, aware that any attempt to supply Sumter might spark war, sought the advice of his general-in-chief Winfield Scott. Sumter's evacuation, Scott informed Lincoln, was 'almost inevitable': it could not be held without a large fleet and 25,000 soldiers, neither of which the USA possessed. On 15 March Lincoln brought the matter before his cabinet. Most favoured withdrawal. Lincoln put off making an immediate decision. In the meantime he sent trusted observers to Charleston to assess the situation.

In late March, Lincoln called another cabinet meeting to discuss the crisis. By now, the fact-finding mission to Charleston had returned and reported finding no support for the Union whatsoever; the hope that unionist sentiment would prevail was thus gone. Moreover, northern newspapers were now demanding that Sumter be held. Heedful of northern opinion, most of the cabinet favoured re-supplying Sumter.

ACTIVITY

Hold a class debate about what might have been done between November 1860 and April 1861 to prevent Civil War. One group will argue that a compromise solution could and should have been found. The other group will argue that no compromise solution was possible.

Lincoln acts

On 4 April 1861 Lincoln informed Anderson that a relief expedition would soon be coming and that he should try to hold out. Two days later he sent a letter to South Carolina's governor telling him that he intended to re-supply Sumter. A small naval expedition (three ships and some 500 men) left for Charleston on 9 April. It has been claimed that Lincoln deliberately manoeuvred the Confederacy into firing the first shots. More likely, he was simply trying to keep as many options open as possible. He hoped to preserve peace, but was willing to risk war. By attempting to re-supply Sumter, he put the responsibility for starting a conflict onto Davis. The Confederate leader now had to decide what to do. If he gave orders to fire on boats carrying food for hungry men, this was likely to unite northern opinion and possibly keep the upper South loyal.

On 9 April Davis' cabinet met. Most members thought that the time had come to take action against Fort Sumter. Moreover, a crisis might bring the upper South into the Confederacy. Thus Davis ordered that Sumter must be taken before it was re-supplied. General Beauregard, commander of Confederate forces in Charleston, was to demand that Anderson evacuate the fort. If Anderson refused, then Beauregard's orders were to 'reduce' Sumter.

The first shots of the war

On 11 April Beauregard demanded Sumter's surrender. Anderson refused. Negotiations dragged on for several hours but got nowhere. And so, at 4.30 a.m. on 12 April, the opening shots of the Civil War were fired. For 33 hours Sumter's defenders exchanged artillery fire with Confederate land batteries. Extraordinarily there were no deaths. The relief expedition arrived too late and was too small, to affect proceedings. On 13 April, with fires raging through the fort, Anderson surrendered.

The attack on Sumter angered and aroused the North. In New York, a city which had previously tended to be pro-Southern, 250,000 people turned out for a union rally. 'There can be no neutrals in this war, only patriots – or traitors', thundered Senator Douglas. On 15 April Lincoln issued a **Call to Arms**. He asked for 75,000 men for 90 days; Davis called for 100,000 men. Such was the enthusiasm that men rushed to join the Union and Confederate armies.

KEY TERM

Call to Arms A presidential order calling up troops and putting the USA on a war-footing.

Secession: the second wave

Given that Lincoln called on all Union states to send men to put down the rebellion, the upper South states had to commit themselves. Virginia's decision was crucial. Its industrial capacity was as great as the seven original Confederate states combined. A state convention voted by 88 votes to 55 to support its Southern 'brothers'. A referendum in May ratified this decision, with Virginians voting by 128,884 votes to 32,134 to secede. Richmond, Virginia's capital, now became the Confederate capital. In May Arkansas and North Carolina joined the Confederacy. In June, Tennessee voted by 104,913 votes to 47,238 to secede. However, support for the Confederacy in the upper South was far from total. West Virginia now seceded from Virginia and remained in the Union. More importantly, four slave states – Delaware, Maryland, Missouri and Kentucky – did not secede.

ACTIVITY

Did Davis's order to attack Fort Sumter have the outcome he expected?

SOURCE K

A contemporary photograph showing Confederate forces occupying Fort Sumter after its surrender. Note the Confederate flag, the 'stars and bars', flying from the makeshift flagpole.

Photographs were expensive to take in 1861. Why do you think the photograph in Source K was taken?

SOURCE L

An extract from Lincoln's second inaugural address, 1865

On the occasion corresponding this four years ago all thoughts were anxiously directed to an impending civil war ....

One eighth of the whole population was coloured slaves, not distributed generally over the union, but localised in the southern part of it. These slaves constituted a peculiar and powerful interest. All knew that this interest was somehow the cause of the war. To strengthen, perpetuate, and extend this interest was the object for which the insurgents would rend the union even by war, while the government claimed no right to do more than to restrict the territorial enlargement of it.

How did Lincoln explain the origins of the Civil War in Source L?

Summary

For many southerners the election of a Republican president in 1860 was the last straw – an affront to their honour. So, following the example of South Carolina, the seven states of the Deep South seceded. They formed the Confederacy and Jefferson Davis became their president. He hoped that the North would accept the new state but expected that the Confederacy would have to fight to establish its independence. Lincoln did not accept that the southern states could secede. All efforts at compromise failed. War came when Confederate guns opened fire on Fort Sumter in April 1861. Four of the upper South states now joined the Confederacy. Four others remained in the Union.

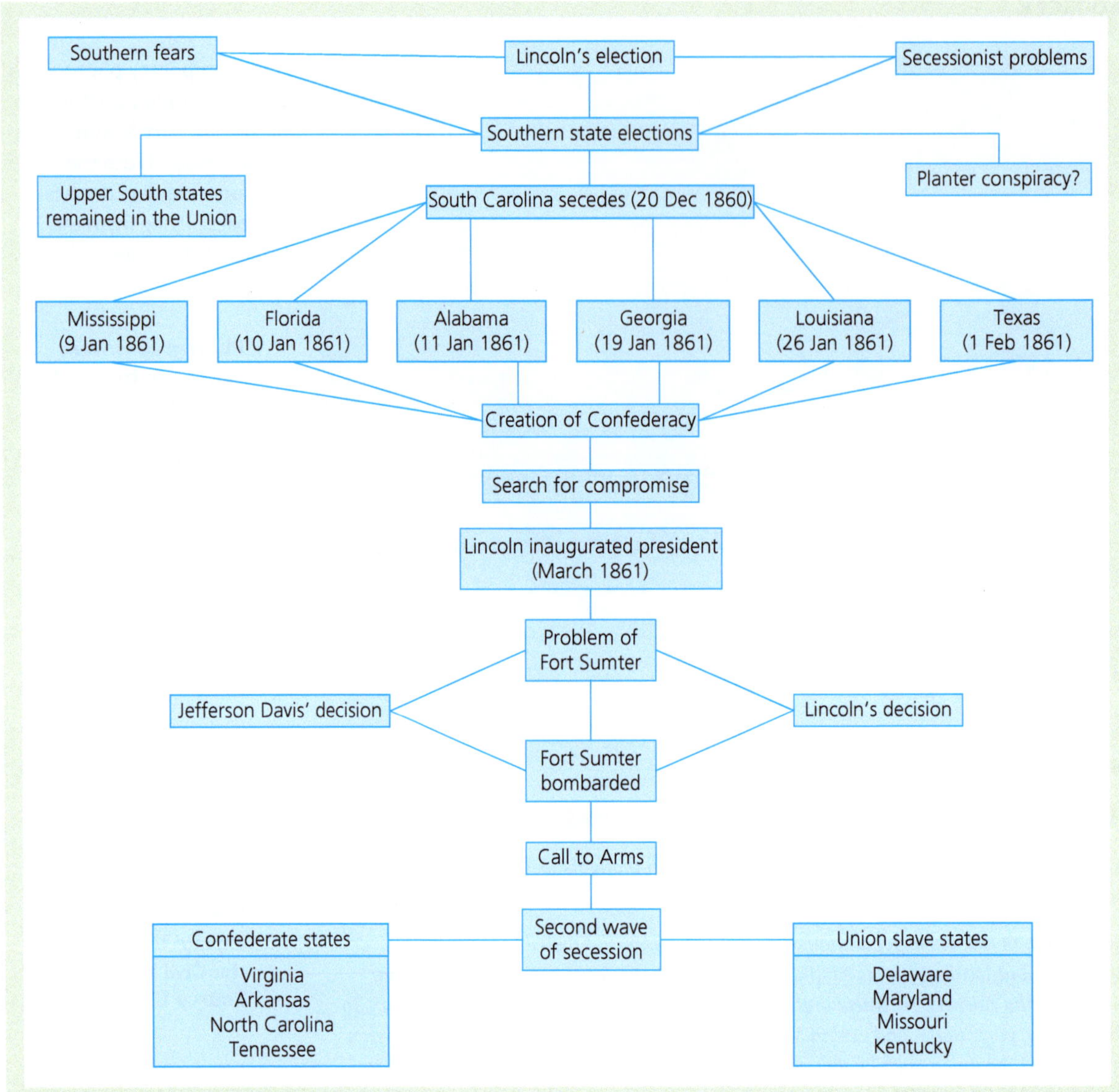

SUMMARY DIAGRAM

Why did Civil War break out in April 1861?

Was the Civil War mainly brought about by slavery?

In March 1865 Lincoln, in his second inaugural address, gave a short explanation of how and why the war came (see Source K). Today, few historians disagree with Lincoln's view that slavery was 'somehow' the cause of the war. Slavery defined the South, permeating almost every aspect of its life. The market value of the South's four million enslaved people in 1860 was \$3 billion – more than the value of land and cotton. Slavery, moreover, was more than an economic system. It was a means of maintaining racial control. While only a quarter of southern white people were slave owners in 1860, most non-slaveholding white people supported slavery.

The rise of militant abolitionism in the North increased tension. Although the abolitionists did not get far with their message of racial equality, the belief that slavery was unjust and obsolete entered mainstream northern politics. But it was the issue of slavery expansion, rather than the existence of slavery itself, that split the nation. Most of the crises that threatened the bonds of union arose over this matter. Convinced that a Slave Power conspiracy was at work, northerners came to support the Republican Party, which was pledged to stop slavery expansion. While the Confederacy might claim its justification to be the protection of states' rights, it was one state right, the right to preserve slavery, that led to the Confederate states' separation.

The importance of nationalism

In 1861 Lincoln was pledged to preserve the Union, not end slavery. Most northerners fought to save the Union. The Confederate states fought for the right to self-determination (the right to decide their own government). Thus nationalism (loyalty and commitment to a country) became the central issue. Pre-1860 most southerners saw themselves as loyal Americans: fire-eaters were a distinct minority. The creation of the Confederacy was a refuge to which many southerners felt driven, not a national destiny that they eagerly embraced. The Civil War did more to produce southern nationalism than southern nationalism did to produce war. In so far as there was a sense of southern-ness in 1861, it had arisen because of slavery.

Who was to blame?

With hindsight, it is clear that southerners got things wrong. Slavery was not in immediate peril in 1860–61. Given that the Republicans did not have a majority in Congress, there was little Lincoln could do to threaten slavery. Indeed, he was prepared to make some concessions to the South. From November 1860 to April 1861 Lincoln acted reasonably and rationally. The same cannot be said for southerners and their leaders. The maintenance of slavery did not require the creation of an independent southern nation. For much of the pre-war period most southerners regarded the fire-eaters as lunatics. Unfortunately, in the emotionally charged atmosphere of 1860–61, lunatic ideas, rather than the lunatics themselves, took over the South. Secession was a reckless decision. The North, so much stronger in terms of population and industrial strength, was always likely to win a civil war – and Confederate defeat could result in the end of slavery. The fact that this was not obvious to most southerners is symptomatic of the hysteria that swept the South in 1860–61.

Chapter summary

The USA was far from united in the mid-nineteenth-century. Slavery was the key divisive issue. Southerners defended their 'peculiar institution'. Northern abolitionists condemned it. Western expansion was a crucial issue. Problems arising from western expansion, particularly resulting from the Mexican War, led to serious sectional confrontations. The 1850 Compromise contained the immediate danger. However, the Kansas–Nebraska Act (1854) reignited sectional tensions. Events in 'Bleeding Kansas' ensured that the Republican Party emerged as the main opponent of the Democrats. The election of Democrat James Buchanan as president in 1856 averted sectional crisis. But Buchanan's leadership, especially with regard to Kansas, alienated northerners. John Brown's raid on Harper's Ferry (1859) raised tensions to new heights. Following the election of Republican Abraham Lincoln in 1860, seven lower South states seceded from the Union and created the Confederacy. The Confederacy's attack on Fort Sumter led to the outbreak of civil war in April 1861. Four upper South states now joined the Confederacy.

Refresher questions

1 What were the main differences between North and South in the mid-nineteenth century?
2 Why were southerners so committed to slavery?
3 Why was western expansion a threat to the Union?
4 How successful was the 1850 Compromise?
5 What were the effects of the Kansas–Nebraska Act?
6 Why did the Republicans emerge as the Democrats' main rivals?
7 Why were sectional tensions so high in 1860?
8 Why did Lincoln win the 1860 presidential election?
9 Why did the lower South states secede in 1860–61?
10 Why did four upper South states secede in mid-1861?

Study skills

Paper 1 guidance: Source questions

Understanding and interpreting sources

In your examination for Paper 1 you will be presented with four sources and a question made up of two parts. You will have to answer both parts of the question. The first question will ask you to read two sources and compare and contrast them – see where they agree and disagree or assess how useful they are as evidence. For the second question you will need to read all four sources and consider how they support a particular view.

In the examination, you need to show key skills in approaching evidence.

- You have to interpret evidence. You need to link it to the issue in the question and decide what the evidence is saying about the issue. In the example below the issue is:

  How far was the Civil War caused by the issue of slavery?

- You will need to consider how useful the evidence is. This involves thinking carefully about who wrote it, why it was written and how typical it might be.
- This really involves knowledge of the whole situation in 1860–61, but it is also important to look at the type of evidence you are dealing with. The use of knowledge is a skill that will be developed in the next two chapters. Here it is important to ask 'How is this source linked to the issue in the question?' and 'Was the person who produced this source in a position to know, and is there a reason why he or she might hold that view?'

However, you can only move on to these questions once you are sure you understand the relevance of the sources to the question. The activity on the next page will help you to establish the basic relevance of the four sources. You do not need to create a table in an examination but the activity will help you with the vital first step – the skill of interpreting the sources.

Activity

1 Look at Sources A, B, C and D. Make a copy of the table below. You will see that one part has been done for you. Now fill the rest in for Sources B to D.

Source	What is this source saying about the key issue?	What evidence from the source shows this?
A	Indicates that South Carolina seceded because the northern states threatened the institution of slavery. It implies that most northerners supported the abolition of slavery and were trying to bring about a slave revolt in the state.	Northern states 'have denied the rights of property [slavery]', 'denounced' slavery as 'sinful' and encouraged enslaved people to flee or rebel by sending 'emissaries, books and pictures' to the South.
B		
C		
D		

2 On the basis of what they say about the importance of slavery, group the sources. Which ones are most obviously saying that slavery is the key and which ones suggest that it is not just slavery but other issues?

SOURCE A

Part of South Carolina's Declaration of the Causes of Secession

We affirm that these ends for which this [United States] Government was instituted have been defeated; and the Government itself has been destructive of them by the action of the non-slaveholding States. Those States have assumed the right of deciding upon the propriety of our domestic institutions; and have denied the rights of property established in fifteen of the States and recognised by the Constitution; they have denounced as sinful the institution of Slavery ... They have encouraged and assisted thousands of our slaves to leave their homes; and those who remain, have been incited by emissaries, books and pictures, to servile insurrection.

This was issued on 24 December 1860, four days after South Carolina voted to secede

SOURCE B

Part of Jefferson Davis' inauguration speech. Davis was the Confederate President

We have entered upon the career of independence, and it must be inflexibly pursued. Through many years of controversy with our late associates of the Northern States, we have vainly endeavoured to secure tranquillity and obtain respect for the rights to which we were entitled. As a necessity, not a choice, we have resorted to the remedy of separation, and henceforward our energies must be directed to the conduct of our own affairs and the perpetuity of the Confederacy which we have formed.

The inauguration speech was delivered on 18 February 1861 in Montgomery

SOURCE C

From a speech by Alexander Stephens. Stephens was Vice-President of the Confederacy

The new Constitution has put at rest forever all the agitating questions relating to our peculiar institution – African slavery as it exists among us – the proper status of the negro in our form of civilization. This was the immediate cause of the late rupture and present revolution ...

Our new Government's ... foundations are laid, its cornerstone rests, upon the great truth that the negro is not equal to the white man; that slavery, subordination to the superior race, is his natural and moral condition.

Stephens delivered this speech on 21 March 1861

SOURCE D

From the *Boston Transcript*, a Northern newspaper

Alleged grievances in regard to slavery were originally the causes of the separation of the cotton states; but the mask has been thrown off, and it is apparent that the people of the principal seceding states are now in favour of commercial independence. They dream that the centres of traffic can be changed from northern to southern ports. The merchants of New Orleans, Charleston and Savannah are possessed with the idea that New York, Boston and Philadelphia may be deprived of their mercantile greatness by a revenue system verging upon free trade.

March 1861

Comparing and contrasting two sources

In the examination you may be asked to compare and contrast two sources. It is important not just to describe what one says and follow it by describing what the other says.

- There should be a point-by-point comparison (where the sources agree) and contrast (where the sources disagree).
- The comparisons should be illustrated by brief quotations from both texts.
- There should be some explanation of the differences by looking at who was writing and why.

To help practise the skill of comparing and contrasting sources and planning an answer it might be helpful to draw up a table like the one below:

Activity

Practise this skill by filling in the table for Sources E and F on page 35.

Points on which the sources agree	Parts of each source which show this	Reasons as to why the sources might agree (provenance)	Points on which the sources disagree	Parts of each source which show this	Reasons as to why the sources might disagree (provenance)

Paper 2 guidance: essay questions

In Paper 2 of your examination you will have to answer two types of essay question for two topics. The first question is a short answer essay which will ask you to explain an issue or event, the second is a long essay. Most of the advice here applies to answering the long essays but there is also guidance on how to tackle the 'explain' or short essay questions.

Understanding the wording of the question

It is very important that you read the wording of the question you are answering very carefully. You must focus on the key words and phrases in the question; these may be dates, the names of leading figures or phrases such as 'How successful ...?' Unless you directly address the demands of the question you will not score highly.

The first thing to do is to identify the command words; these will give you the instructions about what you have to do.

In question (a) you will be asked to explain an event or why something happened.

In question (b) you may be asked one of the following.

- To make a judgement about the causes or consequences of an event.
- To consider to what extent or how far a particular factor was the most important in bringing about an event.
- To make a judgement about a particular government or president.

Here are two examples.

'The most important reason for the southern states' secession in 1860–61 was the issue of states' rights.' How far do you agree?

This question requires you to consider reasons. You must consider that the most important states' right in the view of most southerners was the right to own enslaved people and write a paragraph on it, even if you argue that it was not the most important reason for secession. However, even if you think it was the most important, you must still explain why other factors were less important.

To what extent was Abraham Lincoln responsible for the outbreak of the American Civil War?

In this essay you would need to analyse why Lincoln might be held responsible, for example, his election as president in November 1860, his failure to reach a compromise with the Confederate states, and his decision to re-supply Fort Sumter. However, in order to reach the highest levels you would need to judge the relative importance of Lincoln's actions in order to reach a balanced conclusion, not simply produce a list of what he did in 1860–61.

Planning an answer

Once you have understood the demands of the question, the next step is planning your answer. The plan should outline your line of argument. This means that you will need to think about what you are going to argue before you start writing. This should help you to maintain a consistent line of argument throughout your answer. It also means that your plan will be a list of reasons about the issue or issues in the question which will ensure an analytical response. Simply having a list of dates would encourage you to write a narrative or descriptive answer and this would result in an unsuccessful essay.

Consider the first example on the previous page.

Your plan should be structured around issues like:

- Why were states' rights important?
- What other reasons are there?
- Why are these reasons important?
- Are they more or less important than the issue of states' rights?
- What is your overall view having looked at the key factor and the other causes?

A plan for this essay might take the following form.

- What were states' rights? Why did southerners regard states' rights as more important than northerners? You must make the point that the most important right in the view of most southerners was their right to own enslaved people. Many felt that this right was challenged by abolitionist northerners – and the fact that northerners outnumbered southerners and thus threatened to control political power in Washington.
- Other factors: tension brought about by the problems of western expansion which increased sectional tension.
- The rise of the Republican Party in the late 1850s. Why was this party seen as a threat by southerners?
- The 1860 election: Lincoln's success and the southern states' reaction.
- The failure to reach a compromise over the winter of 1860–61 – and the problem of Fort Sumter.
- Conclusion weighs up the relative importance of the issue of states' rights and brings together interim conclusions in previous paragraphs. You might argue that although southern politicians supported the principle of states' rights, there was only one states' right that really concerned them – the right to own enslaved people. Slavery was the major issue that aroused tensions between northerners and southerners in the early and mid-nineteenth century, largely as a result of problems arising from westward

expansion. Politicians had found compromises for southern–northern disputes in 1820 and 1850. They failed to reach a settlement in 1860–61 and the result was civil war.

Planning answers to these questions will help you put together a structured answer and avoid the common mistake of listing reasons with each paragraph essentially saying 'Another reason for the Civil War was.'

Planning an answer will help you focus on the actual question and not simply write about the topic. In the second question you might write all you know about Abraham Lincoln but not explain why he was or was not responsible for the outbreak of the Civil War. Under the pressure of time in the examination room, it is easy to forget the importance of planning and just to start writing; but this will usually result in an essay that does not have a clear line of argument, or changes its line of argument half-way through, making it less convincing and so scoring fewer marks.

QUESTION PRACTICE

The focus of this section has been on planning. Use the information in this chapter to plan answers to the following questions.

1 'Misjudgements by politicians explain why the issue of western expansion divided North and South so sharply in the years 1845–54.' How far do you agree with this view?

2 To what extent did the Republican Party support abolitionism in the period 1856–60?

3 'Lincoln's election in 1860 made civil war almost inevitable.' How far do you agree?

4 To what extent was there any hope of compromise between the Union and the Confederacy in the period December 1860 to April 1861?

EXPLAIN QUESTIONS

The following are examples of short answer essay questions for this chapter.

1 Explain why western expansion in the early nineteenth century resulted in sectional tension.

2 Explain why the USA's victory in the Mexican War 1846–48 helped divide northerners from southerners.

3 Explain why the Kansas–Nebraska Act (1854) created further tensions instead of resolving problems.

4 Explain why the lower South states seceded over the winter of 1860–61.

CHAPTER 2

Civil War and Reconstruction, 1861–77

Given its 'big battalions', the Union was always favourite to win the Civil War. It eventually did so but only after a bitter struggle. Union victory led to the emancipation of American enslaved people. The impact of emancipation was a major problem in terms of reconstructing the nation. How to restore the Confederate states to the Union was another. This chapter will consider the following themes:

- ★ Why did the Civil War last four years?
- ★ How great was the immediate impact of the Civil War (1861–65)?
- ★ What were the aims and outcomes of Reconstruction?
- ★ How successful was Reconstruction?

KEY DATES

1861		First Manassas
1862		Battle of Antietam
1863	**January**	Emancipation Proclamation
	July	Battle of Gettysburg
	July	Capture of Vicksburg
1864	**September**	Fall of Atlanta
	November	Lincoln re-elected president
1865	**April**	Lee surrendered at Appomattox
		Lincoln assassinated. Andrew Johnson became president
	December	Thirteenth Amendment
1867		Military Reconstruction Act
1868	**July**	Fourteenth Amendment
	November	Ulysses S. Grant elected president
1870		Fifteenth Amendment
1877		Rutherford Hayes inaugurated president

1 Why did the Civil War last four years?

Thousands of Americans rushed to volunteer to fight in 1861, anticipating one glorious battle. Instead, the war dragged on for four terrible years during which 620,000 men died. There were a number of reasons why the war lasted so long including lack of preparedness, the nature of mid-nineteenth-century warfare, changing military strategies, resources, and political and military leadership.

Changing military strategies

Neither side was ready for war in 1861. This had an important effect on the length of the war. So did the military strategies of both sides. Those strategies were determined by the nature of mid-nineteenth-century warfare and by the changing military situation. The biggest change in strategy was the combination of dividing the Confederacy by control of the Mississippi River by Union forces and the subsequent damaging of Confederate resources by a deliberate policy of destruction in Georgia and in the Shenandoah Valley in Virginia. The war became one of attrition and victory went to the side that could absorb more losses and bring more resources to bear.

The military situation in 1861–62

In April 1861 the Union had only a 16,000-strong regular army. The War Department totalled 90 men. Lincoln had no military experience. Winfield Scott, the leading Union general, had no carefully prepared plans and no programme for **mobilization**. It was soon obvious that Lincoln's appeal in April 1861 for 75,000 volunteers to serve for three months was insufficient. In July Congress agreed to raise 500,000 men who would serve for three years.

KEY TERM

Mobilization Preparing for war, especially by raising troops.

The Confederacy had to start its military organization from scratch. Davis at least had some military experience. Trained at the military academy at West Point, he had fought in the Mexican War and been secretary of war. The 300 southern officers who resigned from the regular army provided a useful pool of talent. In February 1861 the Confederate Congress authorized the raising of 100,000 volunteers for up to a year's service. In May it authorized an additional 400,000 troops for three years' service. Given its limited manufacturing capacity, the south's main problem was equipping the volunteers.

Compared with European armies, Union and Confederate forces were amateurish.

- Lincoln and Davis had the job of appointing the chief officers. Political criteria, not just military concerns, played a role in these appointments. While some 'political' generals became first-rate soldiers, many were incompetent.
- Only a few junior officers had any military experience. Many were elected by the men under their command or were appointed by state governors because of their social or political standing.
- Most ordinary soldiers were unused to military discipline.

SOURCE A

Confederate soldiers posing outside their tent in 1861

What does Source A suggest about the nature of the Confederate army?

Conscription

The war would have ended much sooner if both sides had continued to rely on men volunteering for the armed forces. By early 1862, as initial enthusiasm faded, the flood of recruits had become a trickle in both the Confederacy and the Union. In March 1862 Davis decided he had no option but to introduce conscription. Every white male aged 18 to 35 (soon raised to 45) was liable for military service. The length of service was extended to the duration of the war.

Most northern states adopted a carrot and stick approach (a combination of incentive and force) to recruiting soldiers. The carrot was bounties – large sums of money offered to men who enlisted. The stick, initially, was the Militia Law (July 1862). This empowered Lincoln to call state militias into Union service. Most states managed to enrol enough men but some had to introduce a **militia draft** to fill their quotas. In March 1863 the Union introduced conscription for able-bodied men aged 20 to 45. As in the South, it was possible to avoid the draft by hiring a substitute. By 1865 900,000 men had fought for the Confederacy; the Union enlisted 2.1 million men.

KEY TERM

Militia draft Conscription of men in the state militias.

The nature of warfare

Improvements in military technology in the mid-nineteenth century changed the nature of warfare, in favour of the defender. This helped to prolong the conflict. It was hard for attacking forces to make a breakthrough. There were few decisive military successes until 1863 and even after that battles were characterized by heavy losses on both sides. This meant that the war turned into a **war of attrition** in which the Union ground down Confederate forces and destroyed resources. By 1861 the **smoothbore musket**, which had an effective range of less than 100 yards, had been replaced – in theory – by the **rifle-musket**. (The latter's production was so limited that not until 1863 did nearly all the infantry on both sides have the weapon.) Rifle-muskets, while **muzzle-loading**, were accurate at up to 600 yards. This meant that battle tactics now favoured the defending force which could fire several rounds at the attackers before they could get close enough to thrust bayonets. Infantry attacks were even more costly if the defenders dug trenches. Battles usually disintegrated into a series of engagements during which infantry traded volleys, charged and counter-charged. Both sides, but especially the attacker, sustained heavy losses. This made it difficult for the successful army to follow up its victory. Usually the beaten army retreated a few miles to recover; the winners stayed in place to rest and to tend the wounded.

Initially, both sides imported weapons from Europe, especially Britain, on a huge scale. The Union eventually had the industrial capacity to produce virtually all the weapons its armies required, though it took time for factories to convert from producing peacetime goods to war materials. The Confederacy also managed to establish an effective system of weapons production (see page 87). While Union armies were generally better-armed than Confederate ones, this did not have much effect until 1865. In 1861–62, Union ordnance chief Ripley opposed the introduction of repeating rifles, on the grounds that soldiers might waste ammunition, which was in short supply. In 1864–65 repeating rifles, used mainly by cavalry units, gave Union armies an important advantage. If Ripley had contracted for repeating rifles in 1861–62, the war might have ended sooner.

KEY TERMS

War of attrition Relentless wearing down of an enemy's morale and strength using continual attacks.

Smoothbore musket These firearms had been in use from the seventeenth century. The barrels of the guns had no grooves. This reduced the accuracy of fire.

Rifle-musket The barrel of this type of firearm was grooved. The lead bullet expanded into the grooves when fired and the spin made the weapon far more accurate than the smoothbore musket.

Muzzle-loading Loaded down the barrel.

Military strategies

Given that the Civil War dragged on for so long, political and military leaders on both sides adopted different strategies at different times in an effort to win the conflict. The Confederacy was essentially on the defensive throughout the war. However, by 1862 many Confederate leaders, including President Davis and General Robert E Lee, believed that attack might well be the best form of defence. President Lincoln realized that the Union's best hope of victory was to make use of its greater numbers of men and materials by attacking on all fronts.

The military situation in 1861–62

The campaigns of 1861–62 were indecisive. The first major battle saw a Union defeat but achieved little for the Confederacy. A weak and over-cautious Union commander achieved little and the Union failed to achieve its main objective of taking the Confederate capital in Richmond. A Confederate attack failed to achieve a decisive result. The armies were too evenly matched in weaponry and the tactic of frontal assault was ineffective. Neither side produced a strategy or tactics that were decisive.

In 1861 Winfield Scott, Union general-in-chief, who thought it would take many months to train and equip the armies needed to crush the insurrection, supported the so-called Anaconda Plan. Its aim was to squeeze the life out of the Confederacy by naval blockade and by winning control of the Mississippi. But Lincoln favoured a quick decisive blow. He accepted that Union troops were untrained but as he wrote to General McDowell, who commanded Union forces around Washington: 'You are green [inexperienced], it is true, but they are green; you are all green alike'. Lincoln urged McDowell to march on Richmond. On 21 July 1861 McDowell, with 30,000 men, was defeated by Confederate forces at First Manassas (or Bull Run). The victorious Confederate army was in no condition to follow up its victory by marching on Washington.

KEY FIGURES

George McClellan (1826–85) McClellan served during the Mexican War. Effectively commander-in-chief of Union forces in 1861–62, he played an important role in organizing the Army of the Potomac. Disappointed by his military performance in 1862, Lincoln removed him from command. Standing as Democratic presidential candidate in 1864, McClellan was defeated by Lincoln.

Thomas 'Stonewall' Jackson (1824–63) Born in West Virginia, Jackson graduated from West Point and fought gallantly in the Mexican War. A deeply religious man and a firm disciplinarian, he became the Confederacy's most acclaimed soldier in 1862–63. He was fatally wounded at the Battle of Chancellorsville.

General McClellan

After Manassas, McDowell was replaced by General **George McClellan**. An able administrator, McClellan restored the morale of the main Union army, now called the Army of the Potomac. Anxious not to create scars that might take a generation to heal, he hoped to win the war by manoeuvre, bringing it to an end without too much gore. The main charge levied against McClellan is that, having built a fine army, he was too reluctant to use it. Over the winter of 1861–62 Lincoln and the northern public grew impatient as McClellan refused to move.

The Peninsula campaign

In April 1862 the Army of Potomac, 121,000 strong, was transported to Fortress Monroe, planning to attack Richmond up the peninsula between the York and James rivers. McClellan advanced slowly, not reaching Richmond's outskirts until late May. Although he had twice as many men as the Confederates, he believed he was outnumbered and awaited reinforcements. General **'Stonewall' Jackson**, who fought a brilliant campaign in the Shenandoah Valley, ensured that McClellan's reinforcements did not arrive. Lincoln, worried at the threat that Jackson posed to Washington, did not send men to help McClellan.

Figure 2.1 The war in the East 1861–62

Robert E Lee

In June 1862 Virginian **Robert E Lee** took command of the Confederate forces defending Richmond. Renaming his army the Army of Northern Virginia, Lee determined to seize the initiative. He believed that a war fought purely on the defensive was unlikely to be successful. The Union would pick off the South almost at will. Hoping to win a major victory, Lee attacked at the end of June. The week of battles that followed is known as 'The Seven Days'. Lee's hopes were not fully realized but at least his actions saved Richmond, forcing McClellan to retreat down the peninsula.

Robert Lee

Lee continued to attack. Advancing north, he defeated Union forces at Second Manassas (29–30 August) and invaded Maryland. On 17 September,

KEY FIGURE

Robert E Lee (1807–70)
Lee, who first won renown in the Mexican War, was the Confederacy's leading general. Appointed commander of the Army of Northern Virginia in 1862, he won a series of major battles against Union armies larger than his own. On several occasions he came tantalisingly close to success. Despite being outnumbered in every campaign, Lee won victories which depressed Union and bolstered Confederate morale. Some historians think that without Lee's work as general the Confederacy would have crumbled earlier.

Lee's army, outnumbered two-to-one, fought a Union army, commanded by McClellan, at Antietam. Lee managed to hold his ground, losing 10,000 men but inflicting 14,000 casualties on Union forces. On 18 September Lee retreated into Virginia. McClellan failed to follow up his 'victory'. Exasperated with his excuses for inactivity, Lincoln relieved him of command, replacing him with General Burnside. On 13 December 1862 Burnside, commanding 100,000 men, launched attacks on Lee's 75,000 men, well-positioned at Fredericksburg. Union losses amounted to 11,000 men. Lee lost less than 5000.

Was the photographer who took the picture in Source B most likely to have been a northerner or southerner? Explain your answer.

SOURCE B

Confederate soldiers, killed at the Battle of Antietam (1862), lie along a dirt road

KEY FIGURE

General Ulysses S Grant (1822–85) Appointed general-in-chief of the Union army in 1864 (after a string of successes in the West), Grant brought the war to a successful conclusion, receiving Lee's surrender at Appomattox in 1865. 'The art of war is simple enough', said Grant. 'Find out where your enemy is. Get at him as soon as you can. Strike at him as hard as you can and as often as you can, and keep moving on.' In 1868 Grant was elected US president. He was re-elected in 1872.

The war in the West 1861–62

The West's lack of natural lines of defence, and the fact that the main rivers flowed into the Confederacy's heartland, meant that the West was the South's 'soft underbelly'. In February 1862 Union forces under **Ulysses S Grant**, helped by Union gunboats, captured the key river forts of Fort Henry and Fort Donelson, forcing Confederate forces to abandon Kentucky and much of Tennessee. In March Grant pushed into south-west Tennessee. A brutal two-day battle at Shiloh (6–7 April) ended with Confederate forces in retreat.

From August 1862 Union forces under Grant tried to take the fortified town of Vicksburg, which prevented Union control of the Mississippi. In Davis' view Vicksburg was 'the nail-head that held the South's two halves together'. The town was probably not as important as Davis thought. By this stage there was little Confederate traffic across the Mississippi. Nevertheless Vicksburg was important symbolically. Its capture would demoralize the South and bolster the North. Despite all Grant's efforts, Vicksburg continued to hold out.

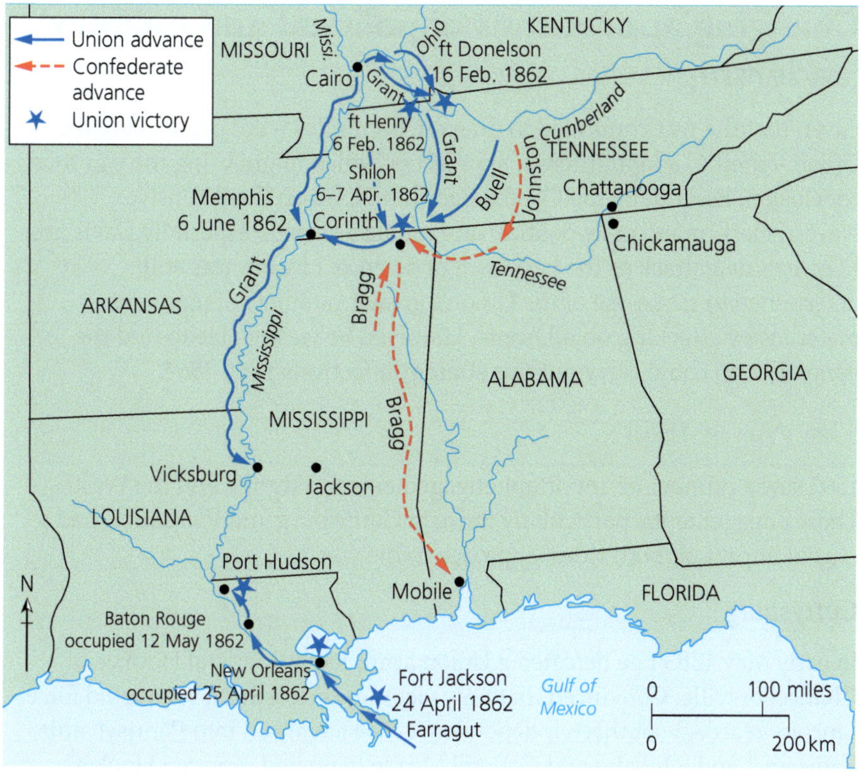

Figure 2.2 The war in the West 1861–62

Ulysses S Grant

The Naval War

In 1861 the Union, on paper, had a fleet of 90 ships but most were obsolete sailing vessels. The Confederacy had no navy at all. Most American shipbuilding capacity was in the North. As soon as the war began the North bought scores of merchant ships, armed them and sent them to do blockade duty. By December 1861 the Union had over 260 warships on duty and 100 more were under construction. Blockading the South was crucial. If the Confederacy could sell its cotton in Europe and purchase weapons and manufactured goods in return, the war might continue indefinitely. Given the 3500 miles (5600 km) of Southern coastline, the blockade was hard to enforce but as the months went by it grew tighter. The Union was also able to use its naval supremacy to transport its troops and to strike at Confederate coastal targets. The loss of many coastal towns, including New Orleans (April 1862), weakened the Confederacy.

Changing approaches of political and military leadership

Given that the war continued to drag on, both sides – but particularly the Union – tried to adopt different approaches which might bring the war to a conclusion. Essentially the Confederacy remained on the defensive. Nevertheless, many of its political and military leaders, especially Davis and Lee, regarded attack as the best form of defence. Lincoln was still determined to make use of the Union's greater numbers of men and materials by attacking on all fronts. However, he was unable to find the generals who could carry out this strategy effectively until 1864.

The War in 1863

1863 saw a number of important engagements in Virginia and the West. These engagements, particularly those at Gettysburg and Vicksburg, had a crucial impact on both sides' approach to the war.

Gettysburg

In early May 1863 Lee defeated a Union army, led by General Hooker, at Chancellorsville. Convinced that only victories on northern soil would force Lincoln to accept southern independence, Lee advanced into Pennsylvania. Between 1 and 3 July he and General Meade (who had replaced Hooker) fought the greatest battle ever fought on the American continent – Gettysburg. Confederate troops had the best of the fighting on 1 and 2 July. On 3 July Lee launched a disastrous attack on the Union centre which came to be known as Pickett's charge. In less than one hour the Confederacy suffered 6500 casualties. In three days Lee lost 28,000 men – one-third of his command. (The Union lost 23,000 men in comparison.) He retreated back to Virginia. Although Meade was unable to follow up his victory, Gettysburg was important. The long-term impact of this battle was greater than its immediate effect as Union forces were not able to follow up and destroy Lee's retreating forces. However, the defeat meant Lee was forced to adopt a largely defensive strategy. The chances of a southern invasion of the North bringing about some sort of negotiated settlement were much reduced. The outcome of the war now depended on whether losses in a war of attrition would wear out the South before it wore out the North.

Vicksburg

In April 1863 Grant marched his army down the west side of the Mississippi, relying on a Union fleet sailing past Vicksburg. This was achieved in mid-April. Two weeks later Grant's men were ferried across the Mississippi. Grant now cut inland, defeating several Confederate forces, and finally besieging Vicksburg. On 4 July the 30,000-strong Confederate garrison surrendered. This was a highly important battle as it divided the Confederacy, gave the Union control of the Mississippi and enabled a Union advance into the South. Grant was able to defeat Confederate forces at Chattanooga and force them to retreat into Georgia.

The war in 1864

Although the defeats at Gettysburg, Vicksburg and Chattanooga were severe blows, the Confederacy was far from beaten. If Lee could continue to inflict heavy casualties on Union forces in Virginia, there was every chance that the northern electorate might oust Lincoln in the 1864 election (see page 92) and support a compromise peace to avoid further losses.

'Simultaneous movement all along the line'

A major development took place in March 1864 when Grant was appointed general-in-chief of all the Union armies. He immediately came east to supervise the effort to destroy Lee. **William Sherman** took over command in the West. Determined to make use of the Union's greater manpower, Grant planned for a 'simultaneous movement all along the line'.

- The 115,000-strong Army of the Potomac would attack Lee.
- Sherman's army would capture Atlanta.
- 30,000 men in Louisiana, led by Banks, would capture Mobile.
- Butler's 30,000-strong army at Yorktown was to threaten Richmond.
- Sigel, with 26,000 men, was to occupy the Shenandoah Valley.

KEY FIGURE

William Tecumseh Sherman (1820–91)
Sherman graduated from West Point in 1840 and served in the Second Seminole War and the Mexican War. Fighting for the Union, he participated in many of the Civil War's main battles. He was given command of the Union's western forces in 1864. After capturing Atlanta, his army marched through Georgia and the Carolinas, weakening the Confederacy's ability to wage war.

Grant's strategy had the backing of Lincoln who had long advocated such an approach. The significance of this change was that the South's resources would be stretched and the North would make best use of its major advantage – greater manpower and war materials. The strategy depended on applying relentless pressure regardless of casualties, so the nature of the war changed. The campaigns in the East became bitter struggles involving attacks which were increasingly costly. There was limited strategic imagination, just a great determination to win at all costs. The war in the South would be waged not just against armies but would affect the civilian population by looting and destroying farms and plantations.

Grant's strategy did not go to plan:

- Banks was defeated in the Red River area.
- Butler failed to exert pressure on Richmond.
- Union forces in the Shenandoah were defeated.

The Army of the Potomac had mixed success. On 5–6 May Union forces suffered 18,000 casualties in the battle of the Wilderness. Nevertheless, Grant's army continued to edge southwards. In the first 30 days of his offensive, Grant lost 50,000 men, twice as many as Lee. But his doggedness paid off. On 12 June Union forces crossed the James river, almost capturing Petersburg, a crucial railway junction. Lee, aware that the loss of Petersburg would result in the loss of Richmond, was forced to defend the town. Both sides dug trenches and the siege of Petersburg began. Although Grant had not defeated Lee, he had forced him onto the defensive.

'Hard war' in Georgia and the Shenandoah Valley

Sherman's capture of Atlanta in autumn 1864 opened the way for a large-scale destructive raid through Georgia. Sherman's aim was to demoralize the South, destroying both its capacity and its will to fight. Leaving a swathe of destruction, Union forces captured Savannah in mid-December.

Sherman was not alone in pursuing 'total' or 'hard' war policies. General Sheridan, after winning battles at Winchester and at Cedar Creek, lay waste to the Shenandoah Valley – an area that provided Lee's army with much of its food. The harsh policies adopted by the Union armies in 1864 were designed to damage property, not kill. While the devastation lacked the ruthlessness and cruelty that characterized twentieth-century wars, it had a damaging effect on southern morale.

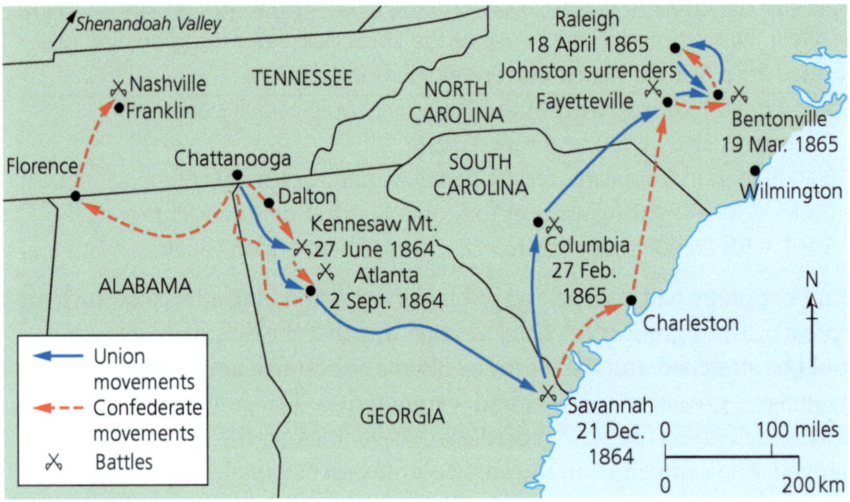

Figure 2.3
Sherman's march through the South

SOURCE C

How useful is Source C for showing the nature of the war by 1864?

A letter written by General Sherman to Confederate officials in Atlanta in September 1864

You cannot qualify war in harsher terms than I will. War is cruelty, and you cannot refine it: and those who brought war into our country deserve all the curses and maledictions a people can pour out ... Once admit the Union, once more acknowledge the authority of the national Government, and instead of devoting your houses and streets and roads to the dread uses of war, I and this army become at once your protectors and supporters, shielding you from danger. You might as well appeal against the thunder-storm as against the terrible hardships of war. They are inevitable and the only way the people of Atlanta can hope once more to live in peace and quiet at home, is to stop the war, which can only be done by admitting that it began in error and is perpetuated in pride.

Confederate surrender

In December 1864 Lincoln spoke confidently of victory. Union resources, he said, were unexhausted and inexhaustible; its military and naval forces were larger than ever, and its economy was prospering. The Confederacy's situation, by contrast, was desperate.

SOURCE D

Part of Lincoln's second inaugural address, 4 March 1865

Fellow Countrymen: At this second appearing to take the oath of the presidential office there is less occasion for an extended address than there was at the first. Then a statement somewhat in detail of a course to be pursued seemed fitting and proper. Now, at the expiration of four years, during which public declarations have been constantly called forth on every point and phase of the great contest which still absorbs the attention and engrosses the energies of the nation, little that is new could be presented. The progress of our arms, upon which all else chiefly depends, is as well known to the public as to myself, and it is, I trust, reasonably satisfactory and encouraging to all. With high hopes for the future, no prediction in regard to it is ventured.

How valid is Lincoln's view in Source D with regard to the military situation in early 1865?

Lee was now given overall command of all that was left of the Confederate armies. There was little he could do. By March 1865 rebel trench lines extended 35 miles (56 km) around Petersburg and Lee had fewer than 50,000 troops to man them. Grant had 125,000 men, not counting Sheridan approaching from the north and Sherman approaching from the south. On 2 April Grant broke through Lee's lines, forcing him to abandon Petersburg and Richmond. Surrounded by Union forces, Lee surrendered to Grant at Appomattox Court House on 10 April. Lee's surrender was effectively the end of the war. On 16 April Johnston surrendered to Sherman. Davis was captured on 10 May.

SOURCE E

Robert E Lee's farewell address to his soldiers, 10 April 1865

After four years' arduous service, marked by unsurpassed courage and fortitude, the Army of Northern Virginia has been compelled to yield to overwhelming numbers and resources. I need not tell the survivors of so many hard-fought battles, who have remained steadfast to the last, that I have consented to this result from no distrust of them: but feeling that valour and devotion could accomplish nothing that could compensate for the loss that would have attended the continuation of the contest, I have determined to avoid the useless sacrifice of those whose past services have endeared them to their countrymen.

According to Source E, why had Lee surrendered?

Summary

Despite the imbalance of manpower, industry and resources between Union and Confederate forces, the war did not produce a rapid and decisive victory. The Union faced a daunting task of reasserting control over a vast area. The

South had to defend itself and the nature of modern weapons gave the defence a great advantage over the attackers as was seen repeatedly. Initially, there was some reluctance to take the fighting to extremes. This was especially true of McLellan in 1862. As the war went on it was fought more bitterly but even with greater determination and willingness to accept casualties, decisive victory eluded both sides. Lee failed to invade the North successfully and while Grant was successful at Vicksburg and Meade at Gettysburg in 1863 neither success brought an immediate end to the war. That was brought about only by intense campaigning in the East and a devastating campaign following control of the West which destroyed large amounts of the southern homeland.

Resources available

The Union had far greater resources at its disposal than the Confederacy. The historian Richard Current (1960), reviewing the statistics of Union strength – two and a half times the South's population, three times its railway capacity, nine times its industrial production, overwhelming naval supremacy – concluded that 'surely in view of the disparity of resources, it would have taken a miracle … to enable the South to win. As usual, God was on the side of the heaviest battalions.' Nevertheless, the Confederacy had a number of advantages which offset those of the Union. This helps explain why the war lasted so long.

Union advantages in 1861

The economic development and population growth of the northern states put the Union in a position to sustain a long war.

- There were 22 million northerners compared with 9 million southerners (only 5.5 million were white).
- Four slave states (Maryland, Kentucky, Delaware and Missouri) remained loyal to the Union. These states would have added 45 per cent to the Confederacy's white population and 80 per cent to its industrial capacity.
- The Union enjoyed huge naval supremacy.
- In 1860 the North had six times as many factories as the South, ten times its industrial productive capacity, and twice as many miles of railway track (see Figure 2.4).
- The North had considerable superiority in railroads. Though there were important rail junctions like Chattanooga, many southern railways were of poor quality and were narrow gauge tracks mainly used for transporting cotton. The North could certainly concentrate forces and supplies better. However, it was not likely that railways would be a decisive issue. They were easily destroyed and railways could not easily reach key battlefields. Most campaigns involved men marching to the battlefield. Thus rail superiority helped to sustain the war effort by linking factories and workshops to military centres but they could not in themselves lead to rapid victories by assembling large forces.

ACTIVITY

In groups, assemble a list of arguments to show that the Confederacy stood little chance of winning the Civil War.

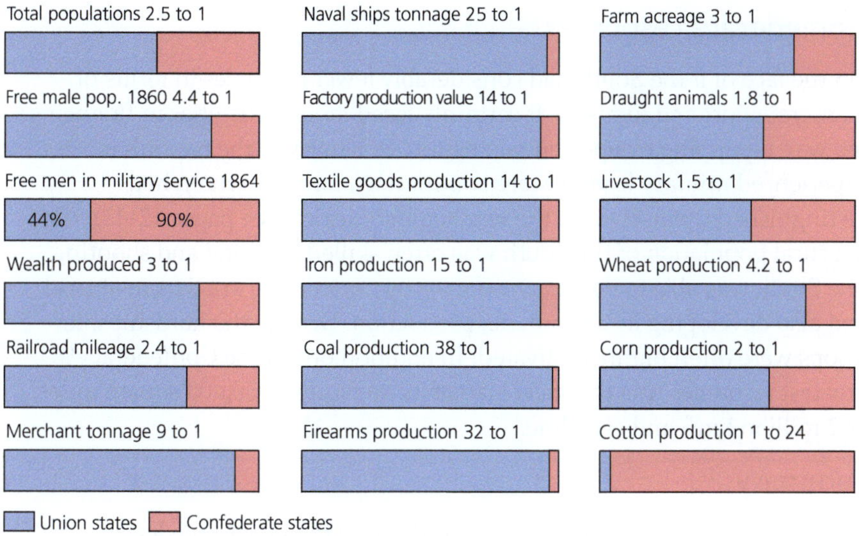

Figure 2.4 Comparative resources of Union and Confederate states

Union financial and economic resources

The Union had considerable advantages in terms of finding the money and materials to wage war. This gave it the capacity to sustain the war without ruining the economy and without causing massive inflation. Northern inflation ran only at 75 per cent whereas the South's currency was rendered virtually worthless by price rises by the end of the war. However, this again was not a factor likely to produce a rapid result and northern financial management gave the North the ability to sustain a long war while southern financial problems were not decisive enough to bring about surrender.

The Union: financing the war

In 1861 the Union had an established treasury, gold reserves and an assured source of revenue from tariffs. Nevertheless, financial problems threatened to overwhelm the Union cause over the winter of 1861–62. Secretary Chase kept the treasury afloat by raising loans and issuing bonds. Two-thirds of the Union's revenue was raised in this way. One-fifth was raised by taxes. An income tax, the first in US history, was enacted in 1861. It imposed a three per cent tax on annual incomes over $800. Far more important was the Internal Revenue Act (1862). This basically taxed everything. In 1862 the Legal Tender Act authorized the issuing of $150 million in paper currency. Ultimately 'greenback' notes to the value of $431 million were pumped into the economy by new national banks. Inflation, over the course of the war, ran at 80 per cent.

Union economic success

The northern economy was able to ensure that Union armies were well equipped and that civilians did not go short of basic commodities. There was little interference by the federal government in the management of the wartime economy. There was no rationing, no attempt to control prices, wages and profits, and no central control of the railways.

ACTIVITY

Prepare a presentation to show that the Confederacy had the means to win the Civil War.

Confederate resources

On the face of it the South had considerably fewer resources in terms of men, transport and industry. It certainly faced more difficulties in financing the war, equipping troops and raising forces. However, the nation's most experienced military leaders were southerners, many of whom had distinguished themselves in the war against Mexico (see pages 12–13). Also the rural population of the South was often skilled in riding and shooting. The South was able to develop resources by purchase of arms from abroad and also developing its armaments production. Despite the hardships, its troops were often highly motivated. In addition one of the Confederacy's greatest resources was the sheer size of its territories (750,000 square miles, or 2 million km^2) and coastline.

Summary

The Union had far greater resources at its disposal than the Confederacy. However, resources alone could not ensure a quick victory. Instead the resources available to both sides allowed them to sustain a long war. The fact that the North could conscript large forces and supply them with well-developed industries allowed them to replenish losses in the costly campaigns and keep the war going. The South could not use one of its key resources – cotton – because of the effects of the northern blockade but it was still able to purchase arms from abroad and to maintain supplies of weapons to its troops. Both sides used their railroads and both sides kept their forces fed and supplied. Of course, it was a greater strain for the Confederacy and there were many troops who were poorly dressed and even without boots. However, it was not until the war became much more of a total war and the Union attacked the southern homeland and forced its armies into punishing campaigns which drained manpower that lack of resources became a decisive factor.

The impact of foreign influences (Britain and France)

Britain, given its naval, economic, financial and imperial strength (including possession of Canada) was the key European power. Davis, aware that alliance with Britain was the Confederacy's best hope of success, did his best to secure British support. Had he succeeded, it may be that the Confederacy would have won independence. Thus the failure to gain recognition helped to prolong the war. Although Britain did not join the war, it did help provide the Confederacy with many of the weapons and supplies that it needed to wage war. This, in part, also helps explain why the war lasted as long as it did.

Britain's attitude to the war

Lord Palmerston, the British prime minister, realized that Britain's interests might well be served by Confederate victory. An independent Confederacy would have strong economic links with Britain, providing raw cotton in return for manufactured goods. Moreover, in order to prevent economic hardship at home, Palmerston realized it might be necessary for Britain to break the Union blockade to acquire southern cotton.

However, Palmerston was aware that there were good reasons for not getting involved in the war:
- Conflict with the Union might result in the loss of Canada.
- War would certainly result in the loss of valuable markets and investments in the North.
- Aware that slavery lay at the heart of the conflict, many Britons supported the Union.

For Palmerston the best solution seemed to be to avoid entanglement.

British neutrality

One immediate problem was whether Britain should recognize the Confederacy as a sovereign state. Lincoln's administration made it clear that the conflict was a rebellion. Thus, recognition of the Confederacy was tantamount to a declaration of war against the USA. However, the situation was confused because Lincoln had proclaimed a blockade against the Confederacy. A blockade was an instrument of war. If a state of war existed, Britain could make a reasonable case for recognizing the Confederacy. In May 1861 the British government adopted a compromise position. While declaring its neutrality and not recognizing the Confederacy as a sovereign state, Britain accepted its **belligerent status**. Under international law belligerents had the right to contract loans and purchase arms. However, Britain's neutrality proclamation prevented the Confederacy fitting out its warships in British ports.

KEY TERM

Belligerent status Recognized legally as waging war.

The Trent affair

There was a major incident in November 1861 which might have led to Britain recognizing the Confederacy, but by resolving it diplomatically the chances of any change in British policy were reduced.

In November 1861 James Mason and John Slidell, Confederate commissioners to Britain and France respectively, left Cuba for Europe in the Trent, a British steamer. Soon after leaving Havana, the Trent was stopped by Captain Wilkes, commanding the USS San Jacinto. Wilkes forcibly removed Mason and Slidell from the Trent. Palmerston's government, angered by this violation of international law, demanded that:
- Mason and Slidell should be released
- the USA should make a public apology.

To back up the threat, the British fleet prepared for action and soldiers were sent to Canada. The Trent affair posed a problem for Lincoln. While there was a danger of war if his government did not satisfy Britain, Union opinion would be outraged if he surrendered. A compromise was eventually found. The US government, while not apologizing for Wilkes's action, admitted he had committed an illegal act and freed Mason and Slidell. This was enough to satisfy Palmerston.

French policy

From the outset, the French Emperor Napoleon III was more keen than Palmerston to get involved in the American Civil War. France had similar cotton interests to Britain. More importantly, Napoleon also had ambitions in Mexico. He was aware that he stood a better chance of realizing his dream if the United States splintered. Napoleon, however, was not prepared to fight the Union without British support. Palmerston, suspicious of Napoleon's global designs, was not keen to work closely with him.

British mediation?

The closest the Confederacy came to getting British recognition was in August–September 1862 after Lee's triumph at Second Manassas (page 65). Napoleon III's proposal that Britain and France should attempt to mediate in the conflict was seriously considered by Palmerston. Given that mediation meant recognition of the Confederacy, Britain and France might have found themselves at war with the Union. However, the failure of Lee's Maryland invasion convinced Palmerston that it would be unwise to intervene. After Lincoln's Emancipation Proclamation (page 82), it was even more unlikely that Britain would risk war against the Union.

What impression of British foreign policy is given by Source F? Explain the reasons for your view.

SOURCE F

A letter from British Foreign Secretary Lord John Russell to Lord Palmerston, written on 17 September 1862

I agree with you that the time is coming for offering mediation to the United States Government, with a view to the recognition of the independence of the Confederates. I agree further that, in case of failure, we ought ourselves to recognise the southern states as an independent State. For the purpose of taking so important a step, I think we must have a meeting of the Cabinet. The 23rd or 30th would suit me for the meeting. We ought then, if we agree on such a step, to propose it first to France, and then on the part of England and France, to Russia and other powers as a measure decided upon by us.

Blockade-runners

Britain supplied the Confederacy with huge amounts of military supplies of all kinds. These goods were smuggled into the Confederacy by ships known as blockade-runners (because they had to avoid the Union naval blockade). Almost all the ships were built in Britain. Most were based in the Bahamas and in Bermuda. They had the advantage of surprise and speed. It is estimated that they stood a 75 per cent chance of success. This high success rate continued until the last months of the war, despite an increasingly tighter Union blockade. Overall, the Confederacy imported 60 per cent of its small arms, 30 per cent of its lead, 75 per cent of its saltpetre (essential for making gunpowder) and nearly all its paper for making cartridges.

Commerce raiders

The Confederacy also purchased **commerce raiders**. While British law forbad the construction of warships for a belligerent power, Confederate agents got round this by purchasing unarmed ships and adding guns elsewhere. Commerce raiders caused considerable damage to Union merchant shipping. The Alabama, for example, took 64 ships before finally being sunk.

The Laird rams

In 1863, Charles Adams, the US minister in London, aware that Laird Brothers were building two ironclad 'rams', threatened war if the boats were sold to the Confederacy. Palmerston, as Adams was aware, had no intention of allowing the **Laird rams** to be sold and the crisis fizzled out.

KEY TERMS

Commerce raiders Confederate warships that attacked Union merchant ships.

Laird rams These vessels had an iron ram projecting from the bow, enabling them to sink an enemy by smashing its hull.

France and Mexico

By 1862 thousands of French soldiers were fighting in Mexico, their avowed purpose being to enforce the collection of Mexican debts. The real purpose, however, was to turn the country into a French colony. In 1864 French troops helped install Austrian Archduke Maximillian, a French puppet ruler, as Emperor of Mexico. Lincoln's administration was furious at France's action but decided there was little it could do. 'One war at a time' was Lincoln's maxim. The Confederate government, hoping for French support, was prepared to tolerate French action in Mexico. But Napoleon, unprepared to take on the Union without British support, refused to recognize the Confederacy.

Conclusion

Given Palmerston's caution, it was always likely that Britain would remain neutral. While Seward, Lincoln and Adams deserve some credit for their diplomacy, their skill should not be over-rated. Nor should Confederate diplomacy be too heavily criticized. Only if the Confederacy looked like winning would Britain have recognized it. Yet only if Britain recognized the Confederacy and went to war on its side, was it likely that the Confederacy would win. Nevertheless, there is no doubt that British supplies, brought in by blockade-runners, enabled the Confederacy to equip its forces. Without this assistance, it is likely that the war would have ended sooner than it did.

Summary

The war lasted longer than expected because the North's superior resources were not a decisive factor in the short term. Even when its generals were well equipped and had full political support and naval backing as with McClellan, the North could not win decisive victories. The war might well have been shortened by foreign intervention and recognition of southern independence by Britain and France but this did not happen. It took both sides time to adjust to the sort of total war that was needed. Not until 1864 did the Union accept the need for a war of attrition. Previously the advantage that the defenders had over the attackers and the relatively limited difference between the tactics and weapons used by both sides had ended in a drawn-out conflict.

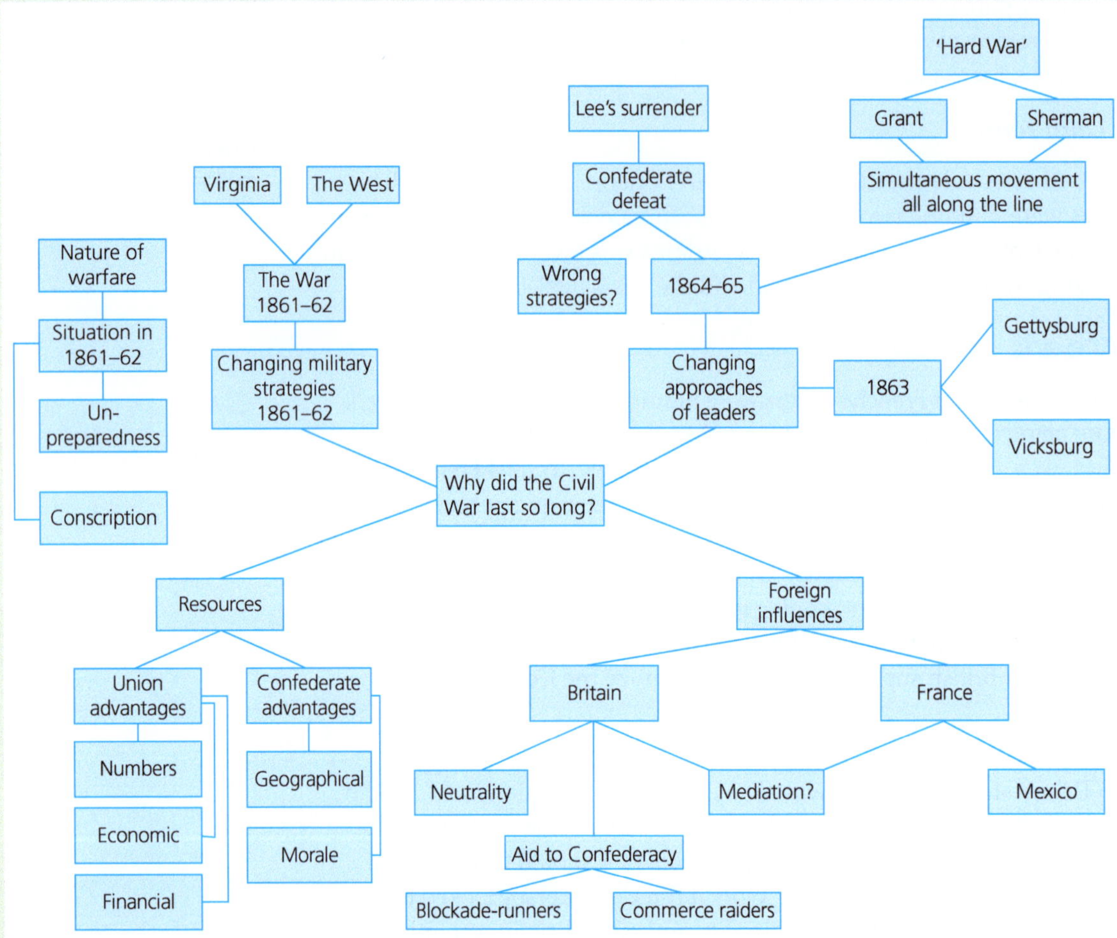

SUMMARY DIAGRAM

Why did the Civil War last four years?

2 How great was the immediate impact of the Civil War?

Limitations on civil liberties during the war

As wartime commanders-in-chief, Lincoln and Davis had greater powers than peacetime presidents. This had repercussions in many areas, not least **civil liberties**.

KEY TERM

Civil liberties The rights of individuals.

Lincoln and civil liberties

Lincoln was willing to suspend civil liberties, including the **writ of *habeas corpus***, freedom of speech and freedom of the press.

KEY TERM

Writ of *habeas corpus*
The right to know why one has been arrested.

The Merryman case

In May 1861 John Merryman from Maryland was imprisoned by military authority at Fort McHenry, Baltimore, for his alleged pro-Confederate activities – destroying railway bridges (on the orders of the Maryland governor). Supreme Court Chief Justice Roger Taney (see page 31) declared that Merryman was illegally detained. General George Cadwalader, in command of Fort McHenry, refused to obey Taney's writ on the basis that Lincoln had suspended *habeas corpus*. Taney then indicted Cadwalader for contempt of court, arguing that only Congress – not the president – had the powers of suspension.

Lincoln justified his action in a message to Congress in July 1861. More importantly, he ignored Taney's opinion and continued to support the suspension of *habeas corpus* throughout the war.

Merryman, although charged with treason, was released on bail (in July 1861) and was never brought to trial. The constitutional question of who has the right to suspend *habeas corpus*, Congress or the President, has never been fully resolved.

Further measures

- In September 1861 Lincoln permitted the arrest of a number of men in Maryland's state legislature on the strength of reports that they were about to co-operate with a Confederate invasion scheme.
- In September 1862 he suspended the writ of *habeas corpus*: anyone could be imprisoned by military authority, for impeding conscription, or affording aid or comfort to the enemy. A horde of petty functionaries decided who was loyal and who was not. Some were over-zealous; others settled old scores. Over 40,000 people were subject to arbitrary arrest.
- In March 1863 Congress passed the Habeas Corpus Suspension Act which confirmed Lincoln's suspension of the writ.

Clement Vallandigham

In early 1863 Union military failures fostered a sense of defeatism. Some Democrats thought it was time to make peace. Clement Vallandigham, campaigning to become governor of Ohio, denounced the war and called upon soldiers to desert. On the orders of General Burnside, Vallandigham was tried by a military court, found guilty of treason and sentenced to imprisonment for the rest of the war. This led to protests from outraged Democrats. Lincoln saw no alternative but to support Burnside. However, anxious to avoid making Vallandigham a martyr, he banished him to the Confederacy.

The Milligan case

In October 1864 several men, including Lambdin P Milligan, Stephen Horsey, William Bowles and Andrew Humphreys, were tried by a military commission in Indiana. The charges against the men included conspiracy against the US government, offering aid and comfort to the Confederacy, and inciting rebellion. In December Milligan, Bowles and Horsey were found guilty and sentenced to hang. Humphreys was found guilty and sentenced to hard labour for the remainder of the war.

In May 1865 Milligan's legal counsel filed a petition for a writ of *habeas corpus*, which called for a justification of Milligan's arrest. (A similar petition was filed on behalf of Bowles and Horsey.) The two judges who reviewed Milligan's petition disagreed about whether the US Constitution prohibited civilians from being tried by a military commission and passed the case to the US Supreme Court. In April 1866, the Court declared that the military commissions did not have the right to try and sentence Milligan and he, Bowles and Horsey were released from prison. Lincoln, the Court decided, had gone beyond his legal powers in trying to suppress dissent.

ACTIVITY

Discussion point: How well did Lincoln deal with the issue of civil liberties?

Conclusion

Military rather than political goals were foremost in Lincoln's mind when he allowed the restriction of civil liberties. Most of those imprisoned without trial came from states such as Missouri, which had many southern sympathizers. Given the grim reality of **guerrilla war, martial law** was essential. Elsewhere moderation was usually the norm. Many of those arrested, for example, blockade-runners, would have been arrested whether the writ of *habeas corpus* had been suspended or not. Moreover, those who were arbitrarily arrested usually found themselves arbitrarily released. Relatively few were brought to trial. Arrests rarely involved Democrat politicians or newspaper editors.

KEY TERMS

Guerrilla war Warfare by which irregular forces harass conventional forces.

Martial law The suspension of ordinary administration and policing and, in its place, the exercise of military power.

Davis and civil liberties

In February 1862 Davis proclaimed that his administration would continue to cherish and preserve the personal liberties of citizens and boasted that, in contrast to the Union, 'there has been no act on our part to impair personal liberty or the freedom of speech, of thought or of the press'. Protecting individual rights might seem an important aim (albeit an unusual one for a state whose cornerstone was slavery). However, historian David Donald (1960) claimed that concern for civil liberties cost the South the war. Unwilling to take tough action against internal dissent, the Confederacy, in Donald's view, 'died of democracy'.

However, the notion that the Confederacy could have created a government machine that could have suppressed civil liberties – and that if it had done so it might have triumphed – is unconvincing. Davis, like most southerners, was fighting for what he saw as traditional American values: abandoning those values would have alienated the public whose support was essential.

Donald's assumption that the Confederacy allowed total individual freedom is also mistaken.

- In 1862 the Confederate Congress authorized Davis to declare martial law in areas threatened by the enemy.
- The widespread opposition to conscription convinced Congress to permit Davis to suspend the right of *habeas corpus* on three separate occasions for a total of 16 months. These suspensions were justified as necessary for apprehending thousands of draft evaders.

Elements of the fiercely independent southern press were critical, not just of the (perceived) violation of civil rights, but of virtually all Davis' policies. Davis did not interfere with the press and seems never to have used his powers to arrest opposition newspaper editors, proprietors or reporters. But to imply that there was total freedom of speech in the Confederacy would be false. Although there was no specific legislation, public pressures (that had long stifled discussion about slavery) generally succeeded in imposing loyalty to the Confederacy. Opposition newspapers could find their presses destroyed by vigilantes. Preachers and teachers who questioned the course of events were liable to lose their jobs, if not their lives.

Reasons for and responses to the Emancipation Proclamation (1863)

In 1861 Lincoln was determined to maintain northern unity. An avowed policy of **emancipation** of the enslaved people would alienate northern Democrats and the Union slave states. It would also leave no possibility of a compromise peace. In April 1861, Lincoln declared, 'I have no purpose, directly or indirectly, to interfere with the institution of slavery in the states where it exists. I believe I have no lawful right to do so, and I have no inclination to do so.' Congress supported this stance.

KEY TERMS

Emancipation The act of setting free from bondage.

Contraband of war Goods which can be confiscated from the enemy.

'Contraband of war'

A set of forces placed pressure on the federal government to take some action with regard to emancipation. One problem was what to do with enslaved refugees who fled to the camps of Union armies occupying areas of the South. By the letter of the Fugitive Slave Act (see page 17), they should have been returned to their owners. Some Union generals did just that. Others, on both humane and practical grounds – the enslaved people would be punished and could also help the rebel war effort – opposed such action. In May 1861 General Butler declared that enslaved people who came to his camp would be confiscated as '**contraband of war**', ensuring they were not returned to their owners. Butler's action was supported by the terms of the Confiscation Act (August 1861) which threatened any property used 'for insurrectionary purposes' with confiscation. It left unsettled the issue of whether 'confiscated' enslaved people became free.

Radical Republicans

As the months went by, radical Republicans began to have more influence in Congress. Radicals wanted to abolish slavery and create a new order in the South. Some, but not all, were genuinely concerned for enslaved people. Most, if not all, loathed slaveholders who they blamed for causing the war. All were concerned that if the Union was restored without slavery being abolished, nothing would have been solved. Most thought that emancipation would weaken the Confederacy. Enslaved people would work to undermine the southern war effort. Moreover, if emancipation became a war aim, there was little chance that Britain would support the Confederacy. Radicals implored Lincoln to declare his support for emancipation. He remained hesitant.

Congressional measures in 1862

In 1862 the Republican-dominated Congress began to take action against slavery.

- In April slavery in Washington DC was abolished.
- In July a much more sweeping Confiscation Act was enacted. This allowed the seizure of all enemy 'property': enslaved people in such cases were to be set 'forever free'. Lincoln also received authority to employ 'persons of African descent' in any capacity deemed necessary for the suppression of the rebellion.

The Emancipation Proclamation

In July 1862 abolitionist William Lloyd Garrison described Lincoln's handling of the slavery issue as, 'stumbling, halting, prevaricating, irresolute, weak, besotted'. However, with the allegiance of the Union slave states now secure, Lincoln was ready to act. He believed that a bold statement on emancipation would weaken the Confederacy.

In July 1862 Lincoln presented an Emancipation Proclamation to his cabinet. It met with general approval. However, Secretary of State Seward recommended that it should only be issued after a military success; otherwise it would seem like an act of desperation born of weakness. Lincoln accepted the logic of this and waited patiently. When newspaper editor Horace Greeley criticized him for not doing more on the slavery front, Lincoln did not reveal his intentions. He responded by saying, 'If I could save the Union without freeing any slave I would do so and if I could save it by freeing all the slaves I would do it; and if I could save it by freeing some and leaving others alone I would also do that.'

SOURCE G

Part of a talk between Lincoln and some Chicago Christian ministers in early September 1862

I am not sure we could do much with the blacks. If we were to arm them, I fear that in a few weeks the arms would be in the hands of the rebels ... I will mention another thing though it meet only your scorn and contempt. There are about fifty thousand bayonets in the Union army from the border slave states. It would be a serious matter if, in consequence of a proclamation such as you desire, they should go over to the rebels. I do not think they all would – not as many indeed as a year ago, or as six months ago – not so many today as yesterday ... Let me say one thing more. I think you should admit that we already have an important principle to rally and unite the people in the fact that constitutional government is at stake. This is a fundamental idea, going down about as deep as anything.

SOURCE H

The Preliminary Emancipation Proclamation, issued by Lincoln on 22 September 1862

And by virtue of the power, and for the purpose aforesaid, I do order and declare that all persons held as slaves within said designated States, and parts of States, are, and henceforward shall be free; and that the Executive government of the United States, including the military and naval authorities thereof, will recognise and maintain the freedom of said persons.

And I hereby enjoin upon the people so declared to be free, to abstain from all violence, unless in necessary self-defence; and I recommend to them that, in all cases when allowed, they labour faithfully for reasonable wages.

And I further declare and make known, that such persons of suitable condition, will be received into the armed service of the United States to garrison forts, positions, stations, and other places, and to man vessels of all sorts in said service.

And upon this act, sincerely believed to be an act of justice, warranted by the Constitution upon military necessity, I invoke the considerate judgement of mankind, and the gracious favour of Almighty God.

Compare the views in Sources G and H with regard to President Lincoln's views on slavery.

The Proclamation was issued on 22 September 1862 after the battle of Antietam (page 66) – a drawn battle which Lincoln chose to regard as a victory. Justified by Lincoln as 'a fit and necessary war measure', the Proclamation seemed, on the surface, to be cautious.

- Slavery was allowed to remain in states that returned to the Union before 1 January 1863.
- Thereafter all enslaved people in enemy territory conquered by Union armies would be 'forever free'.
- The Proclamation had no impact whatsoever in the Union slave states. Nor did it affect slavery in those areas that had already been brought back under Union control.

The Spectator, published in London, said that the principle behind the Proclamation seemed to be 'not that a human being cannot justly own another but that he cannot own him unless he is loyal to the United States'. Nevertheless, most abolitionists were delighted. 'God bless Abraham Lincoln', wrote Greeley. Radical Republicans appreciated that Lincoln had gone as far as his powers allowed in making the war a war to end slavery. As Union forces advanced, slavery in the Confederacy would end – and once it ended there it could not survive elsewhere.

Northern opposition to the Proclamation

Northern Democrats, convinced that the Proclamation would make it impossible to bring the Confederate states back into the Union, denounced the measure. Aware of the fear of a migration of former enslaved people northwards, Democrats made emancipation a central issue in the 1862 mid-term elections. However, Democrat success was limited. The Republicans lost 35 seats but still kept control of the House: they gained five Senate seats.

The impact of the Proclamation

On 1 January 1863 Lincoln proclaimed that the freedom of all enslaved people in rebellious regions was now a Union war aim – 'an act of justice' as well as 'military necessity'. In the short term it may have helped to stiffen Confederate resistance. However, in the long term it weakened the Confederacy which, given the war was now clearly about slavery, stood little chance of winning British support. By encouraging enslaved people to flee to Union lines, the Proclamation also worsened the South's manpower shortage. As Lincoln said: 'Freedom has given us the control of 200,000 able-bodied men … It will give us more yet. Just so much has it subtracted from the strength of our enemies.'

The Thirteenth Amendment

The Emancipation Proclamation was a war measure – not a Congressional act. Given that it only applied during the war, it would be questionable once the conflict ended. Consequently, the Republicans determined to pass a constitutional amendment prohibiting slavery throughout the USA. The Senate passed the amendment in 1864 but it failed to get the necessary two-thirds support in the House of Representatives. The Republican national convention, urged on by Lincoln, agreed to endorse the constitutional amendment. After Republican election success in November (see page 92), Lincoln applied pressure to several Democrats in the House of Representatives (often by threatening to reduce government spending in their states) – to good effect. In January 1865 the House approved the Thirteenth Amendment for ratification by the states. A delighted Lincoln said it was 'a king's cure for all the evils. It winds the whole thing up.' It hardly did that, but it was a major step forward.

Was Lincoln the Great Emancipator?

From January 1863 Union soldiers fought for the revolutionary goal of a new Union without slavery. Many northerners accepted this. Most would not have accepted it in 1861. During the war, opinion changed. Lincoln's policies reflected and influenced that change. He moved cautiously. His main aim was to preserve the Union, not free the enslaved people. But by mid-1862 Lincoln believed that the two issues had become nearly one and the same. By freeing the enslaved people he could help to preserve the Union.

Some historians have claimed that Lincoln did his best to evade the whole question of freedom for black people and that it was enslaved people escaping who forced him to embrace emancipation. However, the argument that the enslaved people freed themselves has probably been pushed too far. Enslaved people lacked the means to win freedom by their own actions. Ultimately enslaved people were freed by the Union army. Lincoln was commander-in-chief of that army. The fact that he was also committed to emancipation was crucial. By 1865 many abolitionists were prepared to give Lincoln credit. Garrison commended Lincoln for having done a 'mighty work for the freedom of millions ... I have the utmost faith in the benevolence of your heart, the purity of your motives and the integrity of your spirit.'

ACTIVITY

In groups, decide how well President Lincoln dealt with the issue of slavery during the Civil War. One group should argue that Lincoln dealt with the issue with considerable skill. The other should argue that Lincoln mis-handled the issue.

The recruitment of black soldiers

In 1861 most northerners opposed recruitment of black men into the Union army. Abolitionists, by contrast, argued that black people should fight in a war that was likely to destroy slavery. Lincoln, anxious to preserve northern unity, initially stood firm against recruitment of black men. The 1862 Confiscation Act gave him the power to use formerly enslaved people as a military force but he interpreted this narrowly, insisting that black people should be employed as army labourers, not front-line troops. After the Emancipation Proclamation, Lincoln's resistance abated and there was a large influx of black people into the Union army.

- 33,000 free northern black people enlisted.
- 100,000 enslaved people were recruited from the Confederacy.
- 42,000 enslaved people from Kentucky, Delaware, Maryland and Missouri enlisted. (This was the swiftest way for Union state enslaved people to get their freedom.)

Within the Union army there was considerable racial discrimination. Regiments were strictly segregated. Regiments of black soldiers received inferior supplies and equipment. What rankled most was the fact that white privates received $13 a month while black privates were only paid $10. Not until mid-1864 did Congress provide equal pay for black soldiers.

The impact of black soldiers on the war's outcome should not be exaggerated. Of the 37,000 black soldiers who died, only 3000 were killed in combat. Nevertheless, troops of black soldiers did help the Union war effort at a critical time. By 1865 there were nearly as many black soldiers in arms against the Confederacy as there were white soldiers defending it.

Life in the Confederate states

In many ways life for most northerners during the war went on as usual. The conflict had a much greater impact on the lives of civilians in the Confederacy – not least economic hardship and Union occupation.

Financing the war

The Confederacy had difficulty financing the war. It had few **gold reserves** and the Union blockade made it difficult to sell cotton and to raise money from tariffs. Taxes on income, profits and property, levied in 1863, were difficult to administer and failed to bring in sufficient revenue. State governments, which collected the taxes, were reluctant to send money to Richmond. Rather than tax their citizens, states often printed state notes to pay their dues, thus worsening **inflationary pressures**. In 1863 Congress passed the:

- Impressment Act, allowing the seizure of goods to support Confederate armies
- Taxation-in-kind Act, authorizing government agents to collect ten per cent of produce from all farmers.

KEY TERMS

Gold reserves Most currencies are based on a country's gold holding.

Inflationary pressure An undue increase in the quantity of money in circulation. The result is that the value of money goes down.

SOURCE I

Extract from the *Richmond Dispatch* newspaper, July 1863, showing inflation in Richmond 1860–63

The state of affairs brought about by the speculating and extortion practiced upon the public cannot be better illustrated than the following grocery bill for one week for a small family, in which prices before the war and those of present are compared:

1860		1863	
Bacon, 10lbs at 12 ½ c	$1.25	Bacon, 10lbs at 1$	$10.00
Flour, 30 lbs at 5c	1.50	Flour, 30 lbs at 12 ½ c	3.75
Sugar, 5lbs at 8c	.40	Sugar, 5lbs at $1.15	5.75
Coffee, 4lbs at 12 ½ c	.50	Coffee, 4 lbs at $5	20.00
Tea (green), ½ lb at $1	.50	Tea (green), ½ lb at $16	8.00
Lard, 4lbs at 12 ½ c	.50	Lard, 4lbs at $1	4.00
Butter, 3 lbs at 25c	.75	Butter, 3 lbs at $1.75	5.25
Meal, 1pk at 25c	.25	Meal, 1pk at $1	1.00
Candles, 2 lbs at 15c	.30	Candles, 2 lbs at $1.25	2.50
Soap, 5lbs at 10cc	.50	Soap, 5lbs at $1.10	5.50
Pepper and salt (about)	.10	Pepper and salt (about)	2.50
Total	$6.55	Total	$68.25

How useful is Source I as evidence for the impact of the war on the Confederacy?

Only eight per cent of the Confederacy's income was derived from taxes. This meant it had to borrow. In 1861 Treasury Secretary Christopher Memminger raised $15 million in bonds and stock certificates. There were initially many buyers, both within the Confederacy and abroad, but after 1863 investors were reluctant to risk loaning money to what seemed like a lost cause. Given that the Confederacy was only able to raise one-third of its war costs through taxes, bonds and loans, Memminger was forced to print vast amounts of treasury paper money. The result was serious inflation. Shortages of basic commodities, resulting from the breakdown of the railway system and from the blockade (see page 67), helped push up prices. By 1865 prices in the eastern Confederacy were 5000 times the 1861 levels. This led to widespread suffering.

The Confederate economy

After 1861 Davis' government acted forcefully to place the Confederacy's economy on a war footing and to expand its industrial base. Government officials intruded into many aspects of economic life, managing manufacturing and transportation. The result was that Davis' government played a greater role in economic matters than Lincoln's government.

- The **Ordnance Bureau**, ably led by Josiah Gorgas, ensured that by 1863 there were enough arsenals, factories and gunpowder works to keep Confederate armies supplied with the basic tools of war.
- The War Department assumed increasing control over the South's railway system.
- Steps were taken to regulate foreign trade. In 1863, for example, a law required all blockade-runners to carry, as at least one-third of their cargo, cotton out and war supplies in.

State governments played a similarly important economic role. Most tried to regulate the distribution of scarce goods, such as salt. They also encouraged farmers to shift from cotton to food production. Nevertheless, by 1865 the Confederate economy was near collapse. Worn-out machinery could not be replaced. Sources of raw materials were lost as Union forces took over large areas of the South. The breakdown of the railway system, much of which was destroyed by advancing Union armies, proved decisive in the Confederacy's defeat.

Poverty and refugees

Shortages of basic commodities, inflation and **impressment of supplies** had a demoralizing effect on the South. Many areas were also occupied or devastated by Union troops. In an effort to tackle the problem of poverty in general and refugees in particular, state governments, local and town authorities, plus private charities and wealthy individuals, organized relief efforts. By the winter of 1864–65, the problem was so great that it overwhelmed the relief activities.

KEY TERMS

Ordnance Bureau The government agency responsible for acquiring war materials.

Impressment of supplies Confiscation of goods by the government.

Women's role

The Confederacy succeeded in mobilizing about 900,000 men – over 40 per cent of white males of fighting age. This had important implications for southern women.

- Wives of farmers had to work longer hours to provide food for their families.
- Wives of planters had to manage plantations and control enslaved people who were restless.
- In towns women took over jobs once done by men.

By mid-1862 fewer women were willingly sending their men off to war. Some attempted to prevent them being drafted or encouraged desertion. Nevertheless, until the winter of 1864–65, most southern women remained committed to the rebel cause.

How useful are the extracts in Source J as evidence for the state of Confederate morale in 1863?

SOURCE J

Extracts on Confederate morale – all from 1863

From an Alabama newspaper

Wives! Mothers! Beware what you write. A thoughtless and imprudent letter may lead to discontent, desertion.

A southern wife writing to her soldier-husband

Our son is lying at death's door ... he is raving distracted. His earnest calls for Pa almost breaks my heart. John, come if you can.

A letter received by a soldier in the 64th North Carolina Volunteers

The people is all turning Union here since the Yankees has got Vicksburg. I want you to come home as soon as you can.

A woman writing to the governor of North Carolina

A crowd of we Poor women went to Greenesborough yesterday for something to eat as we had not a mouthful of meet nor bread in my house what did they do but put us in gail in plase of giving us aney thing to eat ... I have 6 little children and my husband is in the armey and what am I to do?

Slavery in the Confederacy

Given that they comprised more than a third of the Confederacy's population, enslaved people made a major contribution to its war effort:

- They worked in factories and mines, maintained the railways and helped to grow crops.
- Many states passed laws enabling them to conscript enslaved people for military labour.
- In 1863 the Confederate Congress passed a general **impressment law**.

KEY TERM

Impressment law A law allowing the government to confiscate goods – in this case enslaved people.

After 1861 supervision of enslaved people fell to women and young and old men. Most proved less effective taskmasters than their predecessors. Enslaved people took advantage of the situation, working less diligently. By

1864–65 slave owners sometimes had to negotiate in order to get enslaved people to work. Nevertheless, for many enslaved people the war was a time of great hardship. General shortages of goods resulted in planters cutting back on food and clothing given to enslaved people. For impressed enslaved people, labour was usually harder and supervision tighter than on their home plantations. Despite southern white people's fears, there was no slave rebellion. Aware that freedom was coming, enslaved people bided their time. Whenever an opportunity came to escape, most took it.

Confederate will

It is often claimed that the South lost the war on the home front rather than on the battlefield and that southern civilians lacked the will to make the sacrifices necessary for victory. However, many historians disagree. They believe that white southerners, committed to the Confederate cause, endured enormous hardship in defence of that cause. Even in 1864–65, letters, diaries and newspapers reveal a strong resolve to continue to fight. 'The devils seem to have a determination that cannot but be admired', wrote General Sherman in 1864. 'I see no sign of let up – some few deserters – plenty tired of war, but the masses determined to fight it out.'

Lack of nationalism?

Confederate leaders have been charged with failing to generate a strong sense of **nationalism**. Thus, when the going got tough, southerners found it tough to keep going. The lack of nationalism argument, however, is unconvincing. The strength of patriotic feeling in 1861 produced 500,000 volunteers for military service. Confederate politicians, clergymen and newspaper editors did their utmost to create a sense of nationalism. The war, by creating both a unifying hatred of the enemy and new heroes (like Lee), strengthened Confederate nationalism. Far from explaining Confederate defeat, nationalism helps to explain why southerners fought as long as they did. Misery on the home front led, it is claimed, to a growth of defeatism which was conveyed by letters to the soldiers. Some women wanted their men home and told them to put family before national loyalty. But many others encouraged their men to fight to the end. Increased privation and the loss of loved ones often reinforced rather than eroded loyalty to the Confederacy.

KEY TERM

Nationalism Loyalty and commitment to a country.

The war and religion

Given so much death and destruction, some southerners wondered if God was really on their side. But it seems unlikely that these doubts seriously corroded morale. Southern Church leaders supported the Confederate cause until the bitter end. During the war a religious revival movement swept through the Confederacy. Many men were convinced that God was testing the new nation and that out of suffering would come victory.

The nature of democracy in the Union and Confederacy

In many respects, democratic processes continued to operate on both sides during the Civil War.

The situation in the Union

Elections continued to be held at every level – including the 1864 presidential election. However, the war did have an impact on the power of the federal government and the freedom of individual citizens. But criticism of the war was not suppressed and in 1864 George McLellan ran against Lincoln on the basis of ending the war.

The nature of Lincoln's presidency

During the war, Lincoln's Democrat opponents accused him of exerting executive tyranny and abusing the Constitution. There was some truth to these charges. Convinced that waging war was essentially an executive function, Lincoln believed that he must use his presidential powers to best effect. Where no precedent existed, he was prepared to improvise, stretching the authority of his office beyond any previous practice. In April 1861, for example, he called for troops, proclaimed a blockade of the South and ordered military spending of $2 million without Congressional approval.

KEY TERM

Despot Someone who has absolute power and rules like a dictator.

However, while Lincoln was prepared to take tough measures, he was far from being a **despot**. Although he issued decrees without legislative authority, he later secured Congressional approval for many of his actions and the judiciary also accepted much of what he did as public necessity. Overall, therefore, Lincoln remained faithful to the spirit, if not always the letter, of the Constitution, and was committed to the principle of 'government of the people, by the people, for the people'.

Lincoln's cabinet operated effectively with most of the secretaries remaining at their posts for most of the war. Lincoln usually met his secretaries individually. On the rare occasions when the cabinet met *en masse*, Lincoln used the meetings to discuss the timing or language of statements he was about to issue or to get approval for actions he was about to take. Within their departments, most cabinet members performed well. Secretary of State Seward was regarded as Lincoln's right-hand man. Salmon Chase, secretary of the treasury, was the main radical spokesman. Edwin Stanton, an ex-Democrat, who replaced Secretary of War Cameron in 1862, proved himself efficient and incorruptible.

The nature of Congress

In 1861 the House of Representatives was made up of 105 Republicans, 43 Democrats and 28 'Unionists'. Of the 48 Senators, 31 were

Republican. The Republicans retained control after the 1862 mid-term elections. While there was some conflict over the boundaries of executive and legislative power, Congress loyally provided the means for Lincoln to conduct the war.

State government

State governments were mainly Republican-controlled and provided invaluable assistance to Lincoln, especially in raising troops. Democrat-controlled states did little to hinder the Union war effort.

Union opposition to the war

Lincoln, aware of the need to maintain unity, promoted Democrats to his cabinet and to high military command. **War Democrats** totally threw in their lot with Lincoln. But as the war went on, Democratic opposition increased. Democrats particularly disliked:

- the way the war was being handled
- Lincoln's arbitrary measures
- efforts to end slavery.

KEY TERM

War Democrats Those Democrats who were determined to see the war fought to a successful conclusion.

The Copperheads

In the West, Republicans labelled their Democratic opponents 'Copperheads' (after a poisonous snake) and claimed that they belonged to pro-southern secret societies which planned to set up a Northwest Confederacy that would make peace with the South. In reality, pro-Confederate northerners were a small minority. But Republican leaders realized that charges of treason could be used to discredit the Democrat Party as a whole and could serve as an excuse to organize Union Leagues – Republican-led societies pledged to defend the Union.

Democrat dissent reached its height in early 1863 when Union military failures fostered a sense of defeatism. Some Democrats, like Clement Vallandigham (see page 79), thought it was time to make peace. However, the upturn in Union military fortunes after July 1863 undermined the peace-seeking Democrats, most of whom lost election contests thereafter.

The New York draft riots

The most serious internal violence came in New York in July 1863. The New York riots followed the enforcement of the 1863 Conscription Act. When the names of the first draftees were drawn, a mob of mostly Irish workers attacked the recruiting station. The mob then went on the rampage, venting its fury on black people who were blamed for the war. For several days New York was in chaos. Economic, racial and religious factors all played a part in causing the riots. Lincoln sent in 20,000 troops to restore order. At least 120 people died in the process.

The 1864 election

It says much for the strength of northern democracy that the 1864 presidential election went ahead in the midst of the war. The Confederacy's last (and best) hope was that Lincoln would be defeated. This hope was a realistic one. In August, with the war going badly, Lincoln said, 'I am going to be beaten and unless some great change takes place, badly beaten.' The Democrat convention, hoping to capitalize on war weariness, called for a negotiated peace. However, General McClellan, the Democrat presidential candidate, would not agree to the peace platform. This meant that his Party was in something of a muddle.

Lincoln was not popular with all Republicans. Many wanted to nominate General Grant as presidential candidate but he made it clear that he would not stand. In the event, Lincoln was easily re-nominated with Andrew Johnson as his running mate. The fact that Johnson was a southerner and a War Democrat seemed to strengthen the Republican ticket. The Republican platform endorsed a policy of unconditional surrender and supported a constitutional amendment to abolish slavery. In September the war turned in Lincoln's favour. Atlanta fell and Sheridan was successful in the Shenandoah Valley. In November Lincoln won 55 per cent of the popular vote and 212 electoral college votes to McClellan's 45 per cent and 21 electoral votes. The Republicans increased their majorities in both houses of Congress. Native-born Protestants remained loyal to Lincoln. He also won 78 per cent of soldiers' votes. Lincoln's success was the Confederacy's death knell.

SOURCE K

A Union poster from 1864. The Republicans called themselves the National Union Party hoping to encourage Democrats to vote for Lincoln.

What does Source K suggest about Republican propaganda?

President Lincoln

Lincoln is often regarded as the USA's greatest president. Contemporaries would have been staggered by this opinion. Many were critical of his leadership.

The case against Lincoln

- He was a poor bureaucrat.
- He can be accused of meddling and incompetence in military matters. His choice of commanders of the Army of the Potomac up until 1863 was uninspired.
- He can be seen as just a devious politician, a man who spent hours each day dealing with political matters rather than devoting time to the war effort.
- He deserves little credit for foreign policy (handled by Seward), financial measures (handled by Chase) or economic matters (which were left to Congress).
- Democrats accused him of acting tyrannically.
- Lincoln had an easier task than Davis. The Union was favourite to win, regardless of who was president.
- Arguably, it was his murder, rather than his leadership, which assured his reputation.

The case for Lincoln

- Most historians praise Lincoln's diligence, his tenacity, his unassuming style and his deceptive simplicity.
- Generally, he selected able men and delegated well. Ultimately he appointed the winning military team of Grant and Sherman.
- He was able to articulate the Union's war aims.
- He was a consummate politician, keeping in touch with public opinion and devoting time to matters of patronage and party organization. This ensured that there were many loyal men within his party, a fact that served him well in 1864.
- He handled the issue of slavery with great skill (see pages 81–84).
- His views tended to represent the Republican middle ground but he kept open lines of communication with the radical and conservative wings of his party. Sensitive to public opinion, he was concerned with what could, rather than what should, be achieved.

The situation in the Confederacy

The Confederate government tried to ensure that democratic processes in the South were not unduly damaged by the war.

States' rights

The Confederate states had seceded over the issue of states' rights – essentially the right to preserve slavery. After 1861 many southerners continued to claim that most issues should be decided at state level rather than by the government in Richmond.

The nature of Davis' presidency

Davis was chosen to be provisional Confederate president by the constitutional convention which met in Montgomery in February 1861. He was elected to a full six-year term (by the rules of the Confederate Constitution) in November 1861 and was inaugurated as president in February 1862.

Many contemporaries attacked Davis for having despotic tendencies. Historians, by contrast, have often criticized him for exercising his executive powers too sparingly. However, Davis was prepared to support tough measures when necessary, even when these ran contrary to concerns about states' rights. His urgings produced the 1862 Conscription Act which saved the Confederacy as voluntary enlistments dried up. He also supported the impressment of supplies needed by Confederate troops.

In most respects, Davis attempted to rule in a similar manner to former US presidents. In all, he made 16 appointments to head the 6 cabinet departments. Judah Benjamin accounted for three of these as he was appointed, in succession, to justice, war and state. He owed his survival to his ability and to his close relationship with Davis. Benjamin, Stephen Mallory (Navy) and John Reagan (Postmaster General) served in the cabinet from start to finish. The high turnover in the war and state departments resulted not from feuds between Davis and his secretaries, but from Congressional criticisms that sometimes forced Davis to accept resignations. Most of the secretaries were capable men and government operations functioned smoothly for much of the war.

The nature of the Confederate Congress

Congressmen in the Provisional Congress (which met in 1861–62) were selected by their state legislatures. After this, there were two popularly elected Congresses, the first from 1862–64, the second from 1864–65. There was no two-party system. Men who had once been political enemies tried to present a united front. It may be that the absence of an 'official' opposition resulted in less channelling of political activity and more squabbling. Davis, moreover, had no party organization to mobilize support or to help him formulate legislative policy.

In 1861–62 most Congressmen rallied round Davis. Accordingly, the administration's measures, even those seen as anti-states' rights, passed almost intact. However, as morale deteriorated under the impact of military setbacks, inflation and terrible casualty lists, opposition grew, both inside and outside Congress. This was reflected in the 1863 Congressional elections. Almost 40 per cent of the 1864 Congressional members were new and many were opposed to Davis. Some held extreme views on states' rights; others disliked the way the war was being waged. A small minority wanted peace. Not surprisingly the 'opposition' never formed a cohesive voting block. Thus there was no major rift between Congress and Davis.

States' rights

To wage a successful war, the Confederacy needed the full co-operation of all its states. Some states' leaders were not keen to concede too much power to Richmond. Appealing to the principle of states' rights (for which they had seceded), they resisted many of the efforts of Davis' administration to centralize the running of the war. Governors Joseph Brown (Georgia) and Zebulon Vance (North Carolina) are often blamed for not working for the common cause. Brown, for example, opposed conscription and exempted thousands of Georgians from the draft. In reality, however, most state governments co-operated loyally with Davis. All the 28 men who served as governors, including Brown and Vance, were committed to the Confederacy. As commanders-in-chief of their states, they had more power in war than in peace and were not averse to using it. As a result, they often found themselves vying more with their own state legislatures than with Richmond.

Confederate opposition to the War

While many non-slaveholders in upland areas disliked secession, most white southerners rallied to the Confederate cause in 1861: pro-Union sympathizers were a small minority. But opposition grew, particularly with the introduction of conscription in 1862. Lukewarm southerners now faced a choice of military service or overt opposition. In the mountain regions of North Carolina and Alabama, armed men joined together to fight off enrolment officers. Ordinary farmers resented the fact that rich southerners could avoid military service by either hiring substitutes or exempting themselves because they held a managerial role on a plantation. This led to the perception of a 'rich man's war and a poor man's fight'. In reality few wealthy southerners avoided military duty; indeed they were more likely to fight and die than poor southerners.

President Davis

Davis remains a controversial figure. His Vice-President Stephens blamed him for practically everything that went wrong in the war. Yet his supporters claim that his leadership helped the Confederacy to survive for four years.

The case against Davis

- He failed to establish good working relationships with many of his colleagues.
- Some of his military appointments were disastrous.
- Finding it hard to prioritize and to delegate, he got bogged down in detail.
- He was often indecisive.

- He has been charged with failing to mobilize southern opinion and to build a sense of Confederate nationalism.

The case for Davis

- The fact that Davis appointed Lee says much for his military good sense.
- He supported tough measures when necessary, even when these ran contrary to concerns about states' rights and individual liberty.
- Few have questioned his dedication to the Confederate cause or the intense work he put into a difficult job.

Summary

Both sides continued to operate under their respective (and similar) constitutions, the main difference being that Lincoln and Davis, as war presidents, had greater powers. Both men faced the difficult problems of civil liberty and opposition (which could amount to treason) with some skill, remaining faithful to the spirit, if not always the letter, of their Constitutions. The war had a far greater impact on the lives of southerners than northerners. Southerners, white and black alike, suffered from economic and financial hardship. Slavery continued to exist throughout the war but many enslaved people won their freedom as Union armies invaded the South.

SUMMARY DIAGRAM

How great was the immediate impact of the Civil War?

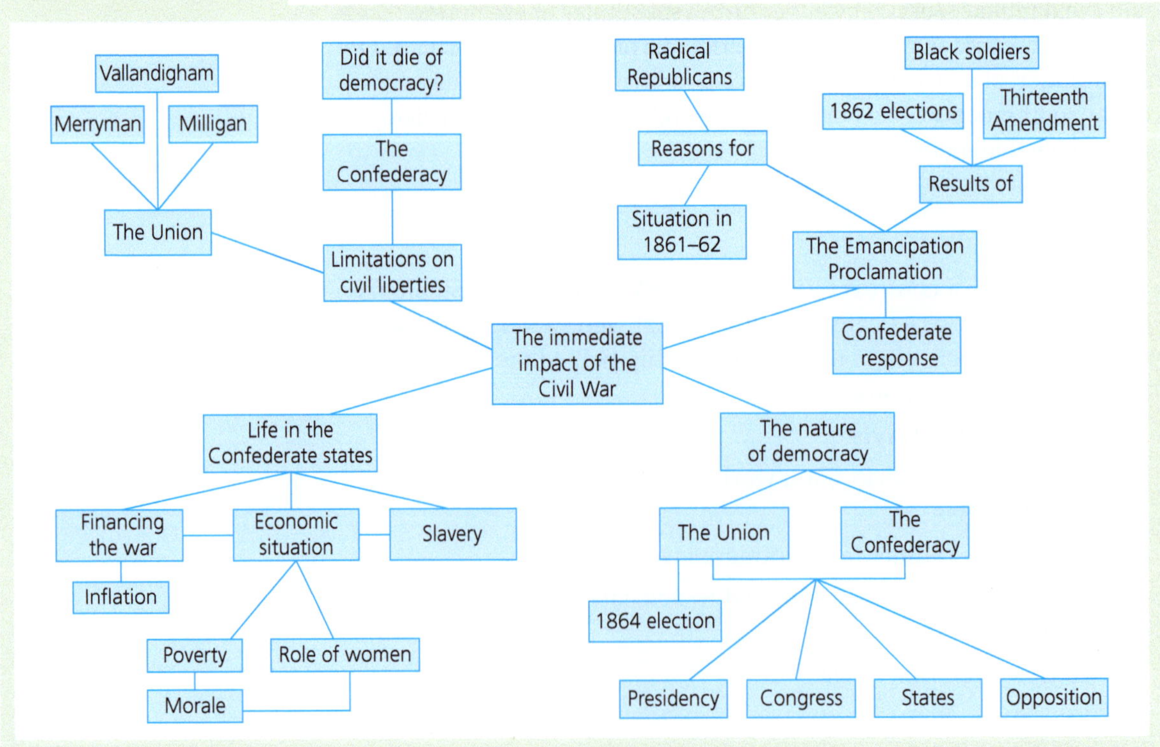

3 What were the aims and outcomes of Reconstruction?

Reconstruction is the name given to the process of bringing the Confederate states back into the Union. The period from 1865 to 1877 is often called the 'age of Reconstruction'. However, Reconstruction was not something that began in 1865: it was an issue from 1861 onwards; it was what the war was all about. Nor did the process of Reconstruction neatly end in 1877: in most southern states it ended much earlier. Virtually every aspect of Reconstruction has been the subject of controversy.

Presidential Reconstruction

From 1861, as Union troops pushed into the South, Lincoln faced the problem of how to restore loyal governments in the rebel states. These problems included:

- On what terms should the states be re-united?
- How should southerners be treated?
- Should Congress or the president decide Reconstruction policy?

Northern opinion was divided on all these matters. As well as differences between Republicans and Democrats, there were differences among Republicans. These differences increased as the war went on and caused problems for both Lincoln and his successor Andrew Johnson.

Lincoln and Reconstruction

Lincoln believed that Reconstruction was a presidential matter. The Constitution gave him the power of pardon: he was also commander-in-chief. Once the war ended, his powers would be reduced. If he was to control Reconstruction he needed to establish firm principles during the war. Lincoln's main aim was consistent: he wanted to restore the Union as quickly as possible. His usual policy was to install military governors in those areas that had been partially reconquered. Lincoln hoped that military government would last only until enough loyal citizens could form a new state government. Lincoln spelt out his Reconstruction ideas in a Proclamation in 1863. He offered pardon to southerners who took an oath of allegiance to the Union. When ten per cent of the 1860 electorate had taken this oath, a new state government could be established. Provided the state then accepted the abolition of slavery, Lincoln agreed to recognize its government. In 1864 Tennessee, Louisiana and Arkansas used this ten per cent plan to create new governments.

ACTIVITY

Discussion point: How valid were the Radical Republican criticisms of Lincoln's Reconstruction plans?

KEY TERM

Disfranchise Deprive someone of the right to vote.

Radical Republican opposition

Radical Republicans disagreed with Lincoln's actions. Most wanted to impose a harsh settlement on the South, punishing the main rebels by confiscating their land. They also believed that people who were formerly enslaved should have the same rights as white Americans. Arguably, radical concern for the rights of black people, particularly suffrage, was the result of political motives rather than idealism. Certainly radicals feared that once the southern states were back within the Union, the Democrats would again be a major threat. There seemed two ways to prevent this: first to ensure that people who were formerly enslaved could vote (they would surely vote Republican); and second, to **disfranchise** large numbers of rebels. Most radicals did not separate idealism and their political aims. They believed that black people should be entitled to vote and hoped that this would ensure Republican ascendancy. Radicals believed that the southern states, by seceding, had reverted to the condition of territories. They were thus subject to Congress's authority, not the president's.

The Wade–Davis bill

Radical dissatisfaction with Lincoln's ten per cent plan was soon apparent. In mid-1864 Congress rejected Louisiana's new constitution and refused admission to its senators. Two radicals, Henry Davis and Benjamin Wade, introduced a bill requiring not 10 but 50 per cent of men from Confederate states to take an oath that they had never voluntarily supported the rebellion before states could re-join the Union. Moreover, anyone who had held Confederate political office or had voluntarily borne arms against the Union was to be excluded from the political process. The bill passed both houses of Congress. Lincoln vetoed it. The federal government thus failed to formulate a definitive method by which former Confederate states would be allowed back into the Union.

The problem of freed slaves

As the war progressed, the Union found itself in control of huge tracts of land, which had either been abandoned by southerners or confiscated from them. What to do with this land, coupled with the organization of its black labour, became issues of debate. Given no firm presidential or Congressional guidance, federal agents created their own solutions. On the Sea Islands (off South Carolina) black people were able to buy plots of land. More often, abandoned plantations were administered by government officials or leased to northern investors who sought financial gain. In these circumstances life for most people who were formerly enslaved did not change very much. They continued to work on the same plantations (for low wages), closely supervised by white managers. Fearing that black and white people could not live peacefully together, Lincoln supported the idea of colonizing people who were formerly enslaved in the Caribbean or Latin America. But attempts to put colonization schemes into effect failed because few black people agreed to participate.

The situation in 1865

- In January 1865 General Sherman declared that freed slaves should receive 40 acres of land and a surplus mule. Sherman was far from a humanitarian reformer: his main concern was to 'dump' the thousands of impoverished black people following his army. Some 40,000 were given land. While Sherman stressed that Congress would have to agree to his plan, his actions raised the expectations of black people.
- By 1865 most Republicans favoured confiscating plantation land and redistributing it among freedmen and loyal white people. However, they were unable to agree on a precise measure.
- In 1865 only five free states allowed black people to vote on equal terms with white people.
- Although Missouri and Maryland freed their enslaved people in 1864, Kentucky still had 65,000 black people in bondage in April 1865. Slavery survived in the state until December 1865.
- In March 1865 Congress set up the Freedmen Bureau. Its aim was to help relieve the suffering of southern black people (and poor white people) by providing food, clothing and medical care.

Lincoln's views in 1865

Lincoln's position on many Reconstruction issues was unclear. While supporting the view that black people should have equality before the law, he seems to have had no desire to punish the South. In his second inauguration speech in March 1865 he talked of 'malice towards none'. Lincoln's intentions will remain forever a mystery. On 14 April 1865 he was murdered by John Wilkes Booth. Booth had long wanted to strike a blow for the southern cause. The irony was that Lincoln's murder did little to help that cause.

SOURCE L

Radical Republican GW Julian of Indiana, April 1865

I spent most of the afternoon in a political caucus, held for the purpose of considering the necessity for a new Cabinet and a line of policy less conciliatory than that of Mr Lincoln: and while everybody was shocked at his murder, the feeling was nearly universal that the accession of Johnson to the presidency would prove a godsend to the country. Aside from Mr Lincoln's known policy of tenderness to the Rebels ... his views of the subject of reconstruction were as distasteful as possible to radical Republicans.

Who do you think was the intended audience for Source L?

Andrew Johnson and Reconstruction

Vice-President Andrew Johnson, an ex-Democrat and former slave owner from Tennessee, now became president. He was the only senator from the Confederate states to stay loyal to the Union. A few radicals were (privately) pleased that Johnson had replaced Lincoln, even if they disliked the circumstances. They hoped he would take a tougher stance against rebel leaders. But the Johnson–radical honeymoon was short-lived.

Johnson, who kept Lincoln's cabinet, claimed his intention was to continue Lincoln's policy. He hoped to restore southern states to the Union before Congress met in December 1865. Keen that the USA should return to its normal functioning as soon as possible, Johnson saw no alternative but to work with former Confederates. He thus favoured leniency. He did not consider black people to be equal to white and was opposed to suffrage for black people. Committed to states' rights, he believed it was not the federal government's responsibility to decide suffrage issues.

In May 1865 Johnson recognized the southern governments created under Lincoln's administration. He also issued a general amnesty to southerners who were willing to swear an oath of allegiance and support emancipation. While major Confederate office-holders were exempted, they could apply for a presidential pardon. Over the summer Johnson granted thousands of pardons, ordering that confiscated land be returned to those pardoned. He also made the process by which southern states would return to the Union easy. He appointed provisional state governors whose main task was to hold elections (in which only white people could vote) for state conventions. The conventions were to draw up new constitutions that accepted that slavery was illegal. Once this was done the states would be re-admitted to the Union.

Andrew Johnson

1808	Born, in extreme poverty, in North Carolina
1826	Moved to Tennessee
1827	Married to Eliza McCardie, who taught him to read and write
1853	Elected governor of Tennessee
1857	Became a senator
1862	Appointed military governor of Tennessee
1864	Nominated as Lincoln's vice-president
1865	Became president
1868	Faced impeachment trial
1875	Died

Throughout his political career, Johnson stressed his working class origins and claimed a special identification with ordinary Americans. In 1865 it seemed likely that he would take a tough stand against the Confederate leaders, especially the great plantation owners whom he had long attacked. This pleased radical Republicans. 'We have faith in you,' Benjamin Wade told Johnson in April 1865. 'By the gods, there will be no trouble now in running the government.' However, Johnson and the radicals quickly fell out.

Historians (for example, HL Trefousse (1989) and A Gordon-Reed (2011)) have generally taken an unfavourable view of Johnson. He has been criticized for sharing the racial views of most white southerners and being unconcerned about the plight of people who were formerly enslaved. He has also been attacked for stubbornly ignoring the northern political mood. While it is possible to argue that Johnson's Reconstruction policies were essentially the same as Lincoln's, it is likely that Lincoln would have displayed more political skill than his successor.

'Reconstruction Confederate style'

White southerners set about implementing Johnson's terms. State conventions acknowledged the end of slavery. States then proceeded to elect legislatures, governors and members of Congress. No state enfranchised black people. All introduced 'black codes', designed to ensure that black people remained second-class citizens. Most required black people to possess contracts which provided evidence of employment. Those who were unemployed or who broke the contracts could be forcibly set to work. Black children could be taken as 'apprentices' and put to work on plantations. Some codes prevented black people from renting or buying land, marrying white people, or serving on juries. The codes were enforced by a legal system that made little pretence of meting out justice fairly. Johnson did not necessarily approve of all these developments but given his belief in states' rights, he had little alternative but to accept what had occurred. In December 1865 he announced that the work of 'restoration' was complete.

Congress versus the South

By the time Congress met in December 1865 there were misgivings about Johnson's leniency. After four years of war northerners still had a profound distrust of the South. The fact that the southern Congressmen who turned up in Washington included Stephens (the Confederate vice-president), four Confederate generals and 58 Confederate Congress members did not reassure northerners of the South's good intent. Nor did the black codes. Moreover, there seemed every likelihood that southerners, with their northern Democrat allies, would soon dominate Congress. Most Republican Congressmen were moderates – not radicals. They had no wish to bring about social revolution in the South. Many were not enthusiastic about suffrage for black people; nor did they wish to greatly expand federal authority but most thought that Confederate leaders should be barred from holding office and that the basic rights of people who were formerly enslaved should be protected. Thus Congress refused to admit the southern Congressmen or to recognize the new southern regimes. A Committee on Reconstruction was formed to recommend a new policy.

ACTIVITY

In relation to Reconstruction, what were the differences between Lincoln's policies and those of Andrew Johnson? Write a paragraph on whether there were more similarities or more differences in relation to their Reconstruction policies.

Congress versus Johnson

Instead of working with moderate Republicans, Johnson chose to side with the Democrats. When Congress tried to enlarge the powers of the Freedmen's Bureau he vetoed it, claiming that it was an unwarranted continuation of war power. Moderate and radical Republicans now joined forces to pass a civil rights bill which aimed to guarantee minimal rights to black people. Johnson, arguing that civil rights were a state matter, vetoed it but in April 1866 a two-thirds majority ensured that Johnson's veto was over-ridden and the Civil Rights Act became law. Congress proceeded to pass a second Freedmen Bureau Act over Johnson's veto.

The Fourteenth Amendment

To ensure that civil rights could not be changed in future, both houses of Congress adopted the Fourteenth Amendment (which embodied the Civil Rights Act). This guaranteed all citizens equality before the law. If individual states tried to abridge the rights of American citizens, the federal government could intervene. It also banned from office Confederates who before the war had taken an oath of allegiance to the Union. This made virtually the entire political leadership of the South ineligible for office. Rejected by all the former Confederate states (except Tennessee), it failed to get the approval of 75 per cent of the states that was necessary for it to become law.

Radical Reconstruction from Congress

In the 1866 mid-term elections Johnson supported – and was supported by – the National Union Convention which hoped to unite Democrats and conservative Republicans. This strategy was a disaster for Johnson. His Republican enemies triumphed. With a two-thirds majority in both houses, they could over-ride any presidential veto. The Republican-dominated Congress now took over the Reconstruction process.

The Military Reconstruction Act

In 1867 Congress passed a Military Reconstruction Act. This stated that:

- No legal government existed in any ex-Confederate state (except Tennessee).
- The ten unreconstructed southern states were to be divided into five military districts, each placed under a federal commander.
- To get back into the Union, southern states had to elect constitutional conventions which would accept suffrage for black people and ratify the Fourteenth Amendment.

The bill was passed despite Johnson's veto. Congress then moved to weaken Johnson's power. A Command of the Army Act reduced his military powers. The Tenure of Office Act barred him from removing a host of office-holders, including members of his cabinet. It was designed to protect Secretary of War Stanton, a fierce critic of Johnson, who had still not resigned from his cabinet. Johnson, unwilling to accept Congressional pressure, dismissed Stanton.

Johnson impeached

Republicans in the House of Representatives, convinced that Johnson had broken the law, determined to impeach him for 'high crimes and misdemeanours'. The **impeachment** proceedings took place in the Senate in the spring of 1868. Johnson was charged essentially with the removal of Stanton from office. After a two-month trial, 35 senators voted against Johnson and 19 for him. This was one vote short of the two-thirds majority needed to impeach him. Although he had survived, for the rest of his term he was a **lame duck president**.

KEY TERM

Impeachment The process by which a president who has been found guilty of grave offences by Congress can be removed from office.

Lame duck president A president who has little power because he does not control Congress or because he will soon be out of power.

President Grant

In 1868 the Republicans chose General Grant as their presidential candidate. Without ever being a fully-fledged radical, he was prepared to support radical Reconstruction. His Democrat opponent, Horatio Seymour, campaigned against equality for black people. Grant easily won the electoral college vote (by 214 votes to 80) but won only 52 per cent of the popular vote.

The Fifteenth Amendment

Given the 1868 election result, Republicans had even better cause to support suffrage for black people. In 1869 the Fifteenth Amendment was introduced. (It was ratified in 1870.) This stated that, 'The right to vote should not be denied … on account of race, colour or previous conditions of servitude'. With civil and political equality seemingly assured, most Republicans believed that black people should no longer be dependent on the federal government. Their place in society would now depend upon themselves.

Summary

Reconstruction was not something which started at the war's end in 1865. The process actually began with the start of the war in 1861. However, apart from the Emancipation Proclamation and the Thirteenth Amendment, little had been set in stone by 1865. Lincoln was at odds with many radicals within his own party on a number of issues. His assassination did not help matters. His successor, Andrew Johnson, soon fell out with Congress by introducing a very 'soft' Reconstruction policy. Congress, dominated by the Republicans after the mid-term 1866 elections, proceeded to introduce its own 'harsher' Reconstruction programme.

SUMMARY DIAGRAM

What were the aims and outcomes of Reconstruction?

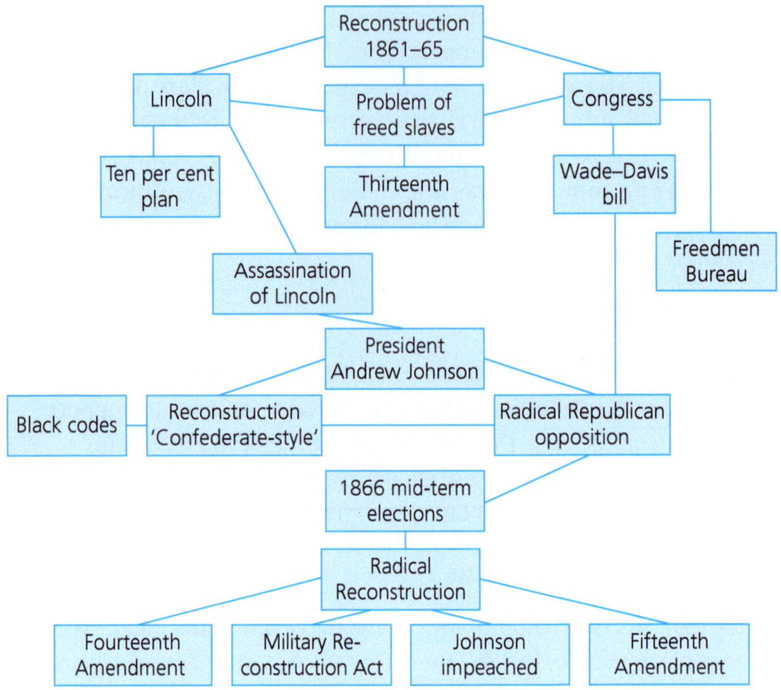

4 How successful was Reconstruction?

Following the Military Reconstruction Act all former Confederate states, except Tennessee, experienced military rule. The extent to which the South was under the heel of a 'military despotism' should not be exaggerated. There were never more than 20,000 troops in the South. Military rule was also short lived. Southern Republicans quickly produced the necessary constitutions and in every state, except Virginia, took over the first restored state governments. By mid-1868, Republican governments in Alabama, Arkansas, Florida, Georgia, Louisiana, North Carolina and South Carolina had ratified the Fourteenth Amendment and been received back into the Union. Texas, Virginia, Georgia and Mississippi were re-admitted in 1870. Just how much success the Republican governments in the South achieved remains a source of considerable debate.

The changing position of people who were formerly enslaved

The position of people who were formerly enslaved seemed to have changed massively by the late 1860s following the Thirteenth, Fourteenth and Fifteenth Amendments. They even seemed to have considerable political power.

The Thirteenth, Fourteenth and Fifteenth Constitutional Amendments

The Thirteenth Amendment abolished slavery and involuntary servitude within the USA. A condition of re-entering the Union was that former confederate states had to ratify the amendment. It was finally ratified in December 1865. It had been introduced to Congress in 1864. Though slavery had been abolished in Washington DC and in rebel-held territories, this was not a guarantee that slavery would end once the war was over. This amendment was therefore highly significant. Lincoln had feared that the Supreme Court could declare the Emancipation Proclamation unconstitutional as it exceeded presidential powers. A return to slavery would reignite old passions and the Republican Party had pressed for it. It was part of Lincoln's election platform in 1864 and he did his best to reduce opposition to it in the House of Representatives. It had a precedent in the Northwestern Ordinance of 1787 and applied to individuals rather than states so was not seen as an attack on states' rights.

The Fourteenth Amendment granted citizenship to all who had been born or naturalized in the USA including people who were formerly enslaved and gave them equal protection under the laws. States that 'abridged' citizens' rights could be punished by having their congressional representation reduced. It also banned those who had been in rebellion against the Union from holding office without two-thirds Congressional approval. It was ratified in July 1868. By that time the Republicans in Congress were angry at the efforts of the Confederate legislatures trying to resist change and to prevent people who were formerly enslaved from voting. The actions of various southern states to prevent black American civil rights led to an amendment which was aimed directly at states which were undermining the progress of the Thirteenth Amendment and Congressional Reconstruction.

The Fifteenth Amendment prohibited states from preventing citizens from voting on grounds of race, clamour or previous involuntary servitude (slavery). However, states could apply voting restrictions provided they applied to everyone regardless of race. This was ratified in February 1870. It aimed to prevent obstacles to voting being imposed by southern legislatures. However, as it did not prevent them imposing general restrictions such as literacy tests or property qualifications which applied to all but would disqualify black people disproportionately, it was not as effective as its Republican supporters hoped.

Republican rule in the South

While often reliant on the support of federal troops, southern Republicans in 1867–68 had a reasonable amount of popular support. This came from three groups: black people, **carpetbaggers** and **scalawags**. They faced fierce opposition from Democrats who sought to **redeem** their states.

KEY TERMS

Carpetbaggers Northern white people who settled in – and were accused of exploiting – the South. (A carpetbag was the suitcase of the time.)

Scalawags Southern white people who supported the Republican Party.

Redeem To restore to white rule.

Black Reconstruction?

The American historian Professor Dunning in the early twentieth century described the period of Republican rule as 'Black Reconstruction'. He thought the new governments represented the worst elements in southern society – illiterate black people, self-seeking carpetbaggers and renegade scalawags – given power by a vengeance-seeking Republican Congress. Dunning depicted 'Black Reconstruction' as undemocratic, with the Republicans ruling against the will of a disfranchised white majority. He also accused the new governments of corruption on a grand scale.

Most of Dunning's views have been challenged, including the term 'Black Reconstruction' which implies that black people dominated the Reconstruction process. Black southerners certainly wielded some political power. Having been given the vote, most black people used it. In South Carolina and Mississippi, black voters constituted a real majority of the electorate. In three other states (by September 1867) black voters outnumbered white because so many rebels were disfranchised. The result was that two black senators and 15 black representatives were elected to Congress before 1877. Far more black people were elected to state legislatures: for a time black people controlled the lower house of South Carolina's legislature. While this was a revolutionary break with the past, black political influence never reflected black numbers. Few of the top positions in state governments went to black people. Divisions within the black community, particularly between free-born black people and those who were formerly enslaved, help explain why black office-holders did not equate with black voters. But perhaps the main reason was the fact that black people were a minority in most states. If Republican governments were to be elected, the Republicans needed to win some support from white voters. Assured of black people's votes, Republicans often put forward white candidates for office hoping to attract white voters. Although power remained largely in the control of white people, the excesses of the Reconstruction governments were usually blamed on black members. Those black people who held office performed as well – and as badly – as white people.

SOURCE M

James Pike of Maine, a famous political journalist of his day, writing of the South Carolina House of Representatives in 1873

The Speaker is black, the Clerk is black, the door-keepers are black, the little pages are black, the Chairman of the Ways and Means is black, and the chaplain is coal-black

... the body is almost literally a Black Parliament, and it is the only one on the face of the earth which is the representative of a white constituency ... [Seven years ago] these men were raising corn and cotton under the whip of the overseer. Today they are raising points of order and privilege. They find they can raise one as well as the other. They prefer the latter. It is easier and better paid ... It means escape and defense from old oppressors. It means liberty.

Look at Source M. What is Pike's view of the fact that the South Carolina House of Representatives had such a large number of black members?

Carpetbaggers and scalawags

Without winning some support from southern-born white people, few Republican governments would have been elected. The scalawags came from diverse backgrounds and voted Republican for a variety of reasons. Some were former Whigs. Others were farmers from upland areas who had opposed the Confederacy. Most did not support full racial equality but they knew that if they were to maintain political control, they must retain black people's vote.

Carpetbagger influence has been much exaggerated. In no state did they constitute two per cent of the population. Nor were they set on fleecing the South economically. Many northerners who went South were young, well-educated and middle class – teachers, clergy, or agents of various benevolent societies engaged in aiding people who were formerly enslaved. Others were army veterans who had served in the South, liked what they saw and remained there. Most supported the Republican Party because they believed that Republican policies were best for the country.

Corruption and inefficiency

Democrats denounced Republican corruption and inefficiency. The Freedmen Bureau, seen as a Republican-sponsored organization, was similarly indicted. Historians have found plenty of evidence to collaborate the charges. Many Republican politicians used their powers of patronage to benefit themselves and their supporters. Bribery, especially by railway companies, was commonplace. Some administrations were also incompetent. Southern state debts multiplied and taxes sharply increased.

However, the late 1860s and 1870s saw corruption and inefficiency everywhere in the USA. Moreover, there had been massive corruption in southern state governments before 1861 and there was similar corruption after the states were 'redeemed'. Southern Republican governments had little option but to raise and spend large sums of money. Most inherited empty treasuries. Much of the southern transportation system had been destroyed during the war. Public buildings needed to be repaired. Schools, hospitals and orphanages had to be built for black people as well as white. The fact that new facilities were built indicates that the money spent was not always wasted. The Freedmen Bureau continued to provide assistance to black people and poor white people.

Economic reconstruction

From 1867 to 1873 the South benefited from high cotton prices. Railways were rebuilt and there was an increase in manufacturing but promising as this was, it did not keep pace with economic progress elsewhere. The South remained an agricultural region, heavily dependent on cotton. In many areas the old plantations remained, sometimes with new owners, sometimes not. During the 1870s most black people became sharecroppers. White landowners provided the land, seed and tools: black tenants supplied the labour. Whatever crop was produced was divided in a fixed ratio – often half to the landowner and half to the tenant. Sharecropping provided black farmers with freedom from supervision by white people day to day and some incentive to work hard but neither the freedom nor the incentive should be exaggerated.

In the early 1870s, a worldwide excess of cotton led to a disastrous fall in prices which resulted in most sharecroppers being in a perpetual state of indebtedness to landowners and local storekeepers. In turn, landowners and storekeepers were in debt to southern merchants and bankers who themselves were in debt to northern banks. The South did well in terms of cotton output. In 1860 it had produced 4.5 million bales of cotton: by 1880 it produced 6.3 million bales. However, the increased production simply added to the glut: consequently prices continued to fall. The South was thus the poorest section of the USA.

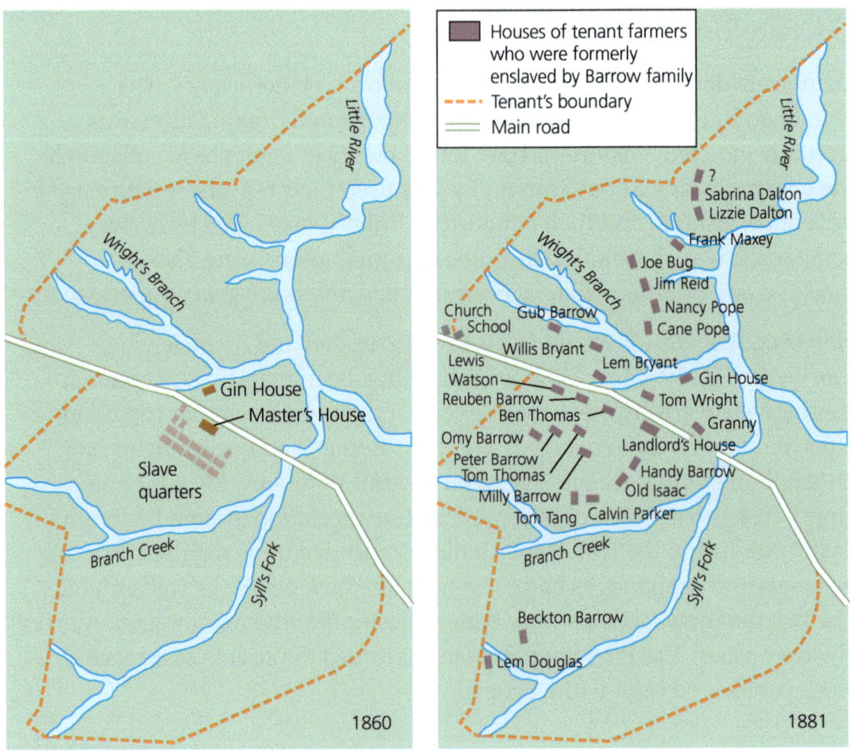

Figure 2.5 Changes on the Barrow Plantation from 1860 to 1881, demonstrating the way that plantation land was divided

Responses of white southerners

Republican rule was loathed by most white southerners.

The Ku Klux Klan

In 1866 **paramilitary groups** formed in most southern states with the aim of restoring white suprem The most notorious was the Ku Klux Klan. The Klan, led for a time by prominent Confederate soldier Nathan Bedford Forrest, spread rapidly, drawing support from many sections of the white community. By 1870 Forrest claimed there were over 500,000 Klansmen. The Klan sought to destroy Republican political organizations by intimidation and force. Its terrorist activities reached their peak in the years 1869–71. Black people who held public office were particular targets. So were schools and churches for black people. Southern Republican governments found it hard to enforce the laws. When Klan suspects were arrested, witnesses were reluctant to testify and Klansmen were ready to lie

KEY TERM

Paramilitary groups Organized along military lines, these groups often engage in rebellion against the government.

SOURCE N

The drawing from 1874 shows members of the White League and the Ku Klux Klan joining hands over a black family.

Examine Source N. What is the message of the source? What do you think was the purpose of the drawing?

in court to provide one another with alibis. Some state governors appealed to Congress for help. Thus, in 1870–71 Congress passed three Force Acts, authorizing President Grant to use the army to break up the Klan. Grant imposed martial law in parts of the South, imprisoning hundreds of suspected Klansmen. While this reduced Klan terrorism, violence and intimidation continued.

The South 'redeemed'

In many southern states radical Reconstruction was over almost before it began. Tennessee was under Democrat control by 1869; Virginia and North Carolina were redeemed in 1870; Georgia in 1871; Texas in 1873; Arkansas and Alabama in 1874; and Mississippi in 1875. By 1876 only Louisiana, Florida and South Carolina were still under Republican control. The Democrat (or Bourbon) regimes, which replaced the Republican governments, shared a commitment to reducing:

- black people's political power
- the scope and expense of government
- taxes.

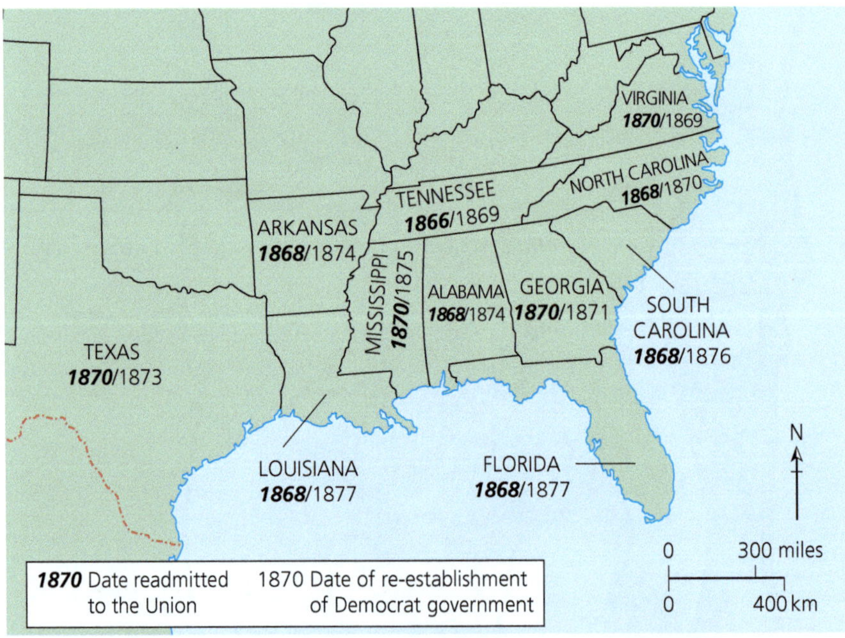

Figure 2.6
The Southern states redeemed. The map shows the date when the states re-joined the Union and when Democrat governments were elected

President Grant's Reconstruction policies

President Grant, who remained in power until 1877, had initially seemed committed to the 'hard' Reconstruction policy of the Republican-dominated Congress. However, as time passed, Grant's enthusiasm for supporting radical/Congressional Reconstruction waned. This was by no means the only reason why Republican rule in the South collapsed.

Reasons for Republican defeat

Several factors played a part in Republican defeat. Intimidation by white people was certainly a factor. So was the effect of factionalism within Republican parties at local level. Racism was a major cause of the in-fighting: scalawags were reluctant allies of black people but there was also rivalry between different groups of scalawags and different groups of black people. Republican policies at state level did not assist the party's cause. Heavy taxation helped to drive white farmers from the party. Southern Republicans were also betrayed by the northern wing of the party. After 1867 radical influence declined as old leaders died or retired. Most northern Republicans had little sympathy for the plight of black southerners. By the early 1870s many Republicans, like President Grant himself, felt the time had come to let the South sort out its own problems. Two actions in 1872 symbolized a desire to build bridges to white southerners.

- An **Amnesty Act** resulted in 150,000 ex-Confederates having their rights returned.
- The Freedmen's Bureau collapsed.

KEY TERM

Amnesty Act A measure granting a general pardon for past crimes.

In 1872 Grant defeated Horace Greeley, winning over 55 per cent of the popular vote. Unfortunately, Grant's second term was dominated by two issues: the economic depression and a spate of scandals which damaged Grant's standing. In the 1874 mid-term elections the Democrats won control of the House of Representatives. Thereafter there was little that the Republican Party or Grant could do to help southern Republicans.

The situation by the mid-1870s

Given Grant's position and the situation in Congress, the end of radical Reconstruction was almost inevitable. The majority of voters in most southern states were white. Those who think that a strong Republican Party might have been founded on policies that appealed to black and poor white people are probably deluding themselves. The reality was that few poor white people identified with poor black people. Given that race was the dominant issue, many of the election campaigns in the South in the 1870s were ugly. White southerners organized new paramilitary groups – Rifle Clubs, Red Shirts, White Leagues – the aim of which was to allegedly maintain public order. Their real mission, however, was to overthrow the Republican governments. Unlike the Klan, these groups paraded openly. On election days, armed white people tried to turn black people away from the polls. Republican leaders tried to ensure that black people did vote – often several times! In Louisiana, for example, every election between 1868 and 1876 was marred by violence and fraud. After 1872, two governments claimed legitimacy. A Republican regime, elected by black people and protected by the federal army, was the legitimate government but a Democrat government, elected by white people, controlled much of the countryside. In 1874 the Republicans stayed in power by throwing out the results from many Democrat areas.

The Compromise of 1877 and the end of Reconstruction

The 1876 presidential election and the 1877 Compromise are often seen as the end of Reconstruction.

The 1876 presidential election

The Republican candidate was Rutherford B Hayes. The Democrats chose Samuel Tilden. Tilden won the popular vote, gaining 4,284,000 votes to Hayes' 4,037,000. But presidential elections are determined by the electoral college, not by the popular vote. While Tilden had 184 electoral college votes to Hayes' 165, the voting returns from Oregon, South Carolina, Louisiana and Florida were contested. These 4 states had 20 electoral college votes. If all 20 went to Hayes he would win. If just one state went to Tilden, he would become president. Hayes was soon assured of Oregon's votes. The real problem lay in the South. It was – and is – impossible to know how far Democrat intimidation offset Republican fraud. The dispute lingered on over the winter. Eventually Congress established a Commission to review the election returns. Eight commissioners were Republicans: seven were Democrats. The Republican-dominated Commission awarded all the disputed elections to Hayes.

The Compromise of 1877

The 1877 Compromise ended the crisis. Given that nothing was agreed in writing, there is still debate about whether anything was actually agreed. The Compromise, in so far as there was one, seems to have been as follows. The Democrats would accept Hayes as president. Hayes, in return, agreed to withdraw all troops from the South, recognize Democrat governments in the three disputed states and appoint a southerner to his cabinet. Hayes, however, denied making any concessions to the South.

Whatever had or had not been agreed, Hayes did withdraw troops from the South with the result that South Carolina, Louisiana and Florida fell under Democrat control. Thus, by 1877 all the ex-Confederate states had returned to white rule. Hayes continued his policy of conciliation, visiting the South on a goodwill tour. While Hayes's presidency is usually seen as marking the end of Reconstruction, his actions did not mark an abrupt change in policy. They only confirmed what had been done earlier by Congress or by Grant.

ACTIVITY

In groups, list five reasons to explain why the South was so quickly 'redeemed'. Then choose the reason you think is the most important and debate your choice with a partner.

Was Reconstruction a tragic failure?

White southern historians (like Dunning) once saw Reconstruction as 'The Tragic Era' – a time when southerners suffered military occupation, when the South was ruled by corrupt governments and when black people proved incapable of exercising the political rights which the North thrust upon them. In Dunning's view the Reconstruction heroes were President Johnson, who tried to continue Lincoln's policies, and southern Democrats who campaigned to redeem the South. The villains were the vindictive radical Republicans.

In the 1950s and 1960s, historians such as Kenneth Stampp depicted Reconstruction very differently. 'Rarely in history', said Stampp, 'have participants in an unsuccessful rebellion endured so mild penalties as those Congress imposed upon the people of the South and particularly upon their leaders.' In Stampp's opinion the villains were Johnson and white southern Democrats. The heroes were the radical Republicans who fought for the rights of people who were formerly enslaved. In this view, black, not white, southerners were the real losers of Reconstruction.

Given the Civil War's scale, the North was remarkably generous to white southerners. Most, even those who had held high Confederate office, were quickly pardoned. Davis spent two years in prison but was then freed. Only one man, Henry Wirz, the commandant of the notorious Andersonville prison camp in which hundreds of Union soldiers had died, was executed for war crimes. Slavery apart, there was no major confiscation of property. The North was less generous to people who were formerly enslaved. Black people came out of slavery with little or no land. By the 1870s most eked out a living as poor sharecroppers.

However, historians (like Eric Foner) have recently been rather more positive about Reconstruction's economic impact on the lives of black people.

- Sharecropping was significantly better than slavery.
- After 1865 black people steadily increased the amount of land they farmed.
- With the end of slavery, black people had mobility. Many moved to southern and northern cities.
- Living standards for black people generally improved after 1865.

A major criticism of Reconstruction is that it failed to guarantee black people's civil rights. By 1900, black people were second-class citizens. Segregation was the norm in virtually every aspect of southern life. While a rigid legalized segregation system did not exist in most states until the 1890s, the so-called **Jim Crow laws** did not represent a shift in the actual degree of segregation. These laws simply confirmed segregation – a fact of southern life since 1865. Moreover, by 1900 southern state governments had introduced a variety of measures – poll tax tests, literacy tests and residence requirements – to ensure that black people could not vote. Black people were also taught to know their place. 'Uppity' black people were likely to receive brutal treatment. **Lynchings** were a common aspect of southern life in the late nineteenth and early twentieth centuries.

However, black southerners were not just victims or objects to be manipulated: they were also important participants in the Reconstruction process. Quite naturally, given their experiences under slavery, many had no wish to mix socially with white people. Like most American ethnic groups they preferred to keep themselves to themselves. Accordingly segregation was often a statement of black community identity. After 1865, for example, there was an almost total withdrawal of black people from 'white' churches as black people tried to achieve **self-determination**.

KEY TERMS

Jim Crow laws Segregation laws, passed in most southern states in the 1890s.

Lynching Executing without the usual forms of law, often by a crowd of people who were angered by the actions of the 'accused'.

ACTIVITY

Make a copy of the table then fill it in to show the arguments for and against the view that Reconstruction was a failure.

Reconstruction failed because...	Reconstruction succeeded because...

KEY TERM

Self-determination The right of a population to decide its own government.

Churches, the first and most important social institutions to be controlled by black people, became a focal point of black people's lives. Black people also established their own trade associations and benevolent societies. The fact that there were institutions for black people, paralleling those of white people, meant there were opportunities for black people to lead. Interestingly, the disfranchisement of black people did not occur on a major scale until the 1890s. During the 1870s and 1880s black people voted in large numbers and were appointed to public office. Historian Eric Foner sees participation of black people in Southern political life after 1867 as 'a massive experiment in interracial democracy'.

KEY FIGURE

Booker T Washington (1856–1915) Born into slavery, Washington was a major black American leader and educator in the late nineteenth and early twentieth centuries. He did not support integration or full political equality but wanted black Americans to rise through education so that they could share in US economic prosperity and take advantage of opportunities.

Some black leaders of the late nineteenth and early twentieth centuries, notably **Booker T Washington**, accepted that black people were second-class citizens. Washington believed that black people must seek to better themselves through hard work and education. His faith in education was shared by many black people. After 1865 many black communities raised money to build their own schools and to pay teachers' salaries. After 1870 most teachers in schools and colleges for black people were themselves black. Education for black people was one of the successes of Reconstruction.

Reconstruction was thus far from a total failure. Crucially black people were no longer enslaved. If Reconstruction did not create an integrated society, it did establish the concept of equal citizenship. If black people were not yet equal citizens, at least the Fourteenth and Fifteenth Amendments could be invoked by later generations of civil rights' activists.

Summary

After 1866, the federal government was successful in bringing the seceded states back into the Union. Few white southerners approved of the Reconstruction process. Black Americans' hopes and expectations, particularly with regard to land ownership, were not realized while white people believed that they had been deprived of their democratic rights and placed under the thumb of corrupt and illegitimate Republican governments. These governments were ultimately dependent on military force. By the mid-1870s Grant's administration and Congress were no longer keen to support the use of force. After 1877, as a result of the 1876 presidential election and the 1877 Compromise, white Democratic administrations controlled all the former Confederate states. Debates about whether Reconstruction was a success or failure look set to continue.

SUMMARY DIAGRAM

How successful was Reconstruction?

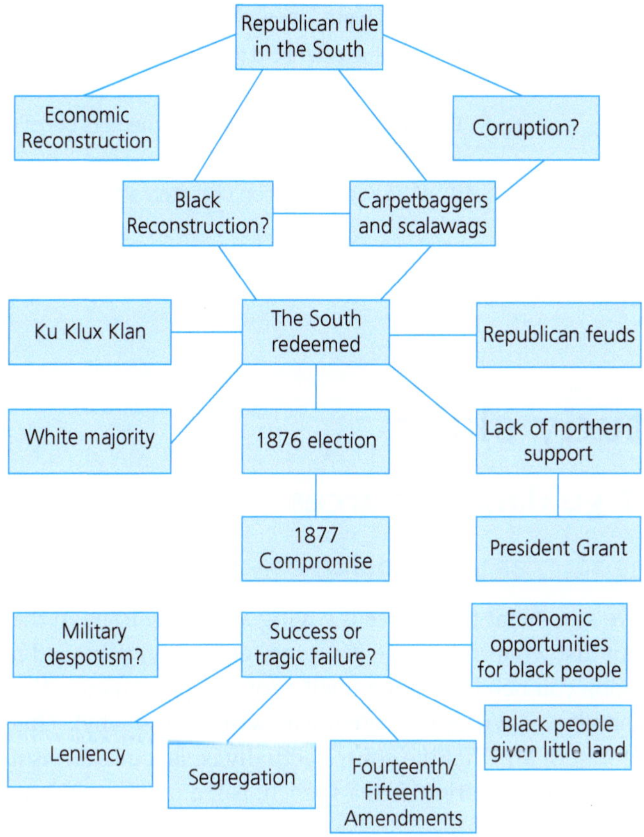

Chapter summary

Although Confederate forces fought well, its armies were outnumbered by better-equipped Union armies. Davis' Confederate government faced problems on the home front as well as on the battlefield. These included states' rights, financial weakness, managing a war economy and domestic opposition. The strength of the northern economy ensured that the Union had little difficulty financing the war. Lincoln, committed to winning the war, had the support of most northerners. Union troops, ably led in the end by Grant and Sherman, eventually forced Lee to surrender in 1865. Lincoln, Johnson and Congress had the difficult task of reconstructing the Union, a process which began in 1861. Apart from the Emancipation Proclamation and the Thirteenth Amendment, little had been established firmly by 1865. Lincoln's assassination did not help matters. Johnson soon fell out with Congress, which then introduced its own Reconstruction programme. Few white southerners approved of Congressional Reconstruction. They believed they had been deprived of their democratic rights and placed under the control of corrupt and illegitimate Republican state governments. Nevertheless, by 1877 white Democrat administrations controlled all former Confederate states. Despite the Thirteenth, Fourteenth and Fifteenth Amendments, the hopes of black southerners were not realized. While freed from slavery, they remained second-class citizens economically, socially and politically.

Refresher questions

1 What were the main Union strengths?
2 What were the main Confederate strengths?
3 Why did Britain not intervene in the Civil War?
4 How did the war affect life in the Confederacy?
5 Why did the war last so long?
6 What were Lincoln's aims with regard to Reconstruction?
7 What were Johnson's aims?
8 To what extent did the South suffer from military despotism?
9 To what extent did black southerners benefit from Reconstruction?
10 Was Reconstruction ultimately a tragic failure?

Study skills

Paper 1 guidance: sources

Evaluating sources using source content and provenance

Once you are sure what the source is saying about the issue in the question (not just what the source is saying, generally) you need to think what questions you need to ask yourself about its provenance (that is who wrote it, when it was written, where it was written and why). This means considering first of all what the source actually is. Is it a letter; is it a report; is it a record of a conversation; is it a speech; is it a memoir, is it a diary; is it a newspaper article?

The danger is that you will just assume that all diaries are reliable because the person involved in the historical events writes them; or all newspaper articles are unreliable because the journalists want to sell papers; or all records of conversations are useless because the person might not remember the exact words. Try not to generalize about sources of this type but instead look at the actual source itself.

After looking to see what the source is, ask yourself some key questions:

- Why was it written? For example, if it is a speech, why was it delivered?
- Who is the intended audience? A diary or a letter will have a different audience from a public report or a newspaper.
- When was it written? Something written in the middle of a historical development, like the situation in the Civil War in 1863 when it is not clear what will happen, is very different from something written later when the outcome is known.
- How typical is it? For example, if a southern politician writes that he wants to get rid of Jefferson Davis was this a usually held view of Confederate politicians?
- How useful is this source as evidence, even if you don't think it is 'true' or 'unbiased'. It might be, for instance, that a source is very critical of Abraham Lincoln for not acting quickly enough on the issue of emancipation.

This might or might not be justified but the source is still likely to be useful as evidence for a widely held view of Lincoln's failing leadership.

Activity

Read sources A, B, C and D that follow this activity box. Having studied them carefully, fill in the table below in order to help plan an answer to the question:

How far do the following sources explain the defeat of the Confederacy?

Source	What is it?	When was it written? Is this important?	Why was it written?	Was the author in a position to know?	Explain why the author might be prejudiced or inaccurate
A					
B					
C					
D					

Which do you think the most useful source here is? Explain your answer.

Most useful source	Explain why

SOURCE A

Part of a letter written by Jonathan Worth, a former Whig politician from North Carolina, writing to his friend Jesse G Henshaw. Worth, the State Treasurer of North Carolina, had opposed secession but nevertheless gone with his state in 1861

I hardly know whether I am in favour of the peace meetings [which had occurred in North Carolina] or not. On the one hand, it is very certain that the President and his advisers will not make peace, if not forced into it by the masses and the privates in the army ...

I am for peace on almost any terms and fear we shall not have it until the Yankees dictate it. Upon the whole I would not go into a peace meeting now or advise others to go into one, particularly in Randolph – but I have no repugnance to them in other places and see no other chance to get to an early end of this wicked war, but by the actions of the masses who have the fighting to do.

The letter was written in August 1863

SOURCE B

Part of President Lincoln's State of the Union Address to Congress

The war continues. Since the last annual message all the important lines and positions then occupied by our forces have been maintained and our arms have steadily advanced, thus liberating the regions left in rear so that Missouri, Kentucky, Tennessee and parts of other states have again produced reasonably fair crops. The most remarkable feature in the military operations of the year is General Sherman's attempted march of 300 miles [480 km] directly through the insurgent region.

Lincoln's speech was delivered on 6 December 1864

SOURCE C

President Davis's final message to the people of the Confederacy

The General-in-Chief of our Army has found it necessary to make such movements of the troops as to uncover the capital and thus involve the withdrawal of the Government from the city of Richmond. It would be unwise, even if it were possible, to conceal the great moral as well as material injury to our cause that must result from the occupation of Richmond by the enemy. It is equally unwise and unworthy of us, as patriots engaged in a most sacred cause, to allow our energies to falter, our spirits to grow faint, or our efforts to become relaxed under reverses, however calamitous.

Davis delivered this message on 4 April 1865

SOURCE D

Robert E Lee's General Order to the Army of Northern Virginia after his surrender at Appomattox

After four years of arduous service marked by unsurpassed courage and fortitude the Army of Northern Virginia has been compelled to yield to overwhelming numbers and resources. I need not tell the survivors of so many hard fought battles, who have remained steadfast to the last, that I have consented to this result from no distrust of them. But feeling that valour and devotion could accomplish nothing that could compensate for the loss that would have accompanied the continuance of the contest, I determined to avoid the useless sacrifice of those whose past services have endeared them to their country.

Lee's order was written on 10 April 1865

Comparing and contrasting two sources

In the previous chapter (page 57) you were given advice on how to compare two sources and a table that you could use to help you approach such a question.

The example on page 119 shows a completed table using the following two sources.

SOURCE A

President Jefferson Davis's final message to the people of the Confederacy, 4 April 1865

The General in Chief of our Army has found it necessary to make such movements of the troops as to uncover the capital and thus involve the withdrawal of the Government from the city of Richmond. It would be unwise, even if it were possible, to conceal the great moral as well as material injury to our cause that must result from the occupation of Richmond by the enemy. It is equally unwise and unworthy of us, as patriots engaged in a most sacred cause, to allow our energies to falter, our spirits to grow faint, or our efforts to become relaxed under reverses, however calamitous...

Animated by the confidence in your spirit and fortitude, which never yet has failed me, I announce to you fellow countrymen, that it is my purpose to maintain your cause with my whole heart and soul; that I will never consent to abandon to the enemy one foot of the soil of any one of the States of the Confederacy...

If by stress of numbers we should ever be compelled to a temporary withdrawal from her limits, or those of any other border state, again and again will we return, until the baffled and exhausted enemy shall abandon in despair his endless and impossible task of making slaves of a people resolved to be free. Let us not despond, my countrymen; but relying on the never-failing mercies and protecting care of our God, let us meet the foe with fresh defiance, with unconquered and unconquerable hearts.

SOURCE B

General Robert E. Lee's General Order No. 9 to the Army of Northern Virginia, 10 April 1865

After four years of arduous service marked by unsurpassed courage and fortitude the Army of Northern Virginia has been compelled to yield to overwhelming numbers and resources.

I need not tell the survivors of so many hard fought battles, who have remained steadfast to the last that I have consented to this result from no distrust of them. But feeling that valor and devotion could accomplish nothing that could compensate for the loss that would have accompanied the continuance of the contest, I determined to avoid the useless sacrifice of those whose past servives have endeared them to their country...

With an unceasing admiration of your consistency and devotion to your country and a grateful remembrance of your kind and generous consideration of myself, I bid you an affectionate farewell.

Source	Points on which sources agree	Points of each source that show this	Reasons as to why sources might agree (Provenance)	Points on which sources disagree	Parts of each source which show this	Reasons as to why the sources might disagree (Provenance)
A	The military situation is not good. Fortitude of the people of the Confederacy.	The Confederate government has been forced to withdraw from Richmond – 'a great moral as well as material injury to our cause'. Davis talks of 'the spirit and fortitude' of his fellow countrymen which 'never yet has failed me'.	Lee's army was in dire straits – defeated, surrounded and short of men. Davis, as president, was well aware of this. Most Southerners had fought hard for the cause. Davis's job, as president, was to try and maintain the moral of his fellow countrymen.	The Confederacy will continue to fight on. The Confederacy will never be defeated.	Davis says he 'will never consent to abandon to the enemy 'one foot' of Confederate soil. The 'baffled and exhausted enemy' would ultimately 'abandon in despair his endless and impossible task of making slaves of a people resolved to be free'.	Davis issued his message on 4 April 1865. There was still a chance that Lee's army might escape to the West – to continue the war. Davis hoped that the Confederacy could continue to fight a guerrilla war.

Source	Points on which sources agree	Points of each source that show this	Reasons as to why sources might agree (Provenance)	Points on which sources disagree	Parts of each source which show this	Reasons as to why the sources might disagree (Provenance)
B	The Confederate army had fought well. The troops continued to show great fortitude.	Lee talks of 'four years of arduous service marked by unsurpassed courage'. They have shown 'consistency and devotion' to the Confederacy. Lee praises his men for remaining 'steadfast to the last'.	As the Confederacy's leading soldier, no one was in a better position to know how well the Army of Northern Virginia had fought. The few thousand soldiers who remained with Lee determined to fight to the end.	Lee accepts defeat. His army was surrounded and outnumbered by the enemy. There is no point in continuing to fight a lost war.	Lee accepts that his army 'has been compelled to yield to overwhelming numbers and resources'. Lee has decided that enough is enough: he determined to avoid further 'useless sacrifice'.	Lee is writing on 10 April. His attempt to march west, find supplies and join up with other Confederate troops has been thwarted. He has been forced to surrender. He sees little point in fighting on. His own army had been forced to surrender and much of the Confederacy was occupied by the enemy.

The key to a good answer would be a point by point comparison of the two sources. In this instance, both sources are in overall agreement that the Confederacy, despite the great courage and fortitude of its people and soldiers, is in a calamitous military position. They differ on what should happen next. This is partly because they were writing at different times. President Davis, who issued his message on 4 April as he abandoned Richmond, hoped that Lee's army might join with Confederate forces to the west and continue the struggle. Lee had attempted to do that. But surrounded by overwhelming numbers of Union troops, he had been forced to surrender to Grant at Appomattox on 10 April. With a heavy heart, he accepts defeat. He believes that Confederate forces have ultimately been defeated by the 'overwhelming numbers and resources' of the Union. It shoud be said that Davis still wanted to continue the struggle after Lee's surrender at Appomattox. He hoped that a guerrilla war might weaken the resolve of the enemy. But most Southerners accepted that Lee's surrender meant that the war was over and they had lost. Davis's brave words were not enough. Further sacrifice would, as Lee suggested, be 'useless'.

Once you have made a point by point comparison which includes a consideration of the provenance of each source and use of some contextual knowledge, you would then make an overall judgement about their views on the Confederate war effort and Confederate defeat.

Paper 2 guidance: essay questions

Writing an introduction

Having planned your answer to the question, as described in the previous chapter (pages 57–59), you are now in a position to write your crucial opening paragraph. This should set out your main line of argument and briefly refer to the issues you are going to cover in the main body of the essay. The essay will require you to reach a judgement about the issue in the question and it is a good idea to state in this vital opening paragraph what overall line of judgement you are going to make. It might also be helpful, depending on the wording of the question, to define in this paragraph any key terms mentioned in the question.

Consider the following question.

> **To what extent does Abraham Lincoln deserve the title 'The Great Emancipator'?**

In the opening paragraph of an answer to this question you should:

- Identify the issues or themes that you will consider. These might be Lincoln's actions in 1861, pressures on Lincoln to take action on the slavery issue, action by others (for example, Congress, army officers and enslaved people themselves), Lincoln's Emancipation Proclamation, and Lincoln's measures after 1863, especially his support for the Thirteenth Amendment.
- State your view as to which of the issues you regard as the most important.

This type of approach will help you to keep focused on the demands of the question rather than writing a general essay about Lincoln's emancipation measures. It might also be helpful to occasionally refer back to the opening paragraph.

This approach will also ensure you avoid writing about the background to the topic, for example, explaining military developments in the Civil War, which has no or little relevance to the question set. Another mistake is to fail to write a crucial first paragraph and rush straight into the question. Readers appreciate knowing the direction the essay is going to take, rather than embarking on a mystery tour where the line of argument becomes apparent only in the conclusion.

The following is a sample of a good introductory paragraph.

In September 1862 President Lincoln issued his Emancipation Proclamation. Justified by Lincoln as 'a fit and necessary war measure', it declared that while slavery was to be left untouched in states that returned to the Union before 1 January 1863, thereafter all enslaved people in enemy territory conquered by Union armies would be 'forever free'. This Proclamation does not sound particularly revolutionary. It had no impact whatsoever in the Union slave states. It did not even affect slavery in those areas that had already been brought back under Union control. It should be said that Lincoln had taken little action on the slavery issue before his Emancipation Proclamation. Individual generals (like General Butler), Congress and the actions of enslaved people themselves had been far more influential on the emancipation front. Indeed, in July 1862 abolitionist William Lloyd Garrison described Lincoln's handling of the slavery issue as 'stumbling, halting, prevaricating, irresolute, weak, besotted'. However, this essay will claim that Lincoln's actions with regard to slavery were skilful and principled – so much so that he does deserve the title the 'Great Emancipator'.

Avoiding irrelevance

You should take care not to write irrelevant material as not only will it not gain marks, but it also wastes your time. In order to avoid this:

- Look carefully at the wording of the question.
- Avoid simply writing all you know about the topic; remember you need to select information relevant to the actual question, use the information to support an argument and reach an overall judgement about the issue in the question.
- Revise all of a topic so that you are not tempted to pad out a response where you do not have enough material directly relevant to the actual question.

Consider the following question.

> **'Reconstruction in the period 1865–77 was a political and economic success.' How far do you agree?**

The following is a sample of an irrelevant paragraph in answer to the question above.

Reconstruction began in 1861. Lincoln was determined to control the process. He believed that the Constitution gave him the power of pardon. He was also commander-in-chief. He was determined to establish firm principles. His aim was consistent. He wanted to restore the Union as quickly as possible. His usual policy was to install military governors in those areas that had been partially reconquered. The governors were expected to work with whatever popular support they could find. Lincoln spelt out his Reconstruction ideas in 1863. He offered pardon to white southerners who would take an oath of allegiance to the Union. When ten per cent of the 1860 electorate had taken this oath, a new state government could be established. Provided the state then accepted the abolition of slavery, Lincoln agreed to recognize its government. However, Congress refused to accept Lincoln's plan. In 1864, Congress passed the Wade–Davis bill which made it far more difficult for the Confederate states to re-join the Union. Lincoln vetoed this bill. Thus the process by which the southern states would return to the Union was unclear in 1865.

Although the paragraph shows some knowledge of Reconstruction, it fails to address the question. The question asks students to comment on the political and economic success from 1865 to 1877. This paragraph examines the situation before 1865. Lincoln was assassinated in 1865. A brief assessment of the situation in 1865 is in order. But most of the detail contained in this paragraph is irrelevant. Moreover, answers to this question need to address whether Reconstruction was a political and economic success. Most paragraphs should be related to this issue and make some comment on success or failure. In short, the answer is not completely descriptive but analysis is only implied and then not focused on the actual question.

QUESTION PRACTICE

The focus of this section has been on avoiding irrelevance and writing a focused vital opening paragraph. Using the information from the chapter, write an opening paragraph to two of the essays below, ensuring that you keep fully focused on the question. It might also be helpful to consolidate the skill developed in the last chapter by planning the answer before you start writing the paragraph.

1 To what extent were northern advantages in manpower and industrial output the deciding factors in the Civil War?

2 How important were Britain's and France's role in the American Civil War?

3 'Both the Union and Confederate governments did their best to protect civil liberties during the American Civil War.' How far do you agree?

4 'Black Americans did not benefit from the process of Reconstruction.' How far do you agree?

Paper 2 guidance: the short questions

It is very important to write analytically in answering both the essay question and also the shorter question which asks for explanation. The short question is not asking you to describe events or developments but is asking you to explain causes or consequences. For higher level marks you need to have a clear understanding of the connections between causes and reach a supported conclusion.

Look at these two extracts from answers. One describes and one explains.

Explain the importance of Grant's military leadership in the Civil War.

Extract A

Grant was born in Ohio in 1822. In 1839 he trained as a soldier at West Point. He served in the Mexican War but then resigned from the army. He proved a failure in civilian life. However, in 1861 he was rapidly promoted to brigadier general. In 1862 he won a major success when he captured Fort Donelson but was almost defeated at the Battle of Shiloh. After months of frustration, he captured Vicksburg in July 1863 and won a major victory at Chattanooga in November 1863. In March 1864 he was appointed general-in-chief of the Union Army. His campaigns in Virginia in 1864–65 against Robert E Lee cost terrible casualties but ensured Union victory. Lee surrendered to Grant at Appomattox in April 1865. Grant went on to become US President between 1869 and 1877.

Extract A is largely descriptive and is very much a 'write all I know about' Grant.

Extract B

Grant made a major contribution to Union success in the Civil War. From 1861 to 1863, he fought in the West, winning success at Fort Donelson, Shiloh (just!), Vicksburg and Chattanooga. His Western victories were crucially important, reviving Union morale at a time when Confederate General Robert Lee enjoyed success against northern armies in Virginia. Grant's capture of Vicksburg in July 1863 was particularly important, ensuring that the Confederacy was effectively cut in two. In March 1864 Lincoln appointed Grant general-in-chief of the Union Army. He immediately came east to supervise the efforts to destroy Lee and capture Richmond. Determined to make use of the Union's greater manpower and resources, he planned for a 'simultaneous movement all along the line'. This was not totally successful. But Sherman's 'hard war' policies in Georgia and South Carolina weakened the Confederacy. Grant, himself, although suffering huge casualties maintained the pressure against Lee forcing him to defend the town of Petersburg. In April 1865 Union forces finally broke through Lee's lines. Lee, abandoning Petersburg and Richmond, headed west but Grant followed him and forced him to surrender at Appomattox. Grant was thus the most successful Union general in the Civil War.

Extract B, by contrast, examines Grant's military role in the West and then as general-in-chief in 1864–65. It stresses his main achievements and does not drift off the question.

EXPLAIN QUESTIONS

Using the information from the chapter, write an opening paragraph to two of the short essay questions below, ensuring that you keep fully focused on the question.

1 Explain why the Union changed its military strategies between 1861 and 1865.
2 Explain the importance of Britain's role in the Civil War.
3 Explain how the Civil War affected life in the Confederate states.
4 Explain the impact of the Thirteenth, Fourteenth and Fifteenth Amendments.

CHAPTER 3

The Gilded Age and Progressive Era, 1870s to 1920

Between 1870 and 1900 the USA experienced phenomenal economic growth. These years are often referred to as the Gilded Age – a derogatory term implying that the period had a shiny exterior but was rotten underneath. The first two decades of the twentieth century, by contrast, are seen as the Progressive Era – a time of reform. This chapter will examine the Age and the Era by considering the following questions:

★ Why was the late nineteenth century an age of rapid industrialization?

★ How great were the consequences of rapid economic growth in the late nineteenth century?

★ What were the main aims and policies of the Progressive Movement and how popular were they?

★ How successful was the Progressive Movement up to 1920?

KEY DATES

1869	Completion of first transcontinental railroad
1876	Alexander Graham Bell invented the telephone
1877	Great Railroad Strike
1887	Interstate Commerce Act
1890	Sherman Anti-trust Act
1892	Formation of Populist Party
1896	William McKinley won presidential election
1901	Theodore Roosevelt became president, following McKinley's assassination
1904	Roosevelt elected president
1908	William Taft elected president
1912	Woodrow Wilson elected president
1913	Seventeenth Amendment added to the Constitution
1917	The USA entered the First World War
1919	Eighteenth Amendment added to the Constitution
1920	Nineteenth Amendment added to the Constitution

1 Why was the late nineteenth century an age of rapid industrialization?

In 1870 the American economy was still essentially agricultural. By 1900, the USA was producing nearly a third of the world's manufactured goods. 'The old nations of the world creep on at a snail's pace', declared Andrew Carnegie (see page 128) in 1886. 'The Republic thunders past with the rush of the express.' By 1900 the USA had taken Britain's place as the leading industrial nation – as can be seen from the iron, coal and steel production shown in Figure 3.1. There were many reasons for this success. This section will focus on four: the growth of big business; technological innovation; the growth of railroads; and US trade policies.

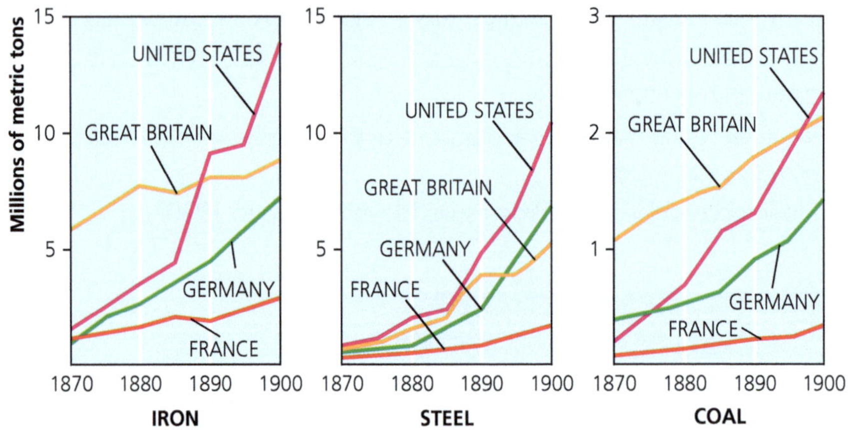

Figure 3.1 Iron, coal and steel production 1870–1900

Factors favouring US industrialization

- With huge natural resources, the USA was virtually self-sufficient in every commodity.
- The demands of the Civil War, coupled with inflation and wartime legislation favourable to business, are often assumed to have triggered industrial growth. Arguably the war encouraged employers to think 'big'. However, it may be that far from advancing industrialization, the war retarded it. The economy grew more slowly in the 1860s than in the 1850s and 1870s.
- Capital, especially from Britain, helped the USA develop its economy.
- Immigrants poured into America in the late nineteenth century, providing cheap labour and a growing home market.

- Social and cultural influences may have been important, especially the emphasis American society placed on hard work and thrift.
- American governments, Republican and Democrat, supported the notion of **laissez-faire**. They allowed big business considerable freedom. Nor did they impose high taxes on businesses or successful businessmen. The latter thus had money to invest in further industrial expansion.

The growth of trusts and corporations (including robber barons)

After 1865 American businesses tended to consolidate into large-scale units. The trend towards 'bigness' was not universal. Textiles, for example, continued to be manufactured by many small and medium-sized firms. But railroads, public utilities, and the processing of minerals came to be dominated by a few giant companies. Near-monopolies also developed in many other industries, including tobacco and sugar-refining. The giant companies were known initially as trusts and then as corporations. The men who owned them were often described as '**robber barons**' – a disparaging term. The robber barons, however, were very influential in promoting industrial expansion.

Industrial consolidation

Businesses devised various forms of combination.

- The first was the 'pool', an informal agreement between firms to limit output or divide markets. Not legally binding, such arrangements had largely disappeared by the 1880s.
- In 1882 the Standard Oil Company created the first 'trust'. This was an arrangement whereby stockholders in different companies deposited their shares with trustees, who then exercised unified control over nominally independent firms. (Thus in the Standard Oil case, stockholders of 77 oil companies, producing 90 per cent of the USA's refined oil, transferred their stock to nine trustees.) Though Americans referred to all forms of combination as trusts, the trust, strictly speaking, had been abandoned by the early 1890s, largely because of attacks in state courts.
- Giant enterprises eventually turned to the holding company. Essentially, this meant a company owned sufficient stock in others to be able to control their operations. In 1899 Standard Oil, for example, held stock in 41 companies. Between 1895 and 1904 there were more than 300 mergers of this kind with a total capital of over $6 billion. About 40 per cent of it was accounted for by the seven largest holding companies – Amalgamated Copper, Consolidated Tobacco, American Smelting and Refining, American Sugar Refining, International Mercantile and Marine, Standard Oil, and United States Steel.

KEY TERMS

Laissez-faire The view that governments should not intervene in economic and social matters.

Robber barons Great industrialists who dominated particular industries and who were seen as exploiting their power – at the public's expense. The first robber barons were railway magnates.

Andrew Carnegie and iron and steel

Iron and steel were vital to American industrialization, providing the nation with its machinery, tools, trains, bridges and railroad tracks. Between 1860 and 1900 US pig-iron production rose from 800,000 tons to 14 million tons. Steel output increased from small proportions to 11 million tons, more than Britain and Germany's combined production. Pittsburgh, surrounded by coalfields and iron-beds, was the main iron and steel centre. The discovery of vast iron ore deposits in northern Michigan and in the Mesabi Range in Minnesota did not lessen Pittsburgh's supremacy since the ore could be brought cheaply to Pennsylvania via the Great Lakes. A variety of new processes enabled manufacturers to boost steel production and to reduce prices from $300 a ton to $35.

The greatest steel master was **Andrew Carnegie**. A man of driving energy, he rode roughshod over competitors and trade unions alike. Surrounding himself with able associates, he created a huge combine, securing control of all the needed sources of supply – coalfields, limestone deposits, iron mines, ore ships and railroads. Carnegie's company made huge profits: $40 million in 1900. In 1901 the company merged with others to form the United States Steel Corporation, a body which controlled 60 per cent of the USA's steel production.

KEY FIGURES

Andrew Carnegie (1835–1919) The son of a Scottish weaver, his parents emigrated to the USA in 1848. After working in a cotton mill, he became a telegraph operator, before turning to railroading, then iron manufacturing, and finally to steel. He became one of America's richest men. After his retirement, he devoted himself to philanthropy, giving $350 million to libraries and educational institutions.

John D Rockefeller (1839–1937) Rockefeller dominated the American petroleum industry. He developed management techniques that revolutionized US business. In his later years, he contributed $550 million to philanthropic institutions.

John D Rockefeller and oil

The petroleum industry expanded rapidly after oil was discovered in Pennsylvania in 1859. Petroleum products found a variety of uses: heat, lubrication, medicine and light. Since little capital was needed for drilling or refining, thousands of small operators entered the business. In the competitive conditions that ensued, prices and profits fluctuated wildly. In 1865 a young Cleveland merchant **John D Rockefeller** turned his attention to the oil business. Rockefeller, a brilliant organizer, aimed to eliminate competition and to impose order and stability. In 1872 he and his associates founded the Standard Oil Company. In 1882 it became the first of the trusts, overseeing 90 per cent of America's oil production. Like Carnegie, Rockefeller ensured he controlled most of his company's needs, building his own pipelines, warehouses and containers. A ruthless entrepreneur, he resorted to blackmail, espionage and price-slashing to drive competitors into bankruptcy or to force them to merge with him.

John D Rockefeller

JP Morgan and investment banking

What Carnegie was to steel and Rockefeller to oil, **John Pierpont Morgan** was to investment banking. The son of a rich banker, Morgan was a co-founder of the New York banking-house Drexel, Morgan, re-organized in 1895 as JP Morgan and Co. Possessing enormous financial ability, Morgan came to symbolize the growing influence of investment bankers over corporation management. Morgan bought corporate shares and bonds, and then sold them at a profit – having helped to improve companies' management methods. Morgan used his financial power to force warring companies to abandon their mutually destructive practices. In the 1890s he played a major part in reorganizing railroads which had been reduced to bankruptcy by over-expansion. He then turned his attention to promoting combinations in other industries, the most spectacular being the formation of United States Steel.

KEY FIGURE

John Pierpont Morgan (1837–1913) Morgan was America's greatest banker and financier. He had enormous economic power. Some see him as ruthless, secretive and acquisitive. Others believe he made a major contribution to the USA's corporate growth, philanthropy and culture.

For and against big business

The system which produced Carnegie, Rockefeller, Morgan and a host of other so-called robber barons had its supporters. Conservatives, influenced by the ideas of English philosopher Herbert Spencer, defended laissez-faire. Competitive struggle, Spencer believed, made for human progress: state interference on behalf of the weak and unfit merely impeded it. Many nineteenth-century politicians also supported big business and big businessmen. They claimed, with considerable justification, that their achievements played a vital role in the USA's economic growth.

However, other Americans opposed laissez-faire doctrines and Spencer's notion of survival of the fittest. In the 1880s popular hostility to the railroads broadened into a more general attack on trusts. To some extent the public was simply worried that **monopoly** might lead to higher prices and to consumer exploitation. (Criticism on this score was difficult to sustain since most prices fell continuously.) But the anti-trust movement derived most of its strength from the belief that the growth of big corporations would result in an end to economic opportunity for other Americans.

KEY TERMS

Monopoly A situation where someone or some company has sole command or possession of something.

Curbing the trusts?

In the 1880s 27 states and territories passed laws prohibiting trusts and other forms of combination. But local regulation was never very effective because trusts simply transferred their headquarters to trust-supporting states like New Jersey. In the 1888 presidential election, Republicans and Democrats pledged support for federal action. Thus in 1890 Congress passed the Sherman Anti-trust Act. This declared that 'every contract, combination in the form of trust or otherwise, or conspiracy, in restraint of trade or commerce among the several states or with foreign nations ... is illegal'. People forming such combinations were declared to be guilty of a misdemeanour punishable by fines of $5000 and a year in prison.

Some historians claim that the Sherman Act was a cynical gesture, designed only to make the public believe that something was being done. In fact most Congressmen shared the popular concern about monopoly and seem to have acted in good faith. However, ambiguous phrasing enabled conservative-dominated courts to reduce the effectiveness of the Sherman Act when suits were brought under it. The critical decision came in *United States v E.C. Knight Co* (1895). Though the defendants controlled 98 per cent of the manufacture of refined sugar, the Supreme Court held that this monopoly

ACTIVITY

Write a brief explanation (in your own words) of the following terms:

- laissez-faire
- trusts
- monopoly
- inflation
- protectionism.

was not a violation of the Sherman Act because manufacturing was not 'trade' within the meaning of the law. Given the Knight decision, the late 1890s witnessed a renewed drive towards consolidation.

SOURCE A

What point is the cartoonist trying to make about trusts in Source A?

A cartoon from 1890, preceding the Sherman Act. The cartoon, produced in 1889, portrays what it sees as the alliance between big business leaders and politicians in this period.

SOURCE B

Using your own knowledge, to what extent can you trust the view of business given in Source B?

Samuel Dodd, a company lawyer, writing in the *New York Tribune* in 1890.

The last quarter of a century has been emphatically an era of combination in business. Has competition been destroyed? On the contrary, it was never so strong. Effort impels to effort – combination begets combination. New industries are built up – new markets are opened – new methods of manufacture invented. It is the law of life. By each striving to get ahead, all make better progress. Have prices been increased? On the contrary, combination in business and low prices have ever gone hand in hand ... Has the wage earner suffered? On the contrary, new avenues of labour have been opened; the demand for labour, and particularly skilled labour, has increased, wages are higher, the cost of living is lower and the conditions of the labouring man never so good as today.

Technological innovations

A flood of inventions and technological innovations was vitally important in bringing about rapid industrial growth in the USA. The number of patents soared from an annual average of 2000 in the 1850s to 23,000 in the 1890s.

Communication developments

Dramatic improvements in communications made it possible to operate on a national – indeed international – scale.

- The electric telegraph, which spanned the USA by 1862, was rapidly extended after 1865. In 1866, Cyrus Field laid a successful transatlantic cable.
- In 1876 Alexander Graham Bell invented the telephone. By 1900 the USA had 800,000 phones, twice the total for the whole of Europe.

Edison and electrical developments

The main electrical inventor was Thomas Edison. The research laboratory that he established at Menlo Park, New Jersey in 1876, was a milestone in the history of invention. Hitherto inventors, working on their own, had explored problems at random. But Edison's invention factory was based on the concept of organized team research. Its purpose was to supply the market with new products. Edison's laboratories produced scores of inventions including the phonograph, the motion-picture projector, and the electric locomotive. Perhaps his most significant achievement was the incandescent carbon-filament lamp, patented in 1879. Its cost was negligible and it glowed for up to 170 hours. By 1888 two million electric lights had been installed in American homes and factories.

There were other electrical inventors as well as Edison.

- George Westinghouse developed means by which high-voltage electric current could be transmitted safely and cheaply over long distances.
- Nikola Tesla invented the electric motor in 1888.
- Frank Sprague supervised the building of the first successful electrical streetcar service in Richmond (1887). Sprague's company also developed the electric elevator (1889).

The growth of railroads

The three decades after 1865 witnessed the completion of a national railroad network. Railroad mileage increased from 30,000 in 1860 to 193,000 in 1900.

Transcontinental railroads

In 1862 Congress authorized the building of a transcontinental railroad. The Union Pacific Railroad was built westward from Omaha while the Central Pacific Railroad was built eastwards from Sacramento. Both companies were given land grants and government loans. Railroad construction was difficult. The Central Pacific, which relied mainly on Chinese labour, had to cross the Sierra Nevada Mountains. The Union Pacific, having the advantage of easier terrain, built 1086 miles (1750 km) of track: the Central Pacific 689. The two lines met at Promontory Point, Utah in 1869.

Within a remarkably short time, four other transcontinental roads were built.

- The Northern Pacific (1883) linked St Paul to Portland, Oregon.
- The Southern Pacific (1883) linked New Orleans with San Francisco.
- The Atchison, Topeka and Santa Fe ran from eastern Kansas to San Diego (1884).
- The Great Northern linked Duluth to Seattle (1893).

The five transcontinental lines accounted for only a fraction of western rail construction. Each main line built numerous branch lines. Thus western rail mileage, amounting to only 3000 miles (4800 km) in 1865, had increased to 87,000 miles (140,000 km) by 1900. Although there were no more federal loans after the Crédit Mobilier scandal (see textbox), all the transcontinental lines, with the exception of the Great Northern, received generous land grants. In all, the federal government gave the railroads 131 million acres – a region larger than France. However, most of the capital for railroad building came from private sources, especially from European investors and New York banking houses.

Crédit Mobilier scandal

In 1873 it was revealed that shareholders of the Union Pacific and Central Pacific railroads, rather than inviting competitive bids, had created dummy construction companies. This enabled them to charge very high rates. Thus the Crédit Mobilier company, set up by the Union Pacific, received $94 million for building work that had cost $44 million. This scam, which enriched the company's shareholders, was characteristic of the business practices of the day.

Other developments

The southern railroad system, largely destroyed during the Civil War, was rebuilt. By 1890 the South had 40,000 miles (64,000 km) of track, five times as much as in 1860. In the northeast the major emphasis was on filling in gaps. More importantly, hundreds of small lines were consolidated by lease, purchase, or merger into a handful of large systems. By 1900 two-thirds of the nation's railroad mileage was controlled by seven major groups.

Technological advances made rail travel safer and less of an ordeal.

- The replacement of iron rails by steel rails reduced hazards.
- Steel coaches, which replaced wooden cars, were less likely to fragment in the event of a crash.
- The introduction of new safety devices, like George Westinghouse's air brake (1869), resulted in fewer accidents.
- George Pullman's Palace Car Company, which built dining-cars, became the world's largest railway-car construction company.

What is the message of Source C? What additional knowledge could you use to decide whether the view of the Source is justified?

SOURCE C

From Charles F Adams, Jr, *Railroads: Their Origin and Problems*, 1887

The railroad system of the United States, with all its excellences and all its defects, is thoroughly characteristic of the American people. It grew up untrammelled by any theory as to how it ought to grow; and developed with mushroom rapidity, without reference to government or political systems. In this country alone were the principles of free trade unreservedly and fearlessly applied to it. The result has certainly been wonderful, if not in all respects satisfactory ... If the people, and through the people the government, had faith in competition, the private individuals who constructed the railroads seemed to have no fear of it. They built roads everywhere, apparently in perfect confidence that the country would so develop as to support all the roads that could be built. Consequently railroads sprang up as if by magic, and after they were constructed, as it was impossible to remove them from places where they were not wanted to places where they were wanted, they lived upon the land where they could, and, when the business of the land would not support them, they fought and ruined each other.

The importance of railroads

Railroads were the key to post-Civil War economic growth and constituted the USA's most important single economic interest. In 1890 railroad revenue exceeded $2000 million, twice that of the federal government. The railroads played a major role in the settlement of the West as well as making possible the exploitation of natural resources and the creation of a national market. Their needs largely accounted for the phenomenal expansion of coal and steel production. They were the USA's first big business and the first industry to develop a large-scale management bureaucracy.

Railroad problems

Wasteful construction and overbuilding left many railroads with crushing burdens of debt. Cutthroat competition was accompanied by ruinous rate-wars and the granting of huge rebates – secret reductions below the published rate – in order to secure the business of large shippers.

The financial malpractices of railroad owners gave rise to the label 'robber barons' (a term subsequently applied to successful industrialists like Rockefeller). Not all railway magnates were dishonest. James Hill, owner of the Great Northern, displayed a genuine concern for the region his railroad served but at the other extreme were Jay Gould and Jim Fisk who made the Erie Railway a byword for trickery and fraud. A more representative figure was Cornelius Vanderbilt who expanded the New York Central into a consolidated system. Vanderbilt improved services while reducing rates but he was also a ruthless competitor, prepared to bribe legislators and manipulate stock for his own benefit. When he died in 1877, he had amassed a fortune of $90 million.

Railroad regulation

Many Americans criticized railway malpractices, not least freight rate rebates that favoured large customers at the expense of smaller competitors, and the charging of high prices between places that were dependent on a single line. Starting with Massachusetts (1869), several states established supervisory railroad commissions but the first attempts at thoroughgoing state regulation came in the midwest as a result of agitation by farmers' organizations, especially the Grangers (see page 150). Illinois passed a regulatory measure in 1871: other states soon followed suit. These so-called Granger laws fixed maximum rates for passengers and established railroad commissions to enforce the regulations. The railroads challenged these measures, claiming they were unconstitutional but in *Munn versus Illinois* (1877), the Supreme Court affirmed the right of states to regulate public utilities.

However, state regulation was not very effective.

- Some regulators were incompetent or corrupt.
- Separate state action meant a confusing variety of different rate structures.
- Railroads continued to challenge the regulations in the courts. In *Wabash, St Louis, and Pacific Railroad Company versus Illinois* (1886), a more conservative Supreme Court invalidated an Illinois law prohibiting rate discrimination on routes between New York and Illinois. The decision dealt a body-blow to state regulation.

The federal government thus needed to take action. The Interstate Commerce Act (1887) prohibited rebates, discrimination, and provided that all railroad charges should be 'reasonable and just'. It created an Interstate Commerce Commission with powers to investigate railroad management. The immediate practical results were negligible. Railroads showed great ingenuity in frustrating the Act's provisions and the Supreme Court reversed many of the Commission's decisions. By the 1890s supervision had become largely nominal.

Trade policies and protectionism

Support for laissez-faire did not extend to trade. During the Civil War, tariffs had been raised to an average of 50 per cent per item. They continued to be high thereafter. The extent to which they assisted or hindered American economic growth was debated at the time and continues to be debated today.

The tariff debate

American manufacturers desired tariffs to protect their goods from foreign competition. Most urban workers feared that wage levels would fall sharply if goods produced abroad by cheap labour entered the USA untaxed. However, many (particularly western and southern) farmers thought they picked up the bill for protectionism. Unable to purchase less-expensive foreign items, they had to pay high prices for American-produced goods. Moreover, many countries raised duties against American items in retaliation, making it difficult for farmers to export surplus produce. Democrats professed to believe in moderate tariffs but whenever party leaders tried to revise the tariff downward, Democrat congressmen from industrial states sided with the Republicans. Tariffs thus remained high throughout the 1870s.

Protectionism in the 1880s

In 1882 President Arthur set up a commission to study the tariff issue. It recommended a 20–25 per cent rate reduction, which Arthur supported but

Congress's effort to enact the proposal was counter-productive. The so-called Mongrel Tariff of 1883, which intended to reduce tariff rates, actually raised duties on many products.

In 1887 Democrat President Cleveland launched a campaign for tariff reduction. Existing tariff rates were piling up a revenue surplus, encouraging extravagant and often wasteful public spending. Cleveland also claimed that high tariffs were a form of special privilege, fostered trusts and raised the cost of living. A Democrat bill providing for moderate reductions was blocked by the Republican-controlled Senate. In 1888 the Republicans made protective tariffs the cornerstone of their presidential campaign. Industrialists, fearful of tariff revision, gave huge sums of money to the Republicans. This was used to good effect. While Cleveland won the popular vote, Benjamin Harrison carried the electoral college by 233 to 168 and became president. The Republicans rewarded their industrial backers with the McKinley Tariff Act (1890). This raised duties to prohibitive levels.

The situation in the 1890s

The tariff issue became of major political importance during the serious depression from 1893 to 1897. In 1893 President Cleveland tried to keep his 1892 campaign pledge of tariff reform. A bill providing for a cut in rates passed the House but was so amended in the Senate that in its final form the Wilson–Gorman Tariff Act (1894) was barely distinguishable from the 1890 McKinley Tariff.

In 1896 Republican candidate William McKinley, the man responsible for the 1890 act, won the presidential election (see page 152). McKinley's first action as president was to call a special session of Congress to increase tariffs. The Dingley Tariff (1897) raised duties higher than ever.

In conclusion, high tariffs undoubtedly protected US industry from foreign competition and thus helped American industrialization but they did so at the expense of the American consumer.

Summary

The USA experienced tremendous industrial growth in the late nineteenth century. This growth is generally associated with a number of factors. These include the growth of trusts and corporations (and the rise of so-called robber barons like Carnegie and Rockefeller); technological innovations; the growth of American railroads; and government trade policies – not least the support for high tariffs.

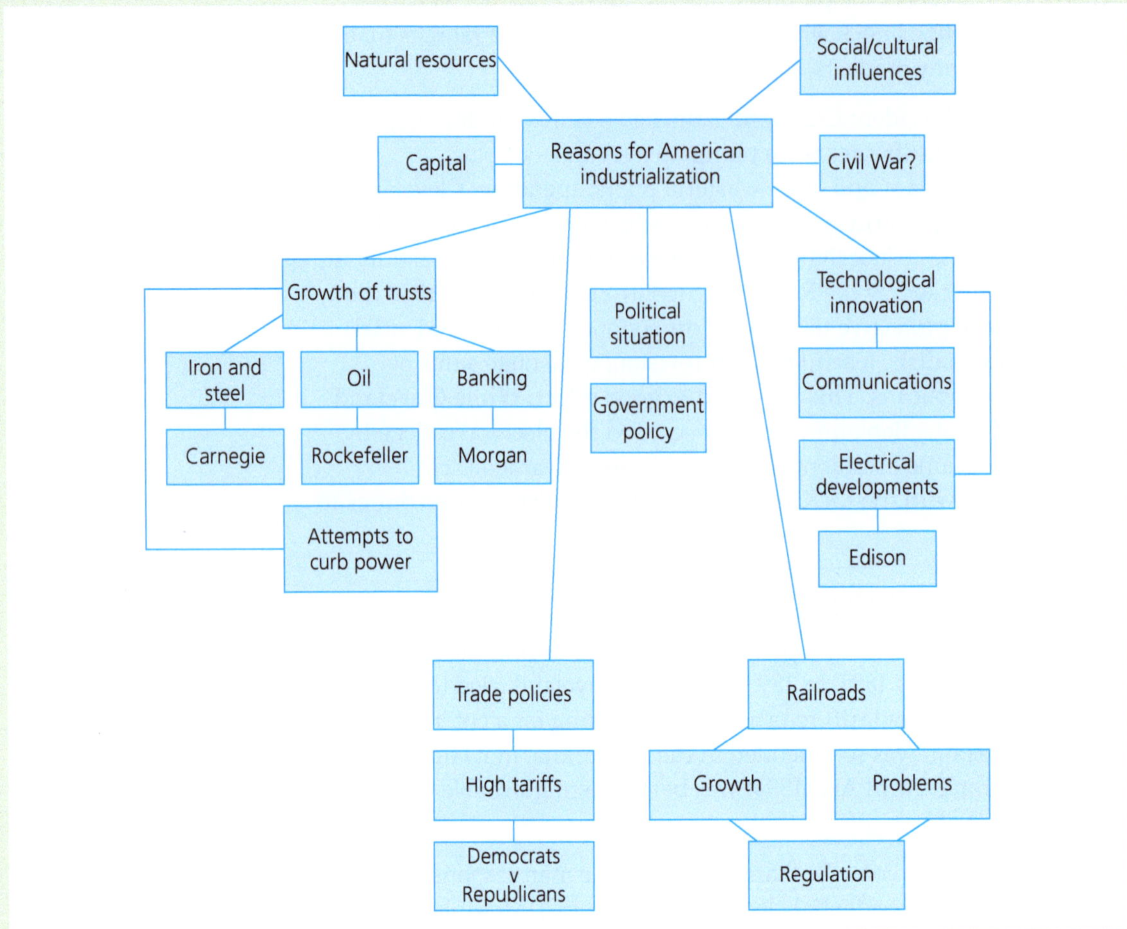

SUMMARY DIAGRAM

Why was the late nineteenth century an age of rapid industrialization?

2 How great were the consequences of rapid economic growth in the late nineteenth century?

Industrialization transformed the USA, affecting every aspect of national life and producing a host of complex social problems.

New immigration from southern and eastern Europe

The USA's population nearly trebled between 1860 and 1910. This was not the result of a rising birth rate: from about 1870 the birth rate declined. It was in part due to a fall in the death rate. Advances in medical knowledge, a more nutritious diet and improved standards of public health were the main reasons why mortality declined. But the main reason for the population growth was the rise in immigration.

ACTIVITY

Hold a class debate about the effects of the influx of new immigrants on the USA in the late nineteenth century. One group will argue the impact was positive. The other will argue that the impact was negative.

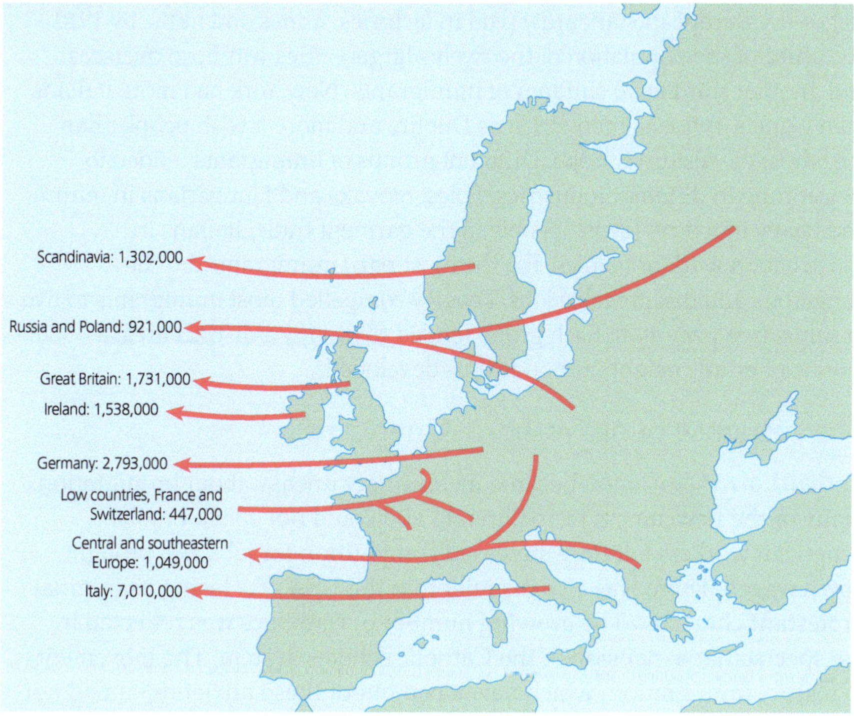

Figure 3.2 European migration to the USA 1870–1900

Causes of the new immigration

In the 50 years after 1865, immigration exceeded 26 million – five times greater than in the previous 50 years. Before 1880 most immigrants came from north-west Europe. Thereafter, a growing number, 85 per cent by 1914, came from southern and eastern Europe. This 'new immigration' brought to the USA large numbers of Italians, Poles, Hungarians, Ukrainians, Croats, Slovaks and Greeks.

Most immigrants probably came to the USA to try to better themselves, pulled by American promise rather than pushed by conditions at home but those conditions encouraged emigration. Most immigrants left behind grinding poverty. Some emigrated to avoid compulsory military service. Others, notably Russian Jews, fled religious persecution. The transition from sail to steamship, virtually complete by 1870, helped swell the exodus. Many immigrants were funded by families and friends already settled in the USA. Others had their passage paid by American employers.

The impact on the USA

To a far greater extent than the old immigrant groups (except Irish), the new immigrants settled in America's cities. They were attracted by the high wages (by European standards) paid in factories, mines and mills. By 1910 one-third of the population of the twelve largest cities was born overseas and another third were children of immigrants. New York had more Italians than Naples, twice as many Irish as Dublin, and more Jewish people than the whole of western Europe. Different groups of immigrants tended to concentrate in different industries: Poles, Slovaks and Hungarians in mining and heavy industry; Jewish people in the garment trade; Italians in construction work or textiles. For the most part, immigrants did the dangerous and disagreeable jobs. Poverty compelled most immigrants to live in slums (see page 143). Each group tended to occupy a distinct area: a mosaic of ethnic neighbourhoods thus developed.

The response of native-born Americans

KEY TERMS

Native-born Americans People born in the USA.

Recession A period when the economy goes into decline.

Native-born Americans became increasingly uneasy about immigration. Many of the newcomers were illiterate and could not speak English. American workers felt they increased competition for jobs and brought down wages. There was also disquiet that the USA was losing its original Protestant character. The growing number of Catholics was reflected in the spectacular expansion of the Catholic schools system. The movement to restrict immigration, which developed out of these anxieties, aimed not at ending immigration but at selective controls to impose restrictions. An immigration law in 1882 debarred convicts, lunatics, paupers and persons likely to become a public charge. The first of a series of Chinese Exclusion Acts was passed in the same year. Thereafter the list of excluded classes was enlarged. By 1907 it included people with contagious diseases and sex workers. Ellis Island, which became New York's immigrant landing depot in 1892, was given the task of detecting undesirables.

Industrial growth and periods of economic recession

For much of the period from 1870 to 1900 the US economy boomed. However, there were two serious economic **recessions** which hit industrial workers. Many farmers experienced hardship even in so-called good times.

Boom and bust 1865–80

The economy prospered after 1865, aided by industrial expansion and the development of the West. However, a stock market panic in 1873 led to economic difficulties for the rest of the decade.

Heated controversies now arose over the tariff (see page 134) and over the currency. The Coinage Act of 1873 took silver out of the coinage. Western silver-mining interests denounced the measure. So did southern and western farmers. They wanted to increase the amount of money in circulation, believing this would help them pay off debt and raise farm prices. In 1877 the House of Representatives passed a bill providing for the unlimited coinage of silver at a 16 to 1 ratio with gold. Senate amendments weakened the measure and the Bland–Allison Act (1878) provided only for the monthly purchase of between \$2 and \$4 million worth of silver bullion to be coined into dollars at the 16 to 1 ratio. Given that successive secretaries of the treasury purchased only the minimum requirements, the 1878 Act had little impact. The return of prosperity in 1879 quietened the silver agitation for more than a decade.

The Free Silver issue

In the late nineteenth century, the US currency was based on gold – the so-called **gold standard**. This limited the number of dollars in circulation because each dollar was supposedly backed by the USA's gold reserves. Supporters of Free Silver wished to have a currency based on gold and silver. (An ounce of gold would be worth 16 ounces of silver.) This would allow the government to increase the amount of dollars in circulation. This was likely to lead to inflation, helping those (like mid-western and southern farmers) who were in debt.

KEY TERM

Gold standard A monetary system according to which the unit of currency has a precise value in gold.

SOURCE D

From the book *Triumphant Democracy*, first published in 1886, by Andrew Carnegie

Touching the material condition of the great mass of the people ... we may safely say that no nation ever enjoyed such universal prosperity. The producers, in agriculture and manufactures, have not made exceptional gains. Indeed, these have not been as prosperous as usual, owing to the great fall in the prices of products. But the masses of the people have never received compensation so high or purchased commodities so cheaply. Never in any country's history has so great a proportion of the products of labour and capital gone to labour and so little to capital ... It is probable that in many future decades the citizen is to look back upon this as a golden age of the Republic and long for a return of its conditions.

What is the message of Source D?

Boom and bust 1880–1900

Industrial expansion continued at a great pace throughout the 1880s. However, from 1893 to 1897 the USA experienced the longest and worst depression so far in its history. Thousands of firms went bankrupt, hundreds of banks closed, and one railroad in every six went into receivership. By 1894 there were more than 2,500,000 unemployed people. Farm prices plummeted. This was good news for those industrial workers who were in work. It was bad news for American farmers.

President Cleveland (1889–93) believed that the prime cause of depression was the Sherman Silver Purchase Act (1890). This required the Treasury to buy 4,500,000 ounces of silver each month. Convinced that the act had undermined business confidence by causing a drain on the treasury's gold reserves, he demanded its repeal. He got his way in 1893 – with Republican support. Most southern and western Democrats voted against the measure. Cleveland's intervention halted neither the depression nor the drain on the treasury.

Cleveland believed that there was little he could or should do to promote economic recovery. Nor did he accept that it was government's responsibility to relieve distress. Nevertheless, in many cities unemployed people demanded public-relief programmes. To dramatize the demand, Jacob Coxey, a Populist from Ohio (see page 151), organized a march of unemployed people on Washington. Fewer than 500 members of 'Coxey's army' reached Washington (April 1894) and Coxey was arrested for trespassing on the capitol's ground.

The 1896 election (see page 152), won by McKinley who supported the gold standard, indicated that most of the urban working class were frightened by the Democrat support for free silver. They realized that an inflationary policy designed to boost farm prices would probably cut their real wages. Working men also believed that the protective tariff (supported by McKinley) was in their interests. Hence the Republican vote in the northern industrial states increased spectacularly.

The election was soon followed by the return of prosperity. Ironically, this was helped by the inflation of the currency which McKinley's opponents had advocated. This came about, not through silver, but from a new flood of gold into the world's money markets – the result of new discoveries in South Africa, Canada and Alaska. The 1900 Currency Act put the USA firmly on the gold standard.

Farmers' problems

Many farmers suffered worsening economic conditions for much of the late nineteenth century. While US agricultural production was expanding, thanks to mechanization and to millions of additional acres being farmed, vast tracks of new land were also being brought under cultivation in Australia, Canada, Russia and Argentina. Railways and steamships made it possible to transport food and raw materials quickly and cheaply over long distances. Given the glut of produce on the market, there was a fall of prices. This brought distress to farmers in many parts of the world. The worst sufferers in the USA were the growers of staple crops in the South and West who were accustomed to selling their cotton and wheat surplus abroad. As prices dropped, their burden of debt grew. By growing more wheat or cotton to raise the same amount of money, farmers contributed to the vicious cycle of overproduction and price decline.

Few farmers understood how want could be caused by plenty. They shared the puzzlement that Kansas's governor professed at a friend's argument in the 1890s that 'there were hungry people because there was too much bread' and 'so many poorly clad because there was too much cloth'. It seemed impossible to speak of overproduction when many were in desperate need. Critical of the economic system, farmers turned to radical groups, like the Grangers (see page 150) and the Populists (see page 151).

SOURCE E

From an article 'The Farmer's Changed Condition', written by Rodney Welch in 1891

Farmers have long been losing their place and influence in the councils of the State and nation. Our later Congresses have not contained enough farmers from the northern States to constitute the committees on agriculture. Our national law-makers have known so little about what would promote the prosperity of farmers that they have favoured measures that have greatly injured agriculture. They have insisted on developing the national domain in advance of a demand for any more land for cultivation ... they have encouraged tens of thousands of persons to engage in farming who would otherwise have remained in other pursuits. The offer of free land, or of land at a nominal price, has tempted many to leave shops, mines, and vessels, and to engage in agriculture ... They have overstocked the home and foreign markets with grain, meat, vegetables, fruits, dairy products, and honey, and as a consequence the price of nearly every farm product has declined, sometimes below the cost of the labour required to produce it.

According to Source E, what were the main farming problems in 1891?

The impact of urbanization on living conditions

Industrialization and immigration led to the growth of towns and cities – urbanization. Urbanization created a host of social problems. At the same time, however, it benefited large numbers of Americans. It may be that those benefits were more important than the problems.

Urban growth

Railroads, industry and technological advances helped build cities and were in turn stimulated by them. By 1900 one-third of the USA's population were city-dwellers and 40 cities had more than 100,000 inhabitants. New York's population grew from 1 million in 1860 to 3.5 million in 1900. Chicago was the second largest city, its population soaring from 100,000 in 1860 to 1.7 million in 1900. In the same period, the population of Minneapolis rose from 2,500 to 200,000. Although most Americans did not live in urban areas until 1920, the city became the controlling influence on American life, attracting rural and small-town Americans as well as immigrants. The city's appeal was obvious: city work was better-paid and people worked fewer hours than those who toiled on the land.

Transport problems

Transport problems, arising from urban growth, were aided by technological advances.

- Steel bridges helped relieve traffic congestion.
- Elevated steam railways, pioneered by New York in the 1870s, assisted the moving of commuters.
- Cable cars, first introduced by San Francisco in 1873, became commonplace.
- Thanks to the development of the dynamo, electric trolleys soon became the principal mode of urban transport. By 1898, America had 15,000 miles (24,000 km) of electric-trolley line.
- Boston (1897) and New York (1904) introduced underground railways.

Lighting, sewage and water supply

Electric arc lamps, invented by Charles Brush and installed in 1879 in Cleveland, were quickly adopted by other cities. Better lighting made the streets safer at night, allowed shops to stay open longer and gave a stimulus to theatres and restaurants.

Sewage facilities lagged behind the needs of rapidly expanding populations. In the 1870s most cities discharged untreated waste into rivers or the sea. Baltimore and New Orleans relied heavily on open gutters, Philadelphia and Washington on private cesspools. Underground drains were only gradually introduced.

More effort was expanded in enlarging water supplies. The number of public waterworks increased more than fivefold in the 1880s. Attention was paid to water quantity rather than quality. Accordingly, pollution by sewage or industrial waste was common. Only when the connection was grasped between polluted water and typhoid epidemics did cities pay the problem closer attention.

Urban planning and architecture

In the 1880s and 1890s, public parks became a prominent feature of urban life. This was largely the achievement of Frederick Law Olmsted. Appointed chief architect of New York's Central Park in 1858, Olmsted subsequently designed park systems in many other cities. Nevertheless, city planning in the broader sense was virtually unknown before 1900. Hence American cities grew haphazardly.

The concentration of business in inner-city areas led to a distinctively US architectural form – the skyscraper.

Several factors facilitated the skyscraper's development:

- the need to economize on ground area because of high land costs
- the development of steel-frame construction
- the invention of the electric elevator
- the development of the telephone and electric lights.

Much of the pioneer work on skyscrapers was carried out in Chicago in the 1880s by a group of architects led by Louis Sullivan. Sullivan later designed skyscrapers in St Louis (1891) and Buffalo (1895). The skyscraper eventually spread to New York in the twentieth century.

The slum problem

The worst evil of urban expansion was the growth of slums. In mid-nineteenth century America, landlords had converted old mansions and warehouses into tenements and built cheap houses in every inch of space. Conditions deteriorated still further with the introduction in 1879 of the 'dumbbell tenement' – so-called because of the shape of its floor plan. Five or six storeys high, these barrack-like buildings were honeycombed with tiny rooms, many without direct light or drainage. In 1900 Manhattan had 42,700 tenements, housing over 1.5 million people. Not surprisingly, the tenements had high death rates. In 1890, journalist Jacob Riis exposed the terrible conditions of slum life in his book *How the Other Half Lives*. Together with other crusaders for better housing, he secured the appointment of a Tenement House Commission.

SOURCE F

New York's Lower East Side c1886

How useful is Source F for portraying urban conditions in the mid-1880s?

SOURCE G

The Illinois Bureau of Labor Statistics – Report (1884)

PROFESSION: Baker NATIONALITY: Pole

ANNUAL EARNINGS: Of father - $450

CONDITION: Family numbers five – parents and three children, all girls, aged one month, eighteen months and four years. Rent a house containing three rooms for which they pay a rental of $8 per month. Family are very ignorant, dirty and unkempt. The street is narrow and filthy: no pavement: mud knee-deep: no vaults or sewerage. Father works fifty weeks per year, and for a winter day's work he is employed twelve hours, and in summer fourteen. He receives $1.50 for each day's labour. His house is situated so far from his place of work that he cannot go home at noon. Carries no life insurance, and belongs to no unions.

What is the message of Source G with regard to urban living conditions in the 1880s?

FOOD – Breakfast – Coffee, bread and crackers

Dinner – Soup, meat and potatoes

Supper – What is left from dinner

COST OF LIVING	
Rent	$96
Fuel	$15
Meat and groceries	$165
Clothing, boots and shoes	$70
Books, papers, etc.	$3
Sickness	$40
Sundries	$65
Total	$454

Crime

City slums were nurseries of crime. Gangs from the slums committed robbery and assault, battling with the police and with each other. In the 1880s the prison population increased by 50 per cent. Police forces, while growing in size, were frequently corrupt. Investigations in New York in 1894 revealed that policemen regularly received percentages of the earnings of sex workers and thieves.

Settlement houses

As urban problems multiplied, middle-class reformers, especially educated women, established settlement houses in slum areas to provide help and guidance. The first American settlement house (modelled on experiments in London) was opened in New York in 1886. By 1900 there were 100 of them. The most famous was Hull House in Chicago, founded in 1889 by Jane Addams. Besides providing social services and recreational facilities, Addams and her co-workers sought to introduce 'foreign slum-dwellers' to American ways. But settlement houses alone could not deal with urban problems. Addams, with other social workers, campaigned for better housing and improved sanitary conditions.

SOURCE H

Part of an article written by Jane Addams on Hull House in 1893

Hull House stands on South Halsted Street, next door to the corner of Polk ... Between Halsted Street and the river live about ten thousand Italians ... To the south on Twelfth Street are many Germans, and side streets are given over almost entirely to Polish and Russian Jews ...

The policy of the public authorities of never taking an initiative and always waiting to be urged to do their duty is fatal in a ward where there is no initiative among the citizens. The idea underlying our self-government breaks down in such a ward. The streets are inexpressibly dirty, the number of schools inadequate, factory legislation unenforced, the street-lighting bad, the paving miserable and altogether lacking in the alleys and smaller streets and the stables defy all laws of sanitation. Hundreds of houses are unconnected with the street sewer. The older and richer inhabitants seem anxious to move away as rapidly as they can afford it. They make room for newly arrived emigrants who are densely ignorant of civic duties.

How useful is Source H as evidence for conditions in poor urban areas?

City government

Political scientist James Bryce singled out city government as 'the one conspicuous failure of the United States'. Officials were often dishonest or incompetent. With the large-scale expansion of public utilities and the huge increase in other municipal expenditures, corrupt alliances developed between unscrupulous city politicians and business interests eager for contracts. The most notorious example of municipal graft was the Tweed Ring in New York. Following Tweed's fall in 1871, 'Honest John' Kelly, while not deserving his nickname, committed fewer wrongdoings. But corruption reached new depths after 1886 when Kelly was succeeded as boss by Richard Croker, a former prize-fighter and gang-leader. Immigrant votes increased the power of the bosses and their political machines (see pages 159–60). At a time when there were few public welfare agencies, city bosses often provided help, finding jobs and accommodation for newcomers. Immigrants saw nothing wrong in repaying their benefactors with votes.

Social mobility and the standard of living

American society had a reputation for being uniquely fluid. Horatio Alger's widely read novels, such as *Making His Way* and *Frank's Campaign*, popularized the notion that poor boys could achieve success through hard work and luck. But studies of American business and financial leaders indicate that most were born to wealth and privilege. By the late nineteenth century, blue collar workers and their sons rarely became managers. The most common type of occupational mobility was from an unskilled to a semi-skilled job or from semi-skilled to skilled. Native-born working men did better than immigrants. Black Americans did worse than anyone.

Contemporaries often asserted that the rich were getting richer and the poor poorer but the truth was that while the rich were getting richer, so were the poor. Between 1860 and 1890 real wages rose spectacularly. Although they shrank a little in the depression-hit 1890s, they went up again between 1897 and 1914. Moreover, the average working week was reduced from 66 hours in 1860 to 55 hours by 1914. Workers' gains were unevenly distributed. Skilled workers gained more than unskilled. Despite this, large numbers of wage-earning families still lived below the poverty line.

The advantages of urban life

Although there were major social problems in late-nineteenth-century American towns, they nevertheless continued to attract large numbers of people – both new immigrants and native-born Americans. This was largely because they provided jobs. These jobs were usually better paid and less laborious than work on the land. Moreover, towns provided a number of other benefits.

- They provided greater opportunities for sport and leisure.
- They provided better education, both at elementary and high school level.
- Many towns provided public libraries, museums and art galleries.
- Most large towns staged theatre and musical productions.

The impact of technology

For most urban Americans the post-1865 decades were an age of increasing comfort and convenience. A host of inventions, gadgets and techniques transformed the conditions of life, reducing drudgery and enriching the leisure hours of city-dwellers.

- New methods of preserving food made possible a more varied and nutritious diet.
- The sewing machine was a familiar object to most women.
- The modern safety razor was invented by King Gillette (1895).
- Cycling became a popular recreational activity. By 1900, 10 million Americans rode bikes.

The press

By 1900 the USA had 2190 daily newspapers and 15,813 weeklies, more than the rest of the world combined. Rotary presses and other mechanical improvements speeded up and cheapened production. Largely dependent on advertizing, there was intense competition for circulation and a tendency toward consolidation and the development of newspaper chains. Journalistic entrepreneurs, like Joseph Pulitzer, were less concerned with moulding opinion than with making money by catering for the newly created mass literacy. They exploited sport, crime, sex and scandal, while at the same time crusading against political corruption and evils like gambling.

The rise of organized labour in industry

Trade unions developed far more slowly in the USA than in Europe. One reason was that the industrial workforce consisted of large numbers of immigrants divided by ethnic origin and religion. In addition, native-born and immigrant workers often refused to associate with black workers. Employers were thus able to play off one group against another. They also used spies, blackmail and even armed force to thwart union organization. They could generally rely on the support of the law courts. Moreover, many workers had little sympathy with collective action. The opportunities for advancement that existed – or were believed to exist – undermined class consciousness.

Labour unrest in the 1870s

Worker grievances sometimes led to violence.

The Molly Maguires

In the early 1870s a secret Irish group, the Molly Maguires, used violence in the Pennsylvanian coalfields – intimidating, beating and killing in an effort to right perceived wrongs. Mine owners called in the **Pinkerton Detective Agency** which specialized in countering labour unrest. An agent who infiltrated the group produced enough evidence to indict its leaders. Trials in 1876–77 resulted in 24 Molly Maguires being convicted. Ten were hanged.

The 1877 railroad strike

In 1877 the major eastern railroad companies cut workers' wages by ten per cent. Railroad workers at Martinsburg, West Virginia, walked out and blocked the tracks. The strike spread, paralyzing two-thirds of the USA's railroad network. In Pittsburgh a pitched battle between strikers and state militia resulted in 25 deaths and millions of dollars-worth of damage. Order was only restored when President Hayes sent in troops. Eventually, the workers drifted back to work.

The National Labor Union

Local **craft unions** merged to form national organizations in the 1850s and 1860s. In 1866 William Sylvis founded the National Labor Union. It included craft unions, farmer's associations and various reform groups. Though attaining a large membership, the organization lasted only six years. Most of its leaders were more concerned with long-term economic and social reform than working men's immediate problems. Consequently most of the craft unions soon withdrew.

KEY TERMS

Pinkerton Detective Agency Allan Pinkerton, a Scotsman who had emigrated to the USA, set up his Detective Agency in 1850. He organized an intelligence service for the Union in the Civil War. After 1865 his force was often used by business leaders who wished to take action against trade unions.

Craft unions Organizations which were set up by workers to try to improve pay and conditions in particular (often skilled) occupations.

The Knights of Labor

Founded in 1869 by a group of Philadelphia tailors headed by Uriah Stephens, the Knights' organization aimed to unite all 'toilers' in one grand association, irrespective of occupation, race, nationality or sex. The unskilled were welcomed along with craftsmen: so were farmers. The Knights demanded an eight-hour day, equal pay for women and the abolition of child labour. They also put forward a long list of political demands – paper money, an income tax, the nationalization of railroads. Condemning strikes, they sought to achieve their objectives through legislation and, more particularly, through the formation of **producers' co-operatives**.

KEY TERMS

Producers' co-operatives Organizations in which workers or small-scale manufacturers work together to try to help each other in a variety of ways.

Anarchist A person whose ideal of society is one without a government of any kind. Late-nineteenth-century anarchists often sought to bring this about by violent means.

Initially the Knights grew slowly. In 1878 membership was under 10,000. Then in 1879 they elected as Grand Master Workman a Pennsylvanian machinist, Terence Powderly. He persuaded the Knights to abandon secrecy and modify its semi-religious character. The movement soon grew in strength. In 1885 militant local unions, affiliated with the Knights, forced the Wabash railway system, owned by Jay Gould, to restore wage cuts and recognize their union. This victory boosted Knight recruitment. By 1886 it had 700,000 members.

SOURCE I

Some of the main aims of The Knights of Labor in 1878

1 *To bring within the folds of organization every department of productive industry, making knowledge a stand-point for action, and industrial and moral worth, not wealth, the true standard of individual and national greatness.*

2 *To secure to the toilers a proper share of the wealth that they create; more of the leisure that rightfully belongs to them; more societary advantages; more of the benefits, privileges, and emoluments [profits] of the world; in a word, all those rights and privileges necessary to make them capable of enjoying, appreciating, defending and perpetuating the blessings of good government.*

3 *To arrive at the true condition of the producing masses in their educational, moral, and financial condition, by demanding from the various governments the establishment of bureaus of Labour Statistics.*

4 *The establishment of co-operative institutions, productive and distributive.*

Read Source I. How realistic were the aims of the Knights?

The Knights' success was short-lived. Another strike against the Gould system in 1886 failed and union power was broken. The Haymarket Affair in Chicago (1886) further damaged the Knights' prestige. A long-standing strike by workers at McCormick's Harvester plant had led to violence between police and workers. On 4 May a group of **anarchists**, led by German immigrants, called a meeting in Haymarket Square to protest. At the meeting a bomb was thrown, killing 7 people and injuring 67 others. The police rounded up 200 anarchists and charged eight with conspiracy to murder. All were convicted and seven were sentenced to death. One of the condemned, an experienced bomb-maker, blew himself up in his cell, two others had their sentences commuted to life imprisonment and four were hanged.

Though the Knights rejected anarchism and had not been involved in the Haymarket Affair, the public nonetheless connected the organization with violence and **radicalism**. Meanwhile, mismanagement and unfair competition had brought about the failure of most of the Knights' 200 co-operative enterprises. After 1886 the organization quickly crumbled.

The American Federation of Labor

Founded in 1881 by representatives of several craft unions, this organization was reorganized in 1886 under the name of the American Federation of Labor (AFL). The AFL, a federation of national unions, repudiated the Knights' ideal of one big, centrally controlled union. Made up predominantly of skilled workers, its leaders did not share the Knights' aspirations for political reform or the creation of co-operatives. Instead, they focused on improving the lot of their workers. They were prepared to use strikes and boycotts to attain their ends. Samuel Gompers, the AFL's long-standing president, stated that he stood for 'pure and simple' unionism. Accepting capitalism, he fought a bitter battle against socialist influence within the AFL. Avoiding the taint of radicalism, the AFL experienced a steady growth in membership.

Industrial action in the 1890s

There was a series of strikes in the 1890s. Two were particularly important.

The Carnegie Homestead strike

This strike began at Carnegie's Homestead steel plant near Pittsburgh in 1892. A wage dispute escalated into a quarrel over collective bargaining. The plant manager, Henry Clay Frick, used **strike-breakers** and engaged 300 Pinkerton detectives to protect them. On 6 July, as the Pinkerton men approached the plant, they were fired on by strikers. In the ensuing battle six workers and three Pinkerton men died before the Pinkertons were forced to surrender. Frick appealed to the governor of Pennsylvania for help and the National Guard was sent in to restore order. Public opinion, initially on the side of the strikers, seems to have changed after an attempt to murder Frick. The strike was finally broken in November, with the result that unionism in the Carnegie system was destroyed.

The Pullman Strike

Over the winter of 1893–94, the Pullman Palace Car Company cut the wages of its employees by 25 per cent. When the management refused to discuss grievances with a representative committee and sacked some of its members, workers went on strike (May 1894). The strikers' cause was supported by the militant American Railway Union, led by Eugene Debs. The union's decision to boycott railroads using Pullman cars led to a major strike which paralyzed traffic out of Chicago and was accompanied by

KEY TERMS

Radicalism The principles of those who want to bring about massive change in society, usually by overthrowing those in control.

Strike-breakers People who are prepared to work during a strike or who are brought in because they are willing to work during a strike.

KEY TERM

Injunction A court order.

sporadic violence. The railroad companies appealed for federal intervention and secured a federal-court 'blanket' **injunction** restraining anyone from interfering with the railroads or the mails or from seeking to dissuade railway employees from performing their normal duties. President Cleveland then sent in troops, ignoring the protests of the Governor of Illinois Altgeld who sympathized with the striking workers. Federal intervention broke the strike. Debs, who defied the injunction, was imprisoned for six months.

The rise of organized labour in agriculture

Farm discontent arose from adversity. After 1865 the prices of staple crops fell steadily. Wheat, which sold for $1.45 a bushel in 1866, fell to 49c by 1894: cotton fell from 31c a bale to 6c. Western farmers, who had taken mortgages to cover the costs of land and machinery, were unable to meet their obligations. Agricultural discontent was strongest in the South and West. Given the falling farm prices, farmers searched for people to blame.

- The railroads were regarded as the main villains. Railroad rates were higher in the South and West than in the Northeast.
- Banks were blamed for increasing interest rates.
- Corporations were blamed for what were perceived to be high prices.
- Middlemen, who handled the farmers' products, were criticized.
- State and federal governments were blamed for doing nothing to help farmers.

The Granger Movement

In 1867 Oliver Kelley founded the Patrons of Husbandry organization – better known as the Grange (an old word for granary). Starting as a social and educational response to farmers' isolation, it began to promote farmer-owned co-operatives for buying and selling in an effort to eliminate middlemen's profits. By the early 1870s, it had 1.5 million members. It soon had considerable political influence, both within the main parties and through independent third parties. In 1873 and 1874 Grangers won control of 11 Midwestern state legislatures. The Grangers' main political goal was to regulate the rates charged by railroads and warehouses. In five western states they managed to pass 'Granger' laws, attempting to regulate both. Although the Supreme Court in *Munn versus Illinois* (1877) supported the regulatory laws, this was a short-lived victory (see page 133). Moreover, most of the Granger co-operatives failed, owing to managerial inexperience and the hostility of established businesses. A rise in farm prices in the late 1870s led to the demise of Grangerism.

Farmers' Alliances

The Farmers' Alliances grew rapidly with the return of hard times in the late 1880s. By 1890 there were two major groups:

- the Northwestern Alliance whose strength was mainly in wheat-belt states like Kansas and Nebraska
- the Southern Alliance which was larger and claimed some 1.5 million members: a parallel Colored Farmers Alliance claimed 1 million members.

At a meeting in St Louis, Missouri in 1889 leaders of the Alliances tried to form a single organization. But nothing came of the idea because northerners objected to southerners' refusal to admit black people as equals. Nevertheless, the Alliances did agree on common political objectives, including the free and unlimited coinage of silver, nationalization of the means of transportation and communication and the introduction of a graduated income tax. The Southern Alliance also supported a subtreasury plan. They envisaged farmers storing their crops in government warehouses and securing government loans for up to 80 per cent of their crops' value at 1 per cent interest. Rather than having to sell immediately at harvest time, this would give farmers leeway to hold their crops for a good price.

In the 1890 mid-term elections Northern Alliance members supported variously named independent parties. They had some success, electing a governor under the banner of the People's Party in Kansas, taking control of both houses in Nebraska, and gaining a balance of power in the legislatures of South Dakota and Minnesota. Southern Alliance supporters, wresting control of local Democrat party machinery from conservatives, succeeded in electing two state governors and 40 Congressmen.

The Populist Party

In May 1891 a conference of farm, labour and reform organizations in Cincinnati agreed to back the creation of a national third party. In February 1892 a meeting at St Louis, dominated by farmers' representatives, formally organized the Populist or People's Party.

SOURCE J

Part of the Populist Party platform (July 1892)

We meet in the midst of a nation brought to the verge of moral, political and material ruin. Corruption dominates the ballot-box, the legislatures, the Congress, and touches even the ermine of the bench. The newspapers are largely subsidised or muzzled, public opinion silenced, business prostrated, homes covered with mortgages, labour impoverished ... A vast conspiracy against mankind has been organised ... If not met and overthrown at once, it forebodes terrible social convulsions ... or the establishment of an absolute despotism.

How useful is Source J for understanding agricultural grievances in the early 1890s?

Meeting in July at Omaha, the Populist Party chose James Weaver as their presidential candidate. Its platform supported:

- the subtreasury plan
- free and unlimited coinage of silver at the 16 to 1 ratio
- an income tax

- nationalizing the railroad, telegraph and telephone industries
- the secret ballot and direct election of senators
- the eight-hour day and restriction of immigration, in the hope of winning support from urban workers whom Populists regarded as fellow 'producers'.

The 1892 presidential election

Democrat Grover Cleveland won the election but Weaver carried four western states and won eight per cent of the total vote. He did not make much impact in the South where white people continued to vote Democrat and black people Republican. He also failed to win the support of industrial workers. While Populists talked about the 'harmony of labour', farmers and workers had very different concerns.

Populism 1892–96

The 1893 depression, and Cleveland's inability to deal with it, gave the Populists hope of greater success (see page 140). In the 1894 mid-term elections, they polled 1.5 million votes and elected six senators and seven members of the House. As the 1896 presidential election approached, the monetary issue (see page 139) overshadowed all others. The Populist demand for free silver was taken up by sizable factions within both major parties. Western silver-mine owners helped finance the silver campaign. The most effective piece of pro-silver propaganda was William Harvey's Coin's Financial School (1894). Presenting free silver as a cure-all for the USA's economic problems, it sold millions of copies.

ACTIVITY

Discussion point: Why was free silver regarded as such an important issue in late nineteenth century America?

The 1896 presidential election

The major parties took opposite positions on the currency issue. Republican candidate William McKinley supported a gold-standard platform and high tariffs. The Democrats chose 36-year old William Jennings Bryan who supported free silver. The Populists now faced a difficult choice. They could name their own candidate and divide the silver vote or endorse Bryan. Most decided to support Bryan.

Although Bryan barnstormed the country, travelling 18,000 miles (29,000 km) and making 600 speeches, the election was a triumph for the well-organized and well-financed Republican Party. The country was deluged with propaganda identifying Bryan with anarchy and revolution. McKinley carried the popular vote by 7.1 million to 6.5 million and the electoral college by 271 to 176 – the greatest Republican victory since 1872. While the South and West voted for Bryan, the Midwest and East supported McKinley. For the first time in twenty years, the Republicans controlled the presidency and had large majorities in both houses of Congress.

The Populist Party, unable to establish its separate identity, was destroyed. Somewhat ironically, much of the Populists' Omaha platform, which had seemed so radical at the time, was put into effect within the next two decades.

Summary

Some of the consequences of rapid economic growth were beneficial. Others were not. American prosperity encouraged a huge influx of new immigrants from southern and eastern Europe. These people mainly settled in towns. Rapid urbanization resulted in a host of social issues resulting from poor housing, health problems and disregard for the safety of people living and working in slum conditions. Another problem was the fact that while the USA experienced periods of spectacular economic growth, there were also periods of serious economic depression, affecting both industry and agriculture. Economic recession encouraged the rise of organized labour movements, for example, industrial trade unions and aggrieved farmers alliances like the Grangers and the Populists.

SUMMARY DIAGRAM

How great were the consequences of rapid economic growth in the late nineteenth century?

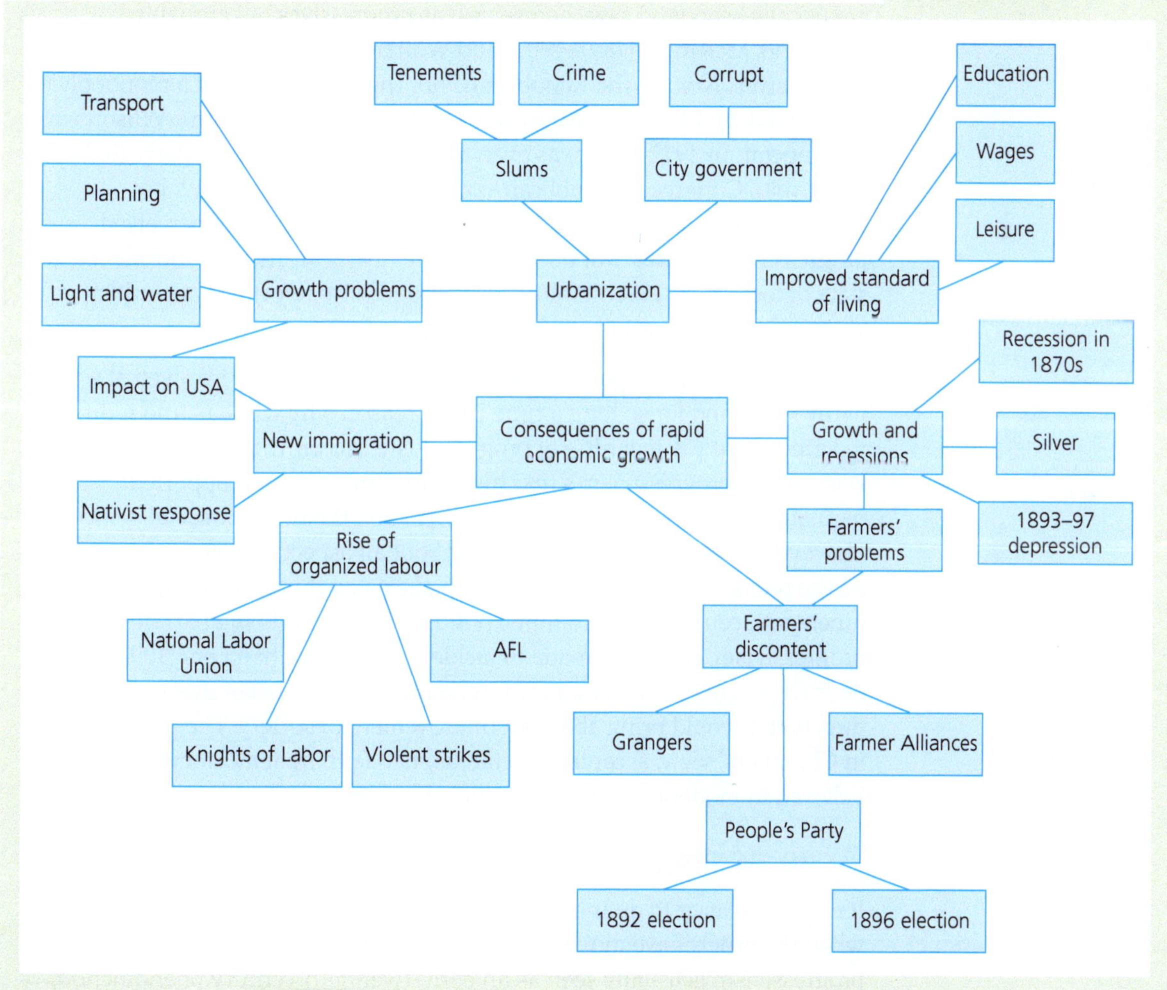

3 What were the main aims and policies of the Progressive Movement and how popular were they?

Historians usually refer to the first two decades of the twentieth century as the 'Progressive Era'. Unfortunately, they do not agree about what caused progressivism, what its aims were or how successful it was.

What was progressivism?

Presidents Theodore Roosevelt (1901–09) and Woodrow Wilson (1913–21) are usually seen (and saw themselves) as progressives but arguably Presidents McKinley (1897–1901) and William Taft (1909–13) were also progressives. Neither the Republicans nor the Democrats had a monopoly of progressivism. McKinley, Roosevelt and Taft were Republicans: Wilson was a Democrat. In 1912 there was even a short-lived Progressive Party (led by Roosevelt). Congress, Republican-controlled from 1896 to 1912, but Democrat-controlled from 1913 to 1916, passed a number of perceived progressive measures. But far more progressive reforms were introduced at state or local level. Historians also see progressive reformers at work in various fields such as the media and education.

The fact that so many politicians, people and groups were involved at so many levels and for so long a time is one reason why scholars find it difficult to agree about the meaning of progressivism. According to Benjamin De Witt, one of progressivism's first historians, progressives supported regulation of big business, political reform and the need for social justice. However, not all progressives agreed about all aspects of reform. Moreover, all the problems De Witt highlighted had existed throughout the late nineteenth century and attempts, not usually seen as being part of progressivism, had been made to tackle them. John Chambers (1992) has defined progressivism as 'a new interventionism' – a belief that intelligent, direct effort could bring about an improvement of society. The progressives, in Chambers' view, accepted capitalism, had faith in democracy, and believed in moderate – not revolutionary – change.

When did progressivism start?

It might be easier to define progressivism if there was agreement about when the progressive movement started. There is no such agreement. While progressivism is usually seen as an early-twentieth-century phenomenon, arguably progressive reform began in the 1890s or even the 1880s (the Sherman Anti-trust Act, for example, was passed in 1890). McKinley is sometimes regarded today as a progressive president. He certainly favoured active federal government of the type provided by Roosevelt and Wilson. Concern with social problems arising from industrialization and urbanization had existed throughout the late nineteenth century and much had been done to tackle the problems at various levels before 1900. These attempts, however, are not usually seen as being part of 'progressivism'.

ACTIVITY

Write a brief explanation of the meaning of the Progressive Movement.

Conclusion

Given that progressivism remains a rather vague concept, it would be unwise to claim that there was a single explanation for progressivism or a single progressive movement. Indeed, it can hardly be called a movement at all. Instead, different progressive groups often had very different aims. Care should thus be taken when speaking of progressives, the Progressive Era or the Progressive Movement. Nevertheless, De Witt (see page 154) was in many respects right. Most progressives were concerned about the regulation of big business and the need for political and social reform.

What caused progressivism?

A number of factors, variously stressed by historians, have been put forward to explain the causes of progressivism.

The need for reform

It is generally accepted that the problems arising from industrialization and urbanization made some kind of reform inevitable.

The need to regulate big business

By 1909 1 per cent of the total of industrial firms produced 44 per cent of the USA's manufactured goods. Big corporations were seen as a threat to free enterprise and the interests of the people. Virtually all progressives wanted to reduce the corporations' power. However, they did not agree about how this should be done.

The need for political reform

Progressives, opposed to corrupt party machines (see page 159), wanted government to be more responsive to the people. Many favoured the use of referendums, direct primary elections (so that voters, not party machines, chose candidates for elections) and female suffrage. But progressives disagreed about the extent of democratic reform. Some, for example, were reluctant to give women the vote.

The need for social justice

There were a host of social problems which needed attention. Progressives wanted government action to help the 'have nots'. They tended to support compensation for injury at work, old age pensions, an end to child labour and factory inspection. But not all progressives agreed on 'social' solutions. For example, while some thought Prohibition (of alcohol) was the solution to all America's problems, others regarded it as a limitation of individuals' rights.

The need to redistribute wealth

In 1890 the wealthiest 1 per cent in the USA owned 51 per cent of the nation's wealth: the poorest 44 per cent owned 1.2 per cent of all property. In 1900 Carnegie's income was $23 million: he paid no income tax. Most progressives supported direct taxation to ensure richer people were more fairly taxed.

Links to populism

Arguably there was a direct link between populism and progressivism. The Populists (see page 151), after all, had demanded political reform, regulation of big business and social/welfare reform. According to journalist WA White, 'The Progressives ... caught the Populists in swimming and stole all their clothing, except for the frayed underdraws of free silver'. However, there were few direct links between progressivism and populism.

- Few Populist leaders were progressives.
- Many progressives had opposed populism.
- Progressivism was free from the taint of radicalism that had damaged populism.
- Populism was limited to certain areas within the USA. Progressivism flourished in every part of the country.
- Populism arose out of distress. Progressivism arose during a time of prosperity. National income increased by nearly a third between 1897 and 1914.
- Unlike populism, progressivism did not (except briefly in 1912) develop into a national political organization. Its supporters operated rather as pressure groups within the two major parties.

The threat of socialism

American socialism was perhaps at its strongest between 1900 and 1920. The Socialist Party of America, founded in 1901, had greater support than at any time before or since. Eugene Debs (see page 149), stood as the Socialist presidential candidate in 1904, 1908 and 1912, winning about six per cent of the vote. In 1910 Milwaukee elected the first Socialist Congressman. By 1912 more than 50 cities had elected Socialist mayors. To many contemporaries, it seemed that socialism was on the march.

Trade unions also grew in strength. By 1904 the moderate American Federation of Labor (AFL) had over 1.4 million members. But some workers supported more militant unions. Violent strikes became common. Union troubles reinforced the suspicion that all was not well with America. It seemed that something had to be done to improve the lot of the 'have-nots' or the USA might face class war. This fear was probably exaggerated. Nevertheless, some progressive leaders supported moderate reform in order to prevent the danger of revolutionary change.

The influence of the middle classes

Progressivism is usually seen as a middle-class movement. Certainly, progressive leaders were often middle-class professionals – lawyers, doctors, small businessmen, clergymen and academics – many of whom were Protestant and 'urban'. Historians, such as George Mowry (1958) and Richard Hofstadter (1955), claimed that such people felt that their status was threatened by big business and political bosses, and that traditional American values were threatened by immigration. Mowry and Hofstadter believed that these middle-class professionals embarked on a political and moral crusade to protect their own position and American values. However, the 'status' theory has been challenged.

- Status anxiety is not usually a primary determinant of political behaviour.
- The social characteristics of progressive leaders were not distinguishable from other non-progressive politicians at the time.

Historians such as Robert H Wiebe (1967), similarly convinced that progressivism was a middle-class phenomenon, believe that it arose out of a desire to bring efficiency and stability to an increasingly chaotic society. Most progressives were confident that scientific methods, especially data gathering and analysis, would ensure that social and economic problems were overcome in an ordered way.

However, it is also arguable that middle-class reformers, rather than suffering from status anxieties or bent on a search for order, were essentially patriots with a social conscience. They simply felt that something should be done to improve the lot of many of their fellow Americans.

Nor was progressivism simply an upper-middle-class movement.

- The lower-middle class – clerical workers, salespeople, teachers – whose numbers were increasing, played a crucial role in terms of supporting progressive reform.
- The urban working class voted for progressive candidates rather than socialists.

The influence of new ideas

Changes in the economic, political and religious ideas may be more important than class-based interpretations of progressivism.

The intellectual climate

While many American intellectuals in the late nineteenth century accepted laissez-faire, some writers did stress the importance of government intervention. Henry George's *Progress and Poverty* (1879) and Edward Bellamy's *Looking Backward* (1888) were particularly influential. Both books suggested poverty could be eliminated if governments purposefully intervened. In the early twentieth century a number of writers examined the consequences of capitalist economic development. While disagreeing about problems and solutions to those problems, most accepted the need for an extension of the role of government in regulating economic and social activity. There was increasing confidence in the idea that social sciences could provide 'laws' which would help human progress.

Changes in religious belief

For most of the nineteenth century, American Protestants stressed the need for individual enterprise and hard work. God, it was usually claimed, had intended that the wealthy should be wealthy. As a result, most churches had shown relatively little interest in helping those in need. However, in the late nineteenth century, some Protestant clergy subscribed to ideas that came to be called the 'Social Gospel'. They believed that Christ's teachings required Christians to promote social and economic reform. Increasingly clergymen argued that adverse social conditions could lead to people becoming evil. Social Gospel clergymen exerted great influence through their sermons, their articles in both religious and secular magazines, and their widely read books.

In the 1890s Protestant Churches organized a variety of philanthropic enterprises and community services to help those in need. In 1908 these bodies united to form the Federal Council of Churches of Christ in America. This organization was vocal in support of social welfare legislation. It can thus be claimed that the Social Gospel movement was an important influence on progressivism. The conviction that laissez-faire led to selfish competitiveness which opposed the teachings of the New Testament underpinned the moral argument of many progressives. Nevertheless, Social Gospel was always a minority element within American Protestantism. Moreover, the Catholic Church showed relatively little interest in secular reform.

A progressive cast of mind?

Progressives tended to be evangelical. They saw political, social and economic issues as crusades. Many encouraged and preached, rather than argued. They were confident that life for all Americans could improve and tended to the view that no evil was too great to be overcome.

The influence of the media

Newspaper exposure of corruption in politics and big business occurred throughout the nineteenth century. The difference was that in the early twentieth century, there was a huge increase in American newspaper circulation. In 1899 some 3 million newspapers were purchased. By 1909 24 million were bought annually. Some newspapers attacked corrupt practices and supported reform. More important in this respect, however, were magazines, read mainly by the educated, urban middle classes. In 1902 SS McClure hit on a winning formula when his magazine's star writer Lincoln Steffens exposed political and business corruption in the USA's main cities. Sales of *McClure's Magazine* rocketed. Other editors rushed to follow McClure's lead. For the next five years '**muckraking**' articles on the evils of business dominated American magazines. The most devastating impact of any of McClure's articles came with Ida Tarbell's, 'The History of the Standard Oil Company', which attacked Rockefeller's business methods.

KEY TERM

Muckraking Focusing attention on unpleasant matters rather than noticing what is good.

The spate of 'muckraking' articles had several effects.

- Public opinion became more 'progressive'.
- Progressive legislation was passed (often at state level).
- Many corrupt politicians suffered defeat at the hands of 'clean' opponents.
- Articles by Steffens in 1904 made Wisconsin's governor, 'Battling Bob' La Follette, a national figure (see page 178).

The articles, full of facts and figures, seemed to have been written from a neutral perspective. In reality, the muckrakers rarely acted as impartial presenters of the truth.

- McClure wanted to arouse readers, in part because he wanted to sell magazines but more importantly because he yearned to exert public influence.
- Other editors and publishers were crassly commercial, their efforts bordering on scandal mongering.
- Some journalists, like Steffens, were committed socialists, anxious to attack the sins of capitalism.
- Tarbell, the daughter of an oil producer who had been ruined by Rockefeller, was hardly unbiased.

ACTIVITY

In pairs list six reasons for the rise of the Progressive Movement. Then choose the reason you think is the most important and debate your choice with a partner.

The heyday of the muckraking magazines lasted just five years (1902–07). Even then magazines devoted only a small percentage of their total space to muckraking articles. After 1907 magazines reverted to a primary emphasis on fiction and non-controversial information. To what extent newspapers and magazines reflected or formed public opinion remains an interesting question.

Limits on party machines and bosses

Progressives had faith in democracy. Their view was that if they could make government more responsive to the people, the reform of evils would follow. State governments adopted various devices to make government more representative and democratic.

Political machines and corruption

Political control in the early twentieth century lay, as it had in the late nineteenth century, with the party bosses and their highly organized machines, which operated at city and state level.

- City bosses, often men of little education and of recent (usually Irish) immigrant origin, preferred not to seek political office themselves but rather to operate behind the scenes.
- State bosses, by contrast, tended to be well-educated and of old American stock. Many were US senators.
- The size and nature of the electorate and the frequency of elections encouraged intensive political organization. Political machines used bribery and a variety of corrupt methods to try to ensure their men were elected.
- Along with machine control of politics went bribery and lobbying, especially by big business. Some state legislatures were in the pay of railroad corporations. Although corruption was more subtle at federal level, it was still widespread.

The direct primary

The most important reform with which the progressives tried to democratize government was the direct primary – the nomination of candidates by the vote of party members. Under the existing convention system, only a small proportion of voters attended the local meetings which sent delegates to county, and in turn to state and national conventions. The system lent itself to domination by political professionals. After South Carolina adopted primary elections in 1896, the movement quickly spread to many other states.

The initiative, referendum and recall

Several devices were adopted by progressives to make government more democratic.

- The initiative gave voters the right to compel consideration of a particular measure.
- The referendum submitted legislative proposals to a direct popular vote.
- The recall was a procedure whereby elected officials could be removed from office by popular vote before the expiry of their terms.

By 1910 some twenty states had adopted the initiative and referendum and nearly a dozen the recall.

Direct election of senators

Selection of senators by state legislatures was notoriously corrupt. Nevada was the first state (in 1899) to let voters express a choice, which state legislators of their party were expected to follow, in selecting senators. By 1912 some 30 states had passed laws virtually requiring legislatures to endorse the popular choice as signified in a preferential primary. The Senate (in 1912) finally accepted the Seventeenth Amendment, authorizing popular election of senators. This was ratified in 1913.

The role of party machines and bosses in progressivism

Recent research has stressed the important role that party machines played in supporting progressive reform at local and state level. On the surface this seems strange. Party bosses and machines were, after all, the enemies of most progressives but some bosses were reform-minded: they genuinely wanted to improve the lot of the working class. Others realized that supporting progressive reform was an effective way of appealing to voters. Thus bosses and political machines often did respond to the people's wishes, especially on the social/welfare front. Nor did bosses necessarily oppose democratic reform. Most found ways to use the new reforms that were meant to weaken them. Direct primaries, for example, did not noticeably change the type of men nominated for office. Given that candidates now had to fight two campaigns rather than one, they needed more publicity and more money. Only well-oiled party machines could turn out voters for referendums and gather signatures for initiatives. Therefore, despite progressives' hopes, political reforms did not destroy the party machines.

Temperance and Prohibition

Agitation for Prohibition gained momentum as a result of the increase in alcohol consumption after 1865.

The development of Prohibition pre-1900

A Prohibition Party was founded in 1869 and achieved some local successes. However, the main spearhead of Prohibition was the Women's Christian Temperance Union (1874), largely a creation of Frances Willard, for whom 'temperance' was essentially a means of protecting the home against male drunkenness. If women were in the van of the movement, they were strongly supported by the Methodist Episcopal Church and the American Antisaloon League, an organization of employers concerned at the impact of drink on industrial efficiency. Prohibitionists won support in the countryside, especially where Protestant fundamentalism was strong. By 1900, five states had adopted Prohibition.

SOURCE K

Samuel Lane Loomis, *Modern Cities and Their Religious Problems*, 1887

Drinking places are also causes of an inestimable deal of ruin. Besides actual drunkenness and the ghastly train of disease and crime that follows it, there is a moral poison about the grog-shops whose deadly power, though less frequently recognised, is scarcely less pernicious. A hellish atmosphere pervades these places. They are full of profanity, indecency, and infidelity, the headquarters of political corruption and the hotbeds of crime. It would be very unjust to put them all on a level. Some are certainly much more respectable than others; but none of them are too good, and the tendency of all is downward.

To what extent can Source K be useful to historians' understanding of the issue of Prohibition?

Progressivism and Prohibition

The war on drink displayed progressivism's characteristic moral fervour and high-minded idealism. Earlier prohibitionists had tried to convince Americans that alcohol was harmful to the individual, damaging health and generating poverty. To progressives it was also the source of numerous social and political ills. Moreover, most believed the liquor industry represented a dangerous concentration of economic power. Progressive prohibitionists had considerable success. Between 1907 and 1915, fourteen states, eight in the South (where anxiety to deny alcohol to black people provided an additional motive) and six in the West became 'dry'. Most of the remaining states enacted local option, a system which allowed counties and cities to decide the issue by popular vote. In the cities, especially those with large German and Irish populations, Prohibition made little progress. Nevertheless by 1916 about two-thirds of the area of the USA was legally 'dry'. Enforcement was difficult, however, so long as drink could be imported into 'dry' territory. Thus Prohibitionists pressed for federal action. In 1913, Congress passed the Webb–Kenyon Act forbidding the importation of intoxicating liquor into areas where its sale was banned.

The Eighteenth Amendment

Prohibitionism was aided by the USA's entry into the First World War in 1917. Prohibitionists claimed that alcohol lowered the efficiency of war workers and the armed forces. The fact that brewing and distilling were virtually German–American monopolies intensified prejudice against the drink trade. The Prohibition Act (1918) forbade the sale or manufacture of intoxicants during wartime. The Eighteenth Amendment, prohibiting the sale, manufacture or transport of alcoholic beverages passed both houses of Congress in December 1917. Ratified by the states in January 1919, it came into force a year later. The Volstead Act (1919) was passed to implement it.

The impact of Prohibition

Prohibition proved difficult to enforce. There were never enough enforcement agents – only 1520 in 1920. Most were poorly paid and susceptible to bribery. A greater problem was the fact that a sizable minority regarded Prohibition as an infringement on personal liberty and simply defied it. In large cities 'speakeasies' (illicit saloons) and night clubs flourished under the protection of political machines. By 1929 New York had 32,000 speakeasies, twice the number of its saloons before Prohibition began.

Female emancipation

By 1900 American women had more independence. An increasing number demanded the right to vote.

Growing female independence

In the late nineteenth century, women's role in society began to change.

- Legislation gave married women control over their earnings and property.
- Industrialization provided women with better opportunities of supporting themselves. The number of working women rose from two million in 1870 (15 per cent of all women) to eight million in 1910 (21 per cent). While domestic service, factory work and teaching accounted for the bulk of female employees, others became shop assistants, typists, telephone operators, social workers, bookkeepers and nurses.
- There were increasing higher education opportunities for women. By 1900 80 per cent of American colleges and universities were open to women. The number of female students had grown to 25,000, a quarter of the total.
- Women's clubs proliferated. While many confined themselves to literary and social activities, others became deeply involved in charities and reform.
- Women played a prominent role in the Progressive Movement, campaigning for Prohibition and the reduction of working hours for women.

Demands for female suffrage

Feminists had tried to secure female suffrage as part of the Fourteenth Amendment (see page 102). After this attempt failed, the National Woman Suffrage Association was founded in 1869. Its leaders were Elizabeth Cady Stanton and Susan Anthony. They regarded suffrage as just one among many feminine causes to be promoted. Almost simultaneously a rival organization was established, the American Woman Suffrage Association, headed by Lucy Stone and Julia Ward Howe. This group focused single-mindedly on equal suffrage through constitutional amendment. In 1890 the two groups merged to form the National American Woman Suffrage Association (NAWSA). NAWSA supporters claimed it was wrong to deny the vote to native-born women while offering it to men born overseas. The movement, largely middle class in membership, was slow to develop. In 1900 only Wyoming (1869), Colorado (1893), Utah (1896) and Idaho (1896) had granted full voting rights to women, although in several other states women could vote in school-board or municipal elections.

Divisions over female suffrage

Many Americans, male and female, were either indifferent or actively hostile to female suffrage. They claimed that:

- involvement in the sordid business of politics would degrade women and undermine family life
- women had no need to vote since they were represented by their menfolk
- women lacked the intellect to comprehend political issues.

American female progressives struck back, claiming that the enfranchisement of women would tend to purify politics and strike a blow at political machines, if only by doubling the size of the electorate. Such causes as Prohibition and the abolition of child labour would also benefit. NAWSA membership soared from 17,000 in 1905 to 2 million in 1917. Between 1910 and 1914 seven additional states, all of them west of the Mississippi, adopted female suffrage. Yet most states continued to oppose giving women the vote. This was in part because of Prohibition. Many men feared (with good cause) that women would support Prohibition. Even where women possessed the vote, they were not the political equals of men. Few were elected to office and none entered Congress before 1914.

KEY TERM

Suffragettes This was the name given to militant women campaigners for the right to vote in Britain. From 1906 to 1914 they used radical tactics including arson and damage to property as well as marches and demonstrations.

In 1912 a handful of radicals, led by Alice Paul, tried to infuse the suffragist movement with the fervour of the British **suffragettes**. But since Dr Anna Howard Shaw and Mrs Carrie Chapman Catt, the dominant figures in the NAWSA, opposed militancy, suffragists did not adopt the law-breaking activities of the suffragettes.

The Nineteenth Amendment

US entry into the First World War in April 1917 undermined opposition to female suffrage. Their contribution to the US war effort made the demand for political equality hard to resist. President Wilson came out in support of female suffrage. In 1917 New York became the first eastern seaboard state to enfranchise women. In January 1918 the House of Representatives adopted the Nineteenth Amendment providing for female suffrage. Southerners blocked it in the Senate for more than a year but it was finally ratified in 1919 and came into force in August 1920.

The regulation of private corporations

Concern over the concentration of economic power had led to the passing of the Sherman Anti-trust Act in 1890 (see page 129). However, the act turned out to be more symbolic than effective. Progressives were keen to take action against corporations.

- Few wished to adopt a socialist programme of public ownership.
- Some hoped to 'trust bust', in the belief that restoring competition would prevent economic abuses. But efforts to restore small-firm competition proved unworkable, largely because splitting up large combinations proved difficult.
- Many progressives, accepting that big business was essential to America's prosperity, believed the best way to prevent abuses was to regulate the corporations. Unfortunately, regulatory agencies often came under the influence or control of those they were supposed to regulate.

Theodore Roosevelt and the corporations

Roosevelt, president from 1901–09, believed that super-corporations were inevitable and essential to America's economic well-being. 'The man who advocates destroying the trusts by measures which would paralyse the industries of this country is at least a quack and at worst an enemy to the Republic', he declared in 1901. His main concerns were to remedy the chief evils by:

- persuading big business to reform itself
- setting up regulatory commissions.

The Bureau of Corporations

In his first message to Congress Roosevelt referred to the 'real and grave evils' of consolidation and urged Congress to set up a federal agency with power to investigate the affairs of big business. He failed but he did manage to get a watered-down Bureau of Corporations in 1903. This had the power to investigate and publicize but not to enforce. The Bureau carried out a number of useful studies into the conduct of several major industries, including oil, steel and tobacco.

The Northern Securities Company

In 1902 Roosevelt showed his determination to discipline industry by invoking the Sherman Anti-trust Act against the Northern Securities Company – a giant railroad holding company, involving JP Morgan among others. Aware that Roosevelt's action posed a threat to big business, Morgan rushed to the White House. 'If we have done anything wrong', he told Roosevelt, 'send your man to my man and they can fix it up'. Roosevelt, who generally supported this sort of agreement, replied: 'That can't be done. We don't want to fix it up. We want to stop it.'

After a long legal battle, the Supreme Court decided (in 1904) that the Northern Securities Company was illegal and it was dissolved. Roosevelt had served notice to the corporations that they could no longer ignore the Sherman Act. After the Northern Securities case, most corporate leaders were prepared to work out 'gentlemen's agreements' with Roosevelt. Trusts that conformed to his somewhat subjective standards could remain as they were. Others must reform or take their chances with the Supreme Court.

Roosevelt's second term 1905–09

Roosevelt's second term saw three important pieces of legislation against corporations.

- The 1906 Hepburn Act gave the Interstate Commerce Commission the power to inspect the books of railway companies and to lay down the maximum rates they could charge. The act marked the start of effective railroad regulation. Within two years the Commission had reduced many rates.
- A 1906 Meat Inspection Act empowered the Department of Agriculture to administer a federal programme of meat inspection and labelling.
- The 1906 Pure Food and Drug Act forbade the manufacture and sale of fraudulently labelled products. The Food and Drug Administration was set up to test and approve drugs before they went on the market.

SOURCE L

Cartoon showing Roosevelt hunting the trusts

Look at Source L. Who do you think was the intended audience for this source?

With Congress unwilling to pass an effective regulatory law, Roosevelt continued to make selective use of the Sherman Act. By 1909, his administration had brought charges against 44 corporations, including some of the largest.

KEY FIGURE

William Howard Taft (1857–1930) A native of Cincinnati, Ohio, Taft became a successful lawyer. Appointed to head the Philippine Commission in 1900, he proved himself an effective colonial administrator. Having served as Roosevelt's secretary of war, he was elected Republican president in 1908. Lacking Roosevelt's political skill, Taft did not enjoy a happy presidency and his actions divided his party. He came third in the 1912 presidential election. In 1921 he was appointed Chief Justice of the United States.

President Taft 1909–13

Although **William Taft** is usually regarded as a conservative, 90 anti-trust prosecutions were brought during his term in office. Taft's prosecutions resulted in the two biggest dissolutions of corporations in US history when in 1911 the Supreme Court ruled in favour of the government against Standard Oil and the American Tobacco Company. The Court ordered both companies to be broken into a number of smaller independent units.

President Wilson's reforms 1913–16

In 1913 Wilson seemed committed to restraining big business.

- The Federal Trade Commission (1913) replaced the Bureau of Corporations. In theory it had more power over trusts but in reality had a limited impact. This was largely because Wilson appointed commissioners who did not pursue vigorous anti-trust policies.
- The Clayton Anti-trust Act (1914) made a number of restrictive business practices illegal, including price discrimination, and also closed some important legal loopholes. Big businessmen could now be held individually responsible when found guilty of violating anti-trust laws. In theory, the act

gave the federal government far more power over corporations than anything passed by Roosevelt or Taft. In practice, however, the act was to have limited impact, disappointing many progressives.

Wilson, rather than attacking big business, acted in a similar way to Roosevelt. Informal agreements with business leaders became the norm.

Big business and progressivism

Left-wing historians, such as Gabriel Kolko (1963), see progressivism as the 'triumph of conservatism'. Despite presidential threats and Congressional acts, big business survived virtually intact. Kolko is critical of this outcome. Conservative historians, by contrast, often praise many of the big business interests for supporting progressivism. They claim that much that was achieved in the workplace was the result of big business putting its own house in order. Corporations supported improvements for a variety of reasons. By no means all big business leaders were uncaring of their worker's interests. Many supported progressive reform, both within society and within their own businesses.

How popular was progressivism?

Most Americans in the years 1900 to 1920 seem to have supported progressive reform. This explains:

- the election of progressive presidents – Roosevelt, Taft and Wilson (see pages 169–80)
- the fact that Congress passed a series of progressive acts
- the even greater amount of progressive action at state and city level
- the Sixteenth, Seventeenth, Eighteenth and Nineteenth Amendments (see page 177) – all of which were regarded as progressive. (It is worth remembering that it is not easy to amend the US Constitution.)

However, there was some resistance to some aspects of progressive reform.

- Some Americans, particularly in the South, continued to support the principle of states' rights and believed that individual states should determine domestic policy – not Congress.
- There was considerable opposition to Prohibition.
- Not all men approved of giving women the vote.
- There was some opposition to the increase in taxes necessary to pay for social/welfare reforms.

Summary

Progressivism remains a rather vague concept. Historians disagree about its main aims – not surprisingly because leading progressives at the time supported different policies at different times. Nevertheless, most progressives wished to limit the power of the party machines and bosses, to regulate private corporations, and to bring about social reform. Some progressives believed that the prohibition of alcohol would have a beneficial effect. Other progressives supported the cause of female emancipation, campaigning particularly for the right of women to vote.

SUMMARY DIAGRAM

What were the main aims and policies of the Progressive Movement and how popular were they?

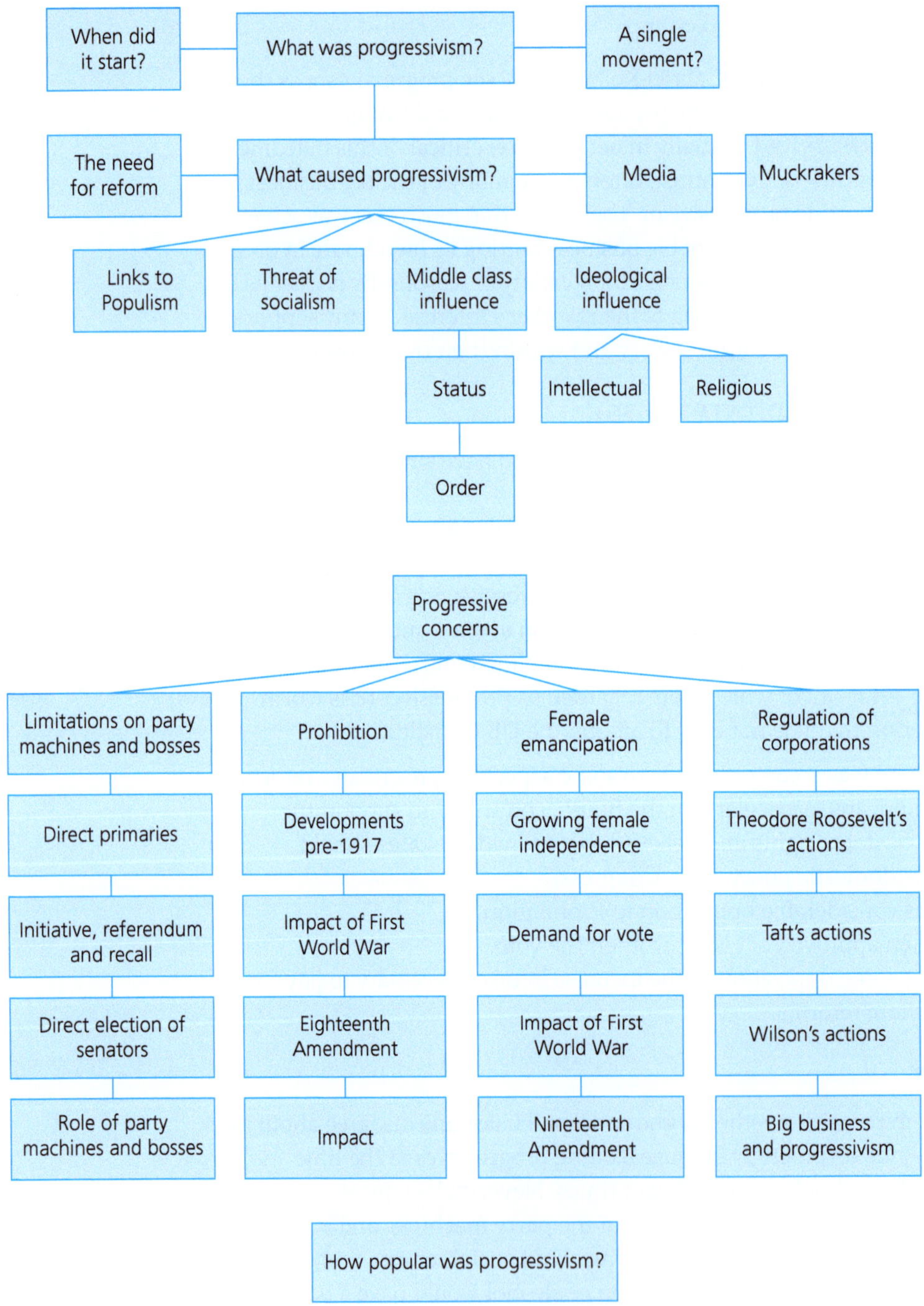

4 How successful was the Progressive Movement up to 1920?

Achievements of the Progressive Presidents

The three presidents between 1901 and 1921 – Roosevelt, Taft and Wilson – all considered themselves progressive. The extent of their progressive achievements on the business regulation, political reform and social justice front continues to generate debate.

Theodore Roosevelt

1858	Born in New York, son of a wealthy merchant
1880	Graduated from Harvard
1880	Married Alice Lee
1881	Elected as a Republican to the New York Assembly
1884	His wife and mother died on the same day: became a Western rancher
1886	Married Edith Kermit Carow
1889–95	Served on the US Civil Service Commission
1895–96	Headed the New York City Police Board
1897	Became Assistant Secretary of the Navy
1898	Led the Rough Riders in the war in Cuba: became a national hero
1898	Elected governor of New York
1900	Became Republican vice-presidential candidate
1901	Became president (on McKinley's assassination)
1904	Won the presidential election in his own right
1905	Won the Nobel Peace Prize
1912	Stood as the Progressive Party's presidential candidate
1919	Died

Historians' views about Roosevelt have tended to mirror those of his contemporaries. A few are critical, seeing him as little more than a windbag who promised more than he achieved. But most historians (like most contemporaries) tend to be positive. Many see him as a showman with something to show. Despite his reputation for hot-headedness, he was a skilled politician. He was also charismatic – a man with whom people could identify. He was an active moralist, lecturing Americans on the proper code of life – hard work, duty, honesty, sobriety and courage. It is difficult to place Roosevelt in a political box. Some historians have argued that he was more pragmatic than principled. This may be unfair. In many respects, his views remained remarkably consistent:

- He demanded a stronger federal executive to deal effectively with national problems. He believed the president should have the right to do anything the nation needed – unless it was specifically forbidden by the Constitution.
- He accepted the need to regulate trusts.
- He believed in democracy and honest and open government.
- He had a genuine concern for people who were poor and needy and favoured moderate social/welfare reform.

ACTIVITY

In groups decide which were the most serious problems facing American presidents in the early twentieth century. Then read the rest of the section and decide which president was most successful at tackling those problems.

Theodore Roosevelt

Roosevelt became president in 1901 after McKinley's assassination. Aged 42 (the USA's youngest president), he was a man with many interests and colossal energy. 'Father always wanted to be the bride at every wedding and the corpse at every funeral', wrote one of his sons. His flamboyant personality and young family helped his vibrant image. His presidency helped to change the concept of what American presidents could and should do.

Roosevelt's first term: 1901–04

Conscious of having become president by accident, Roosevelt was initially cautious. Anxious to be elected in his own right in 1904, he did not wish to antagonize Republican leaders. He declared he would do as McKinley would have done. In reality, he was probably more progressive.

- He set up a Bureau of Corporations (see page 165).
- He took on the Northern Securities Company (see page 165).
- In 1902 there was a serious coal strike after 50,000 miners demanded a pay increase, an eight-hour day and a recognition of their trade union. The mine owners locked out the striking workers. Both sides held firm and coal prices soared. Roosevelt made it clear that he was prepared to intervene on the miners' side, if necessary by sending troops in to operate the mines. The threat was sufficient to persuade the mine owners to accept the findings of a Roosevelt-appointed arbitration board. The miners did the same and the strike ended. In 1903 the board granted the miners a ten per cent wage increase, a nine-hour day but not union recognition.
- Roosevelt, a dedicated conservationist, determined to preserve as much of America's environment as possible. With the support of Chief Forester Gifford Pinchot he made use of the Forest Reserve Act (1891), to add 30 million acres to federal forest reserves. He seemed to be supporting the 'people' against mining, timber and oil 'interests'.

Roosevelt's second term: 1905–09

The Republican 'old guard', while suspicious of Roosevelt's progressivism, realized they had a winner and supported his presidential candidacy in 1904. Offering a 'Square Deal' to Americans, he easily defeated his Democrat opponent, Alton Parker, obtaining over 57 per cent of the vote. Roosevelt's popularity helped the Republicans win their largest majorities in Congress since 1865.

On the eve of his second inauguration, Roosevelt declared, 'Tomorrow I shall come into office in my own right. Then watch out for me!' Many of his ambitious plans, however, came to nothing. The Republican-dominated Congress opposed many of his proposals. He did have some legislative achievements, including the 1906 Hepburn Act, a 1906 Meat Inspection Act, and the 1906 Pure Food and Drug Act (see page 165). In 1908 Roosevelt persuaded Congress to enact an employer's liability law for the District of Columbia. This established a legal basis for workers to seek compensation for injuries sustained at work and illnesses contracted as a result of employment. The law was meant to serve as a model for state measures.

Roosevelt continued to support conservation measures. Some 120 million acres were taken into the public domain between 1905 and 1909. In 1908 he supported a National Conservation Conference attended by 44 governors and 500 other interested parties. As a result of this meeting, many states created conservation commissioners. In two messages to Congress over the winter of 1907–08, he called for the adoption of an income tax and death duties, federal supervision of the stock market, the extension of the eight-hour day and a workmen's compensation law. However, he was unable to persuade Congress to pass more in the way of progressive reform.

Roosevelt's record

It is possible to claim that Roosevelt's commitment to reform was all 'noise and smoke'. He was certainly not against big business. During his presidency, the number of corporations actually increased. He took no action on the tariff question and refused to endorse female suffrage. However, most historians think that Roosevelt deserves credit for helping to dramatize progressive concerns and giving them respectability. The fact that conservatives viewed him with suspicion is testimony to his progressive credentials. His popularity was not in doubt. Had he been prepared to stand again in 1908, he would almost certainly have won. But although he enjoyed being president and was (in his own view) at the height of his mental and physical powers, he respected the two-term tradition, established by George Washington, and refused to run for a third term.

President Taft

Roosevelt's hand-picked successor was William Howard Taft. Taft had been Governor of the Philippines (1900–04), and then secretary of war. Roosevelt very much admired his administrative ability. Taft had never run for office before and was not well-known to the public. However, he seemed to have similar aims to Roosevelt and easily defeated William J Bryan in the 1908 election.

Taft's presidency saw a number of progressive reforms.

- There was more trust-breaking than had occurred under Roosevelt (see page 166).
- Taft continued Roosevelt's conservation policies, adding to the forest reserves.
- The Mann–Elkins Act (1910) enabled the Interstate Commerce Commission to take the initiative in revising railroad rates.
- The Payne–Aldrich Act reduced tariffs – but not by much.
- An eight-hour day was introduced for workers engaged in work on federal government contracts.

In many ways Taft was an able president. However, he lacked Roosevelt's political skills. Most importantly, he failed to handle the progressive-conservative divisions within the Republican Party. Many Republican progressives (or insurgents) soon believed Taft was siding with the conservatives. Their suspicion was in part justified.

- Taft had little sympathy for organized labour.
- He doubted the constitutionality of income tax.
- He did little to prevent conservatives amending the Payne–Aldrich tariff bill, thus ensuring that few tariffs were reduced.
- He sided with his Secretary of the Interior Ballinger (a less than ardent conservationist) who was at odds with Chief Forester Pinchot. He eventually dismissed Pinchot for insubordination.

'Big Bill' Taft – the USA's heaviest if not most progressive president.

Republican division

When Roosevelt returned to the USA after an African safari in 1910, he was still keen to play a role politically but was uncertain what that role should be. In 1910 he delivered an important speech at Osawatomie in which he attacked the 'lawbreakers of great wealth', urged the need for more social reform, and supported the expansion of federal power. His views alienated Republican conservatives. Roosevelt himself was concerned by the 1910 mid-term results. The House of Representatives went Democrat for the first time since 1895. The only Republicans who enjoyed much success were progressives/insurgents in the West. The election results convinced Roosevelt that the Republicans must change or face defeat in 1912.

SOURCE M

Part of Theodore Roosevelt's Osawatomie speech in 1910

I stand for the square deal. But when I say that I am for the square deal, I mean not merely that I stand for fair play under the present rules of the game, but that I stand for having those rules changed so as to work for a more substantial equality of opportunity and of reward for equally good service ... Now this means that our government, national and State, must be freed from the sinister influence or control of special interests ... We must have complete and effective publicity of corporation affairs, so that the people may know beyond peradventure whether the corporations obey the law and whether their management entitles them to the confidence of the public. It is necessary that laws should be passed to prohibit the use of corporate funds directly or indirectly for political purposes: it is still more necessary that such laws should be thoroughly enforced.

According to Source M, what were Roosevelt's main concerns?

In 1912 Roosevelt determined to run against Taft for the Republican presidential nomination. He won the support of the 13 states which held primary elections. But Taft controlled the party machine and his supporters dominated the convention. Roosevelt, claiming that 'special interests' were operating against the people's wishes, quit the convention. He determined to lead a new Progressive Party, launched in August 1912. 'We fight', he said, 'in honourable fashion for the good of mankind.'

The 1912 presidential election

The 1912 election was the first serious three – arguably four – cornered contest since 1860. The presidential candidates – Taft (Republican), Wilson (Democrat), Roosevelt (Progressive) and Debs (Socialist) – while recognizing government's duty to concern itself with the general welfare of people, disagreed about the extent to which it should involve itself in social and economic matters.

Roosevelt and Wilson had different brands of progressivism to offer the voters.

New Nationalism

Roosevelt attacked the evils of 'class government' and 'greedy, short-sighted materialism'. He claimed that trusts should be regulated but not 'busted'. 'Conduct not size' was what mattered. He advocated inheritance and income taxes, the end of child labour, government-backed pensions and worker insurance, a minimum wage for women, female suffrage, government aid to agriculture, national party primaries, and the introduction of the referendum, initiative and recall.

New Freedom

Wilson, with no well-defined programme when the campaign began, developed New Freedom. He attacked the great corporations and supported trustbusting rather than regulatory commissions. He favoured tariff reductions and called for rural credits to assist farmers. He tended to oppose federal government involvement in social/welfare matters on the grounds that these issues should be left to state governments. In Wilson's view, the primary function of government was to destroy the obstacles to opportunity, not to provide positive services for the people.

SOURCE N

Part of an article written by Woodrow Wilson in 1912

The present organisation of business was meant for the big fellows and was not meant for the little fellows: it was meant for those who are at the top and was meant to exclude those who are at the bottom; it was meant to shut out beginners to prevent new entries in the race, to prevent the building up of competitive enterprises that would interfere with the monopolies which the great trusts have built up. What this country needs above everything else is a body of laws which will look after the men who are on the make rather than the men who are already made. Because the men who are already made are not going to live indefinitely, and they are not always kind enough to leave sons as able and as honest as they are.

Compare the views of Roosevelt (Source M) and Wilson (Source N) with regard to progressive reform.

The result

Given the Republican split, Wilson was always favourite to win – and he did so with relative ease, obtaining 41.9 per cent of the total vote and 435 electoral college votes. Roosevelt won 27.4 per cent of the vote and 88 electoral college votes. Taft won 23.2 per cent of the vote but only 8 electoral votes. Debs won 6 per cent of the vote but no electoral college votes. The Democrats also won majorities in both Houses of Congress. Perhaps the most surprising thing about the election result was that there were few surprises. Wilson kept most of the Democrat vote while the Republican vote was split between Taft and Roosevelt.

Woodrow Wilson

1856	Born in Virginia, the son of a Presbyterian clergyman
1875–79	Attended (what became) Princeton University
1885	Married Ellen Axson
1886	Received his PhD
1890	Returned to Princeton as a professor, teaching history and political science
1902	Became president of Princeton
1910	Elected as Democrat Governor of New Jersey
1912	Won the presidential election
1916	Re-elected president
1917	Led the USA into the First World War
1919	Helped draw up the Treaty of Versailles
1919	Suffered a massive stroke
1924	Died

By 1912 Wilson had a great reputation both as a scholar and as a progressive state governor. From the start of his presidency, he was determined to carry out his own ideas, dominating both the formation of policy and the running of the government. His leadership style was far from perfect. He tended to be reserved, aloof, austere, stubborn and, on occasions, vindictive. He was not on close, or even good, terms with many of his colleagues, some of whom disliked his moralizing and patronizing tone. But Wilson proved himself to be efficient, resourceful and single-minded. Moreover, he could be surprisingly flexible. Much of his legislative success resulted from his willingness to change his mind and take advice.

President Woodrow Wilson

Wilson admired the British system of government and saw himself as filling a role similar to that filled by a British prime minister. He would formulate legislation, manage Congress, and lead the nation. In April 1913 he addressed a special session of Congress at which he revealed his plans – something that had not happened since 1801. Thereafter, he followed the government-sponsored bills closely, persuading, threatening and cajoling to ensure his measures passed. He was fortunate that the Democrats had majorities in both houses of Congress.

Wilson's early measures

Wilson's measures in 1913 and 1914 were unprecedented in scope and extent.

- The Underwood–Simmons Tariff (1913) abolished duties on more than 100 goods and reduced them appreciably on a thousand others – the first significant cut since the Civil War.
- In 1913 Wilson introduced the first permanent income tax law in American history. Applying to only five per cent of the population, it was set at a very low rate.
- The Federal Reserve Act (1913) gave the USA a central banking system for the first time since the 1830s. Twelve Federal Reserve Banks were set up (in which the federal government placed its deposits), controlled by a Federal Reserve Board, appointed by the president.
- The Federal Trade Commission (1913) replaced the Bureau of Corporations (see page 166).
- The Clayton Anti-Trust Act (1914) made a number of business practices illegal (see page 166).

By 1914 Wilson was satisfied with his achievements but many Americans thought he had not gone far enough. Little had been done on the social/welfare front, largely because Wilson thought this was a state government responsibility. He refused to back a constitutional amendment giving women the vote, again arguing that this was a state matter. There was no real attack on big business and little was done to help farmers. Wilson's cause was not enhanced by a serious recession in 1913–14, the worst economic downturn since the 1890s. In the 1914 mid-term elections, the Democrat majority in the House fell from 73 to 25.

Wilson's reforms: 1916

In 1916 Wilson introduced a second wave of reforms. Historians have questioned his motives. Some think he may genuinely have become a convert to measures which in many respects were similar to New Nationalism. Others believe that political motives were uppermost in his mind. A presidential election was coming up. Wilson had won in 1912 because the Republicans had split. By 1916 the Progressive Party had disintegrated and Roosevelt looked set to re-join the Republican Party. If Wilson was to win in 1916 he needed to win votes from former Progressive Party supporters. Whatever his motivation, a spate of measures was passed through Congress.

- The Farm Loan Act provided low-cost loans to farmers.
- A Child Labour Act barred goods made by child labour from inter-state commerce.
- A Workmen's Compensation Act ensured that federal employees who were absent from work because of injury or illness received financial assistance.
- The Adamson Act laid down a maximum eight-hour day for railroad workers.
- Income and inheritance taxes were increased (although not by huge amounts) to help pay for the progressive measures.

The 1916 election

The Republicans expected to win the 1916 election. Charles Hughes, an ex-governor of New York with a reputation as a moderate reformer, was the Republican candidate and Roosevelt advised progressives to support him. Wilson, helped by the fact that the First World War had provided a boost to the US economy, campaigned on his record of 'Peace, Progress, Prosperity'. The result was close. Hughes won 254 electoral college votes – 46 per cent of the popular vote. Wilson won 277 electoral votes – 49 per cent of the vote.

The First World War and progressivism

Wilson's victory had been assisted by the fact that he had kept the USA out of war. It was thus somewhat ironic that in April 1917 he took the USA into the First World War. Some scholars think this marked the end of progressivism:

- The war led to greater co-operation between big business and the government.
- US entry into the war resulted in a crackdown on radical groups, especially after the Bolshevik Revolution in Russia. The Espionage Act (1917) was used to smash socialist organizations. Presidential candidate Debs was imprisoned.

- The 'Red Scare' continued after the end of the war. There was a spate of arrests and deportations of immigrants who were suspected of having Bolshevik leanings. It is hard to square this action with progressivism.

However, the war can be seen as the high-water mark of progressivism.

- The ideals which the USA brought to the war ('the war to end war', 'the war to save democracy') can be seen as progressivism applied to foreign policy.
- Most progressives supported American entry into the war.
- During the war, the federal government involved itself in a host of economic and social concerns, including taking over the running of railways and telephone lines.
- There was an increase in income, inheritance and corporate taxes, ensuring that business interests and wealthy Americans paid a large share of the war's cost.
- Nationwide female suffrage came shortly after the war (see page 164).
- The Eighteenth Amendment, which introduced Prohibition, became law after the war (see page 162).

Some see the Democrat defeat in the 1920 presidential election as the symbolic end of progressivism. But others point out that progressive reform continued at state level throughout the 1920s and perhaps returned with Franklin D Roosevelt in 1933.

Constitutional reforms

Four amendments, each perceived to be progressive, were added to the Constitution in the period 1913–20.

1913	The Sixteenth Amendment (The raising of income tax)	The Congress shall have power to lay and collect taxes on incomes, from whatever source derived, without apportionment among the several states, and without regard to any census or enumeration.
1913	The Seventeenth Amendment (Direct election of senators)	The senators of the United States shall be composed of two senators from each state, elected by the people thereof, for six years; and each senator shall have one vote ...
1919	The Eighteenth Amendment (Prohibition of alcohol)	Section 1. After one year from the ratification of this article the manufacture, sale, or transportation of intoxicating liquors within, the importation thereof into, or the exportation thereof from the United States and all territory subject to the jurisdiction thereof for beverage purposes is hereby prohibited. Section 2. The Congress and the several states shall have concurrent power to enforce this article by appropriate legislation.
1920	The Nineteenth Amendment (Votes for women)	The right of citizens of the United States to vote shall not be denied or abridged by the United States or by any state on account of sex. Congress shall have power to enforce this article by appropriate legislation.

State versus federal successes

Although Presidents Roosevelt and Wilson have been praised by some historians for their progressivism, in many respects progressive reform had a greater impact at local and state level.

Municipal reform

Progressives believed that the remedy for boss rule and machine politics was to change the structure of city government. Some worked to replace the traditional form of government – by a mayor, city council and elected administrative officials – with an elective commission, whose members were chosen for their abilities rather than their party affiliations. The commission plan began in Galveston in 1901, in the aftermath of a devastating flood. By 1921, it had been adopted by some 400 cities. A variant of it, the city-manager plan, which involved turning over executive power to a trained expert, was also popular.

Municipal improvement owed much to a new breed of reform mayors. The two most prominent were Tom Johnson of Cleveland and Samuel ('Golden Rule') Jones of Toledo, both of whom turned to politics after having made large fortunes in business. Johnson, according to Lincoln Steffens, made Cleveland 'the best-governed city in America'. Jones increased the wages of municipal employees, campaigned for municipal ownership of all public utilities and established public parks.

Progressivism in the states

Governors John Altgeld of Illinois and Hazen Pingree of Michigan, in power in the 1890s, were early examples of progressives operating effectively at state level. A decade later their example was being followed all over the USA. In California, Governor Hiram Johnson ended the political domination of the Southern Pacific Railroad. In the South, conservative control was undermined by the election of progressive governors like Jeff Davis of Arkansas and Hoke Smith of Georgia. In the East the progressive reputations of Charles Hughes (New York) and Woodrow Wilson (New Jersey) enabled both men to run for the presidency.

Perhaps the most outstanding progressive state governor was Robert La Follette of Wisconsin. During his six years as governor (1900–06), he implemented a sweeping programme of reform, securing from an often reluctant state legislature laws providing for effective railroad regulation, income taxes, regulation of banks, limitation of hours of work for women and children, and primary elections. An important feature of La Follette's administration was the 'Wisconsin Idea', a term denoting the collaboration between the state government and University of Wisconsin experts. The latter provided the legislature with data and advice on economic and social problems and staffed the numerous state commissions appointed to regulate business.

An important feature of the progressive movement was the impulse towards social justice. Reforms invariably began at state level. Those perceived to be successful were copied by other states.

- By 1914 most states banned the labour of underage children and limited the working hours of older children.
- Many states outlawed night work and labour in dangerous occupations for women and children.
- Legislation was introduced to protect workers against accidents at work.

Besides passing laws to regulate corporations and protect wage-earners, state governments adopted various devices to diminish the influence of political bosses. By 1918, twenty states had adopted the initiative and the referendum, twelve the recall (see page 160).

Limits of the Progressive Movement

Historians are divided on the success of the progressive movement.

Critics

Left-wing historians claim that tit-bits of reform were introduced to keep the masses happy – but no more. Poor (especially black) Americans were largely unaffected by progressivism. Compared with Europe, there was little social/welfare legislation nor was there any reorganization of society. Big business survived and prospered. So did political bosses. Much of the emphasis on democracy proved illusory. Progressive reform also seems to have had a darker side of racism, intolerance and repression.

- The Progressive Era saw black people disfranchised in most southern states.
- In 1916 Congress passed a bill requiring all adult immigrants to pass literacy tests in their native languages – the first step towards ending large-scale European immigration.
- Many progressives supported Prohibition, a move abridging the freedom of many Americans.

Right-wing historians are critical of the progressive movement for different reasons. Some hold the view that the real achievements of the progressive decades – wage increases, workers' welfare and pension and profit-sharing schemes – resulted from the voluntary actions of big business, not naïve progressive politicians. Big business generally supported improvements in workers' conditions. Nor was it as bad as it was painted by progressives. Interestingly, many state railroad commissions found that railroads were charging fair rates.

Supporters

A case can be made to support progressive reformers. Historian John Chambers (1992) has claimed that 'within a span of only a few years, progressivism helped make the United States a better country'.

- Progressives should not be blamed for failing to achieve a major reorganization of society. That was not their aim. Indeed, the aim of many was to prevent such a fundamental change. This they achieved.
- Action was taken against corporations to ensure they did not operate to the disadvantage of the public interest. During the Progressive Era, most of the super-corporations lost some of their dominance. For example, in 1901 US Steel had a 62 per cent share of the market. By 1920 this had fallen to 40 per cent. In 1899 Standard Oil produced 90 per cent of US petrol. By 1920 it produced only 50 per cent. **Oligopoly**, by which a handful of large firms dominated the market, characterized American industry – not monopoly.
- Progressive reform reduced the harshness of industrialization. Most states passed laws which ensured at least a basic standard of protection for industrial workers. State and federal action led to a decline in child labour.
- Arguably progressivism created the climate of opinion in which big business was disposed to be humane and party bosses accepted political reform.
- The progressive age saw a considerable rise in American living standards.
- Progressive political reforms made governments more responsible to the people – women as well as men.
- Progressivism kept the American Dream alive. Many progressives believed that with the proper mechanism they could eliminate virtually any social problem – corruption, poverty, drunkenness. This may have been naïve but optimism and faith in the future is better than cynicism and despair.
- The progressive presidents paved the way for later twentieth-century presidents who were similarly activist and reform-minded.

KEY TERM

Oligopoly A situation in which a small number of competitive firms control the market.

ACTIVITY

In which area of progressive activity were government measures most successful? Why do you think this was the case?

Summary

The extent of the success of the Progressive Movement continues to arouse historical debate. Presidents Theodore Roosevelt and Woodrow Wilson are usually seen as successful progressive presidents. Taft, who gravitated towards the conservative wing of the Republican Party, is generally seen as less progressive. During the progressive years, there were a series of important constitutional reforms, especially the Sixteenth, Seventeenth, Eighteenth and Nineteenth Amendments. Much of the progressive success, in both political, social and economic matters, occurred at state rather than federal level. While there was a limit to progressivism's success, the movement can claim some notable achievements.

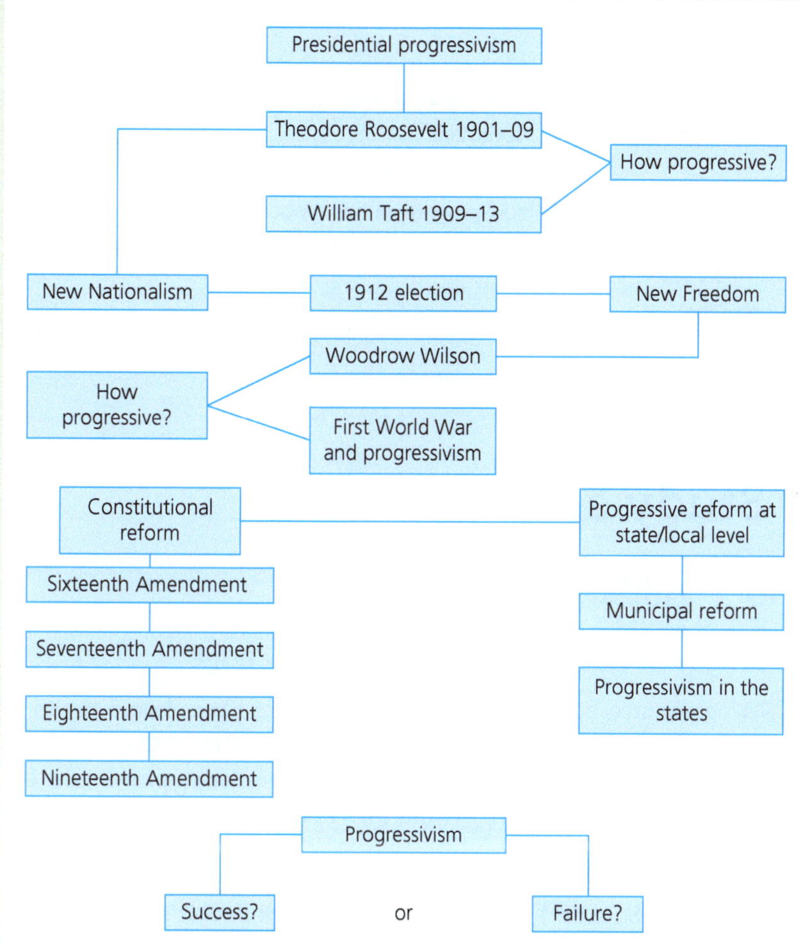

SUMMARY DIAGRAM

How successful was the Progressive Movement up to 1920?

Chapter summary

In the late nineteenth century, the USA became the world's greatest industrial power. Industrialists like Carnegie (steel) and Rockefeller (oil) and bankers like Morgan were better known than the presidents of the time. Industrialization, coupled with a rise in immigration from southern and eastern Europe, created a host of social problems in American cities. Industrial workers experienced good times and bad. Western and southern farmers experienced mainly bad times, due to the fall in prices for wheat and cotton. Militant farmers established radical political parties to try to protect their interests. The most successful was the Populist Party, founded in 1892. In the first two decades of the twentieth century Presidents Roosevelt, Taft and Wilson tried to address some of the economic, social and political problems troubling Americans. A host of so-called progressive reforms were introduced at both federal and state level. Four new amendments were added to the Constitution: the Sixteenth (1913) which declared income tax legal, the Seventeenth (1913) which ensured direct election of senators, the Eighteenth (1919), which brought in Prohibition and the Nineteenth (1920) which guaranteed women the right to vote.

Refresher questions

1 Why did the USA industrialize so quickly between 1870 and 1900?
2 Were the 'robber barons' a good or bad thing for the USA?
3 Why was railroad development so important for the USA?
4 What were the main social problems in the cities?
5 Why were American farmers so militant in the period 1870–1900?
6 What was progressivism?
7 What were the main causes of the Progressive Movement?
8 How progressive was Theodore Roosevelt?
9 How progressive was Woodrow Wilson?
10 How successful was the Progressive Movement?

Study skills

Paper 1 guidance: sources

Evaluating sources using contextual knowledge

In answering a source-based question on a set of sources you should aim to establish what the sources say about the issue in the question and group them. You should consider how useful the evidence is by considering provenance but you also need to test the evidence by your own knowledge of the issue.

To take an example from the chapter.

How useful is Source 1 for informing us of Roosevelt's main concerns in 1910?

SOURCE 1

Part of Theodore Roosevelt's Osawatomie speech in 1910

I stand for the square deal. But when I say that I am for the square deal, I mean not merely that I stand for fair play under the present rules of the game, but that I stand for having those rules changed so as to work for a more substantial equality of opportunity and of reward for equally good service ... Now this means that our government, national and State, must be freed from the sinister influence or control of special interests ... We must have complete and effective publicity of corporation affairs, so that the people may know beyond peradventure whether the corporations obey the law and whether their management entitles them to the confidence of the public. It is necessary that laws should be passed to prohibit the use of corporate funds directly or indirectly for political purposes: it is still more necessary that such laws should be thoroughly enforced.

What contextual knowledge would help you judge this source as evidence for this particular issue?

Let's look at another question and another source.

How convincing is Source 2 as evidence for condition in poor urban areas? You should use your knowledge about its provenance and your own knowledge.

SOURCE 2

An extract from Jane Addams, *Hull House, Chicago: An Effort Toward Social Democracy*, written in 1893. Addams set up the Hull House Settlement – the most famous Settlement house in the USA

Hull House stands on South Halsted Street, next door to the corner of Polk ... Between Halsted Street and the river live about ten thousand Italians ... To the south on Twelfth Street are many Germans, and side streets are given over almost entirely to Polish and Russian Jews ...

The policy of the public authorities of never taking an initiative and always waiting to be urged to do their duty is fatal in a ward where there is no initiative among the citizens. The idea underlying our self-government breaks down in such a ward. The streets are inexpressibly dirty, the number of schools inadequate, factory legislation unenforced, the street-lighting bad, the paving miserable and altogether lacking in the alleys and smaller streets and the stables defy all laws of sanitation. Hundreds of houses are unconnected with the street sewer. The older and richer inhabitants seem anxious to move away as rapidly as they can afford it. They make room for newly arrived emigrants who are densely ignorant of civic duties.

Activity

Look at the sample answer below.

1 Find where the answer has shown what the source is saying about the key issue and highlight.

2 Find any comment on the provenance of the source and highlight in another colour.

3 Find where the answer has used knowledge to assess the source as evidence; highlight in a third colour.

The source shows the conditions in part of Chicago in the early 1890s. According to this source, conditions for many of Chicago's citizens, many of whom were new immigrants from southern and eastern Europe, were dreadful. The streets were dirty, schooling in short supply, factory laws ignored, street-lighting, paving and sanitation bad or non-existent. A major problem was that the municipal government was not prepared to take action to improve matters. As a result, the conditions were unlikely to improve.

The source was produced by Jane Addams, a famous social worker of the time. Addams, daughter of a Quaker businessman who was also a state legislator, was well-educated. She and her friend Ellen Gates Starr purchased Hull House in 1889. The Settlement house, which was supported by wealthy people from Chicago, offered working-class immigrants educational and cultural programmes as well as practical help. Addams had her own progressive agenda: she hoped to improve the social conditions in Chicago and other towns in the USA. She was thus likely to emphasize how bad the conditions were – in an effort to win sympathy and support for the people she hoped to help. The fact that she had strong opinions about a number of issues does not mean that she deliberately misrepresented the situation in Chicago. Moreover, there is evidence from many other sources to suggest that conditions were poor in a host of other cities across the USA.

Addams seems to have been correct in her charge that the Chicago municipal government needed to be prodded into taking more action to improve matters. So did the municipal governments of many towns. Most were controlled by political bosses and machines that won much of their support from the new immigrants. The new immigrants were often helped by the party bosses but this help did not extend to improving housing, work, street and education concerns.

It is all too easy, as Addams shows, to be critical of the situation for many city dwellers in the USA in the early 1890s. However, it is worth stating that city life, however bad by our standards, continued to attract not just immigrants from Europe but also native-born Americans from rural areas who preferred city life – and all its problems – to life on the farm. Thus US cities continued to grow at an astonishing rate, increasing the problems of city governments who had the responsibility to improve matters. In fairness to some municipal governments, great efforts were undertaken to improve transport, housing, education and sanitation. Those efforts should not be overlooked. Given her conviction that far more needed to be done, it is perhaps not surprising that Addams does overlook the fact that improvements had taken place by 1893 and continued to take place thereafter.

Try to make sure that when you answer part (b) questions you incorporate all three elements – interpretation; evaluation by provenance and evaluation by knowledge. Try to offer a distinct view of the usefulness of each source.

Now try to interpret and evaluate all the sources in the question below.

How far do Sources A to D support the view that trusts were unpopular in the USA in the period 1900–17?

SOURCE A

From an article by John Claflin in 1901. Claflin was a famous merchant and banker who was president of the United Dry Goods Company, the largest firm of its type at the time

With a man like Mr Morgan at the head of a great industry, as against the old plan of many diverse interests in it, production would become more regular, labour would be more steadily employed at better wages, and panics caused by overproduction would become a thing of the past.

SOURCE B

Part of Theodore Roosevelt's New Nationalism speech, delivered at Osawatomie in 1910

Combinations in industry are the result of an imperative economic law which cannot be repealed by political legislation. The effort at prohibiting all combination has substantially failed. The way out lies, not in attempting to prevent such combinations, but in completely controlling them in the interest of the public welfare.

SOURCE C

From an article by the *Engineering News*, published in 1911

We are today something like five years behind Germany in iron and steel metallurgy, and such innovations as are being introduced by our iron and steel manufacturers are most of them merely following the lead set by foreigners years ago. We do not believe this is because American engineers are any less ingenious or original than those of Europe ... We believe the main cause is the wholesale consolidation which has taken place in American industry. A huge organisation is too clumsy to take up the development of an original idea. With the market closely controlled and profits certain by following standard methods, those who control our trusts do not want the bother of developing anything new.

SOURCE D

Part of a book, *The New Freedom*, written by Woodrow Wilson in 1912 and published in 1913 by which time he was president

American industry is not free, as once it was free; American enterprise is not free; the man with only a little capital is finding it harder to get into the field, more and more impossible to compete with the big fellow. Why? Because the laws of this country do not prevent the strong from crushing the weak. That is the reason, and because the strong have crushed the weak the strong dominate the industry and the economic life of this country. Nobody can fail to observe that any man who tries to set himself up in competition with any process of manufacture which has been taken under the control of large combinations of capital will presumably find himself either squeezed out or obliged to sell and allow himself to be absorbed.

Comparing and contrasting two sources

It is important not just to describe each source but to explain how they agree and disagree and what might explain that by looking at the provenance of the different passages. Look again at these sources and the question which follows them. Then read the two answers. Which is the better answer and why?

SOURCE A

Part of Theodore Roosevelt's Osawatomie speech in 1910

I stand for the square deal. But when I say that I am for the square deal, I mean not merely that I stand for fair play under the present rules of the game, but that I stand for having those rules changed so as to to work for a more substantial equality

of opportunity and of reward for equally good service...Now this means that our government, national and State, must be freed from the sinister influence or control of special interests...We must have complete and effective publicity of corporation affairs, so that the people may know beyond peradventure whether the corporations obey the law and whether their management entitles them to the confidence of the public. It is necessary that laws should be passed to prohibit the use of corporate funds directly or indirectly for political purposes: it is still more necessary that such laws should be thoroughly enforced.

SOURCE B

Part of an article written by Woodrow Wilson in 1912.

The present organisation of business was meant for the big fellows and was not meant for the little fellows: it was meant for those who are at the top and was meant to exclude those who are at the bottom; it was meant to shut out beginners to prevent new entries in the race, to prevent the building up of competitive enterprises that would interfere with the monopolies which the great trusts have built up. What this country needs above everything else is a body of laws which will look after the men who are on the make rather than the men who are already made. Because the men who are already made are not going to live indefinitely, and they are not always kind enough to leave sons as able and as honest as they are.

What accounts for the different view of the role of corporations (or trusts) in these sources?

Answer 1

Theodore Roosevelt, had been US president from 1901-9. He was generally seen as 'progressive'. In Source A he says that trusts – he refers to them as 'special interests' – have a sinister influence – even control – over national and state governments. He proposes that the USA should be made fully aware of the influence of great corporations to ensure that they are not breaking the law. He also believes that laws should be passed to ensure that corporations should not use their funds for political purposes. He adds that such laws need to be 'thoroughly enforced'. Woodrow Wilson, who became a progressive Democrat president in 1912, is also suspicious of trusts. In Source B he suggests that large corporations are so powerful they effectively prevent smaller businesses from competing with them, thus limiting free enterprise. Consequently, laws need to be passed to reduce the power of the trusts in favour of smaller businesses – 'men who are on the make' rather than 'men who are already made'.

Answer 2

The two sources take a not dissimilar view with regard to the problem of trusts/corporations in the USA. While not anxious to abolish large corporations, both Theodore Roosevelt and Woodrow Wilson suggest that action needs to be taken to regulate them in order to limit their power and influence. Roosevelt, a progressive Republican president from 1901-9, had taken some action against trusts (for example, he had created a Bureau of Corporations and also ensured the break-up of the Northern Securities Company). However, in his important Osawatomie speech in 1910, he claimed that more needed to be done against the 'lawbreakers of great wealth'. In this extract, he suggests that trusts are not allowing 'equality of opportunity' and 'fair play'. He is particularly concerned with corporations' political – rather than economic - power, both at state and national level. He argues that laws needed to be introduced to prohibit the use of corporation funds 'directly or indirectly' for political purposes. Such laws, moreover, needed to be thoroughly enforced. Roosevelt was fully aware that big corporations were often able to avoid anti-trust laws.

Woodrow Wilson, Democrat presidential candidate in 1912, had similar progressive views to Roosevelt. It was somewhat ironic that the two men, along with Republican candidate Taft, stood against each other in 1912 – Roosevelt as the Progressive Party candidate. In 1912 Roosevelt's platform was called New Nationalism. Wilson's, by contrast, was called New Freedom. While it is possible to claim that there were major differences between the two platforms, most American voters at the time seem to have seen little difference between them. Wilson, like Roosevelt, was keen to reduce the trusts' influence. His main concern in Source B is with trusts' economic (as opposed to political) power. He believed that trusts stifled free enterprise and were thus a threat to capitalism. He is rather vague in this extract (as he was in the 1912 campaign generally) as to how he would set about reducing their power. He asserts that something needs to be done to ensure that small businesses are able to compete against the 'big fellows'. A 'body of laws' need to be passed to deal with this situation and to help the 'men on the make'. But Wilson is not specific about what those laws should be. Nor was he in the 1912 campaign. Nevertheless, he was elected president in 1912, largely because the Republican vote was split between Roosevelt and Taft. As president, Wilson did introduce some important anti-trust legislation, for example, the creation of the Federal Trade Commission and the Clayton Anti-Trust Act – measures very similar to those which Roosevelt had long supported. Nevertheless, Wilson (like Roosevelt before him) did little to reduce the economic power of trusts. It was easy to attack corporations' influence to win popular support and show 'progressive' credentials – as Roosevelt and Wilson demonstrate in these two sources. But it was far harder – even for strong progressive presidents as Roosevelt and Wilson both were - to do much in reality.

Activity

Show in the table which answer has:

Point by point differences	
Point by point similarities	
Explanation of differences by the use of reference to who was writing	
Explanation by the use of knowledge of what was happening at the time	

Paper 2 guidance: essay questions

Avoiding descriptive answers and writing analytically

What is meant by a descriptive answer? This is when an answer has relevant supporting knowledge, but it is not directly linked to the actual question. Sometimes the argument is implicit, but even here the reader has to work out how the material is linked to the actual question. Instead of actually answering the question, it simply describes what happened.

In order to do well you must write an analytical answer and not simply tell the story. This means you must focus on the key words and phrases in the question and link your material back to them, which is why your essay plan (see pages 58–59) is crucial as it allows you to check you are doing it. You can avoid a narrative answer by referring back to the question as this should prevent you from just providing information about the topic. If you find analytical writing difficult it might be helpful to ensure that the last sentence of each paragraph links back directly to the question.

Consider the following question.

To what extent did the Progressive Movement achieve its aims?

In order to answer this question you would need to consider the following issues:

- What was the Progressive Movement?
- What were the aims of the Progressives?
- What were the successes of the Progressives?
- What did the Progressive Movement fail to achieve?

Then you would need to consider progressive reform in the following areas:

- Political reform – including votes for women.
- Reform of big business – especially the curbing of the power of 'trusts'.
- Social/welfare reform – including the introduction of Prohibition.

A very strong answer will weigh up the Progressive Movement's success in each area as it is discussed, a weaker answer will not reach a judgement until the conclusion, and the weakest answers will just describe what the Progressives did.

The following is part of a descriptive answer for the question above.

The Progressives introduced a number of political reforms. These were designed to make governments more responsible to the people. The Seventeenth Amendment ensured the direct election of Senators. The Nineteenth Amendment gave votes to women. At state level, progressives introduced the initiative, the referendum and recall – measures designed to reduce the power and influence of political bosses and their machines.

This paragraph outlines some of the facts about progressive reform and is quite well informed but there is little explanation or weighing up of its success. How many states introduced the initiative, referendum and recall? To what extent did the various measures actually reduce the influence and power of the political bosses? To what extent did political bosses actually support – and were responsible for – many of the so-called progressive reforms?

The opening sentence of each paragraph

One way that you can avoid a narrative approach is to focus on the opening sentence of each paragraph. A good opening sentence will offer a view or idea about an issue relevant to the question, not describe an event or person. With a very good answer you should be able to read the opening sentence of each paragraph and see the line of argument that has been taken in the essay. It is therefore worth spending time practising this skill.

'The growth of trusts and corporations played a major role in the USA's rapid industrialization in the late nineteenth century.' How far do you agree?

Activity

Look at the following ten opening sentences. Which of these offer an idea that directly answers the exam-style question above and which simply give facts?

1. By 1900 Carnegie dominated the US iron and steel industry.
2. Trusts were only one cause of the USA's industrial growth.
3. Many Americans disliked the growth of trusts.
4. Railroads were vital in the process of American industrialization. Run by 'robber barons', they were, in many respects, the first great trusts.
5. Big businessmen, like Carnegie, ensured that US industry was the most efficient in the world.
6. Technological innovation played a crucial role in the industrialization process.
7. Many 'robber barons' supported and quickly adopted new inventions and new methods of production.
8. JP Morgan, a financier, played a major role in the USA's industrial growth.
9. Although the USA's big businessmen supported laissez-faire policies, they were against free trade.
10. High tariffs helped protect US industry from foreign competition.

QUESTION PRACTICE

In order to practise the skill of directly answering the question, write opening sentences for the following essays:

1. How successfully did the USA deal with the consequences of rapid urbanization between 1870 and 1900?
2. How successful were the groups that were set up to protect the interests of American workers and farmers between 1870 and 1900?

EXPLAIN QUESTIONS

It might be helpful to also write opening sentences for the short answer essays below.

1. Explain why the Granger Movement failed.
2. Explain why free silver was such an important issue in the early 1890s.
3. Explain why the new immigration affected the process of urbanization.
4. Explain why the Knights of Labor movement rose and fell.

CHAPTER 4

The Great Crash, the Depression and the New Deal Policies, 1920–41

In October 1929 the prices of stocks and shares on Wall Street crashed. Stock prices on the New York Exchange fell in value by 37 per cent. The Great Crash was followed by the Great Depression. By the winter of 1932–33 some 13 million Americans were unemployed. In 1932, Franklin Roosevelt was elected president, promising a New Deal for the American people. This chapter will examine the Great Crash, the Great Depression, and the extent to which the New Deal might be considered great by examining the following questions:

★ What were the causes of the Great Crash?

★ What were the causes and impact of the Depression?

★ How effective were Roosevelt's strategies to deal with the domestic problems facing the USA in the 1930s?

★ Why was there opposition to the New Deal and what impact did it have?

KEY DATES

1920	Warren Harding elected president	**1933**	The Hundred Days
1923	Harding died: Calvin Coolidge became president	**1934**	Democrat success in mid-term elections
1924	Coolidge elected president	**1935**	The Second New Deal
1928	Herbert Hoover elected president	**1936**	Roosevelt re-elected president
1929	Wall Street Crash	**1937**	Supreme Court battle
1929–32	Great Depression	**1937–38**	Roosevelt Recession
1932	Franklin Roosevelt elected president	**1940**	Roosevelt elected president for the third time
		1941	The USA entered the Second World War

1 What were the causes of the Great Crash?

Few Americans predicted the Great Crash or the Great Depression which followed. For most of the 1920s, the US economy boomed and Americans were the most prosperous people in the world. However, there were serious structural weaknesses in the US economy which were liable to bring an end to the prosperity.

Prosperity

After 1921 the US seemed to enter a period of unparalleled prosperity, though this was not shared by many rural areas. However, the US gave the impression that there was an unprecedented economic boom.

Increase in productivity

The key to the boom was a great increase in productivity resulting from technological innovation. The 1920s spawned new inventions and processes of great commercial importance. While the population increased by 16 per cent, industrial production almost doubled. By 1927 42 per cent of all that was produced in the world was American-produced. Between 1921 and 1928 annual income increased on average by 30 per cent. With more money in their pockets, Americans were able to go on a buying spree that kept factory orders and profits high. Americans produced more and earned more in the 1920s not because they worked harder or longer, but because they worked smarter. 'The explosive growth in GNP, real wages and profits rested on the simple fact that each hour of labour and each dollar of capital was used more productively than in the past', says historian Michael Parrish (1992).

The electricity industry

Electricity consumption more than doubled during the 1920s. Increased demands for electricity led to the construction of huge generators. Some were coal-powered. Others were fuelled by oil from newly developed fields in Louisiana, Texas, Oklahoma and California. Electrification brought mass production techniques to new levels of sophistication, cut production costs and created markets for new electrical appliances. By 1929 over 16 million homes, housing two-thirds of the population, had electricity. By 1929 16 companies controlled over 90 per cent of America's electric power production. The great electricity boss was Samuel Insull, once Thomas Edison's (see page 131) private secretary. He used the holding company (see page 127) to maximum effect, absorbing a host of smaller utility companies. By 1928 his utilities empire was valued at $3 billion.

The automobile industry

The automobile revolution contributed most to the business boom. Its architect was Henry Ford. By adapting assembly line techniques and concentrating on a single, standardized vehicle, the Model T, Ford brought the car to the masses. Easy to maintain and repair, the Model T could be driven on almost any surface – a good thing given the state of the nation's (mainly dirt) roads. By 1925 his factories were producing a car every 10 seconds. (In 1911 it had taken 14 hours to assemble a car.) Ford faced competition from other manufacturers, notably General Motors and Chrysler. Ford's initial strategy was to sell an increasing volume of similar, long-lasting vehicles at decreasing prices. Alfred Sloan, head of General Motors, adopted a different strategy. He assumed that automobile production could be sustained in the long term only by persuading Americans to buy a new, more stylish model every three or four years. This approach to producing and selling cars required enormous investment in research and development to generate frequent changes in design. It also required huge spending on advertising to convince motorists that they needed a new car. By 1929 General Motors was the third largest enterprise in the USA.

In 1920 9 million cars were registered in the USA. By 1929 there were nearly 27 million – one car for every five Americans. In 1929 the USA produced 5 million motor vehicles (10 times the number produced by Britain, France and Germany combined) and its car industry employed 447,000 workers – 7 per cent of all manufacturing wage-earners. The automobile industry stimulated a host of other industries – petroleum, steel, glass, rubber, leather, oil and road building.

Construction

There was a huge increase in house building as people moved from the countryside to towns and from towns to suburbs. Industrial and commercial construction also went on apace. By 1929 the USA had some 400 skyscrapers – buildings over 20 storeys high. The 102-storey Empire State Building in New York, completed in 1931 and providing office space for 25,000 people, became the tallest building in the world at 1250 feet high.

Cinema

The Hollywood film industry prospered. Many of the film magnates were first- or second-generation immigrants: Goldwyn (Polish), Mayer (Lithuanian), Fox (Hungarian) and the Warner brothers (Polish). By 1927 the USA made 80 per cent of the world's films. Silent films were the staple fare for most of the 1920s but the success of *The Jazz Singer* in 1927 led to the rise of 'talkies'.

Radio

The first broadcasting station in the USA, KDKA in Pittsburgh, began regular services in 1920. The earliest stations were set up by the manufacturers of radio equipment but broadcasting companies, financed by advertisers, soon dominated the field. Radio stations multiplied. By 1927 hundreds of them had been welded together in two gigantic chains controlled by the National Broadcasting Company and the Columbia Broadcasting System. By 1930, half of all American families possessed a radio.

Consolidation

The movement toward consolidation in industry resumed during the 1920s. By 1929 the 200 largest corporations controlled nearly half the USA's corporate assets. General Motors, Ford and Chrysler manufactured nearly 90 per cent of American cars and trucks. Four tobacco companies produced over 90 per cent of cigarettes. Even retail merchandising, traditionally the domain of small shopkeepers, reflected the trend. The A & P food chain expanded from 400 stores in 1912 to 17,500 in 1928. The Woolworth chain of five-and ten-cent stores flourished.

Most great manufacturers sought stability and 'fair' prices rather than the maximum profit possible. 'Regulated' competition was the order of the day, oligopoly (not monopoly) the typical situation. Producers in various industries formed voluntary organizations – trade associations – to exchange information, discuss common issues and 'administer' prices. Usually the largest corporation became the 'price leader', its competitors following its lead.

Structural weaknesses in the US economy

Unfortunately, the 1920s boom rested upon unstable foundations.

Poverty

Not all Americans enjoyed prosperity. By 1929, according to the Bureau of Labor Statistics, an income of $2,500 a year was needed to maintain a 'decent standard of living' for a family of two adults and two children. But 12 million of 27 million families who filed income tax returns that year earned $1,500 or less. Thus, many households endured economic hardship.

Agricultural problems

More than one in five working Americans still worked on the land. During the First World War, American farmers had prospered, supplying the world's disrupted markets with foodstuffs. They had ploughed marginal lands and increased yields from all acreage with more intensive cultivation. Many farmers borrowed heavily in order to buy more land and machinery, especially tractors. Net farm income more than doubled during the war years from $4 billion to $10 billion. For those who owned their farms, real income grew by 30 per cent.

Falling prices

The bubble burst in 1920. The price of wheat plunged from $2.50 a bushel to less than $1. Cotton slumped from a wartime high of 35 cents per pound to

16 cents. Farmers who had experienced nearly two decades of prosperity entered a long period of decline. There were a number of reasons.

- The recovery of European agriculture after 1918 reduced demand.
- There was a glut of produce on the world markets. Farmers in the USA and elsewhere produced more as a consequence of technical and scientific innovations. Fertilisers, pesticides, hybrid seeds and improved breeding techniques doubled and in some cases tripled the production of grains, cotton and livestock. Mechanization also helped increase production. Five per cent fewer workers earned their living on American farms in 1929 than in 1919. Nearly 13 million acres of land were no longer used. Yet farm output grew by 10 per cent. Increased production meant lower prices.
- Prohibition hit cereal producers. The production of synthetic materials (for example, rayon) hit cotton.
- Shrinking export markets and a slowing down of population growth (as a result of immigration restriction in the early 1920s) resulted in limited growth in demand for agricultural produce.

Over the course of the 1920s the net income of farmers declined by 25 per cent from 1917. Many, burdened by debt, were forced to sell their land. Farm problems particularly hit the most vulnerable groups in agriculture – wage labourers, tenants and sharecroppers (see page 108).

Efforts to obtain government support

Farmers looked to Congress to improve matters. In 1920 a Farm Bloc, a coalition of western Republicans and southern Democrats, was formed to try to protect farmers' interests. It had some success. Congress strengthened the laws regulating railroad rates and grain exchanges and made it easier for farmers to borrow money. However, such measures did nothing to increase agricultural income nor did the high tariffs on agricultural produce have much effect. World prices were so depressed that farmers found it hard to sell abroad and cheap foreign produce forced American farmers to reduce their prices despite the protective tariffs.

In 1921 George Peek, a plough manufacturer, put forward a scheme to help farmers. He proposed that federal government should agree to purchase surplus farm products at prices similar to those in 1917. The government could then sell – or 'dump' – the surpluses abroad at lower world prices, recovering its losses by assessing an 'equalization fee' on American farmers. Farm Bloc congressmen supported the scheme and in 1927 the McNary–Haugen bill was passed by Congress. It was immediately vetoed by President Coolidge (see page 200). Congress passed a similar bill in 1928: Coolidge again rejected it. He did so on ideological and practical grounds. 'A healthy economic climate', he declared, 'is best maintained through a free play of competition.' But he also realized that the scheme would be a bureaucratic nightmare. The measure virtually guaranteed ever bigger farm surpluses. With a subsidized high domestic price, farmers would produce more not less. The government would have to purchase endless tons of farm produce at the 'parity' price. To many Americans this seemed like a raid on the US Treasury by a special interest group. Moreover, dumping surpluses overseas at rock bottom prices would complicate the USA's foreign relations.

Coolidge vetoed a plan which had flaws, but unfortunately, he did not offer an alternative. Accordingly the farmers' share of the national income continued to slide. By 1929, 50 million Americans still lived in rural areas. Of these 45 million had no indoor plumbing and almost none had electricity. There was thus an ever widening gap between country and city life. City-dwellers benefited from the farmers' misery. Overproduction led to lower food prices – good news for urban workers – but farmers suffered. Low agricultural prices meant they lacked the money to buy the goods churned out by the USA's manufacturing industries. This was one of the main structural weaknesses in the US economy.

Disparity between traditional and new industries

Many of the USA's old industries, the industries on which its industrialization had been based, were in difficulty.

- Coal mining, suffering from the competition of oil, entered a period of decline. The industry was plagued by overproduction, falling prices, low wages and frequent periods of high unemployment.
- The woollen and cotton textile industry, facing competition from silk and rayon, suffered from falling profit margins, depressed wages and high unemployment.
- The leather products industry, including boot and shoe manufacturing, declined.

The growth of consumerism

By 1927 Americans seemed to be the world's most prosperous people. Urban workers had more money than ever before and enjoyed an amazing variety of new products on which to spend it. Their homes were full of new appliances – refrigerators, radios, telephones, electric fans, electric razors – that would not become standard elsewhere for a generation or more. Of the nation's 26.8 million households, 11 million had a phonograph (record player), 10 million a car and 17.5 million a telephone. Every year America added more new telephones (781,000 in 1926) than Britain possessed in total. Kansas had more cars than France. Ironically, the growth of consumerism was to be one of the problems that led to the Great Crash.

Advertising

In the 1920s there was an explosive growth of advertising – through newspapers, magazines, billboards, radio and the motion pictures. General Motors alone spent some $20 million a year on advertising in an effort to nurture consumer desires. The reason was simple. By 1929 the big three car makers – Ford, Chrysler and General Motors – all sold vehicles almost identical in quality at about the same price. Advertising and salesmanship replaced engineering and organizational efficiency as the critical variables of competition. The sums allocated to advertising by corporations thus grew each year. Advertising experts sold everything and anything. Spending money was encouraged, thrift ignored. Like the economic boom it helped to nourish, advertising raised expectations and fostered a belief that Americans were entitled as a matter of right and destiny to an ever-increasing standard of living. Consumption became the path to fortune and happiness.

Advertising transferred economic power over basic consumption patterns from wholesalers and retailers, who had previously controlled product distribution, to large-scale manufacturers who made them. Through saturation advertising, manufacturers of items such as breakfast cereals and soup could directly influence the choices consumers made at general stores. By equating their particular brand names with quality, convenience and status, manufacturers sought to cement consumer loyalties. The retailers who failed to carry Kellogg's Corn Flakes or Campbell's Soup might find themselves losing business to those who did.

The Florida land boom

Americans were willing to speculate in the hope of getting rich. Many invested in the Florida land boom in the early 1920s, a boom which reached its height in 1925. But in 1925–26, the boom collapsed. Thousands of investors lost money – a warning of what could happen to speculative ventures.

Hire purchase

Most Americans wished to possess the latest goods pouring from American factories but many did not have sufficient money to purchase them outright. Instead, they developed the habit of buying goods on the instalment system – by hire purchase. The introduction of instalment-buying had been pioneered at General Motors in 1919. The idea was simple. Say a car cost $1000. The customer bought it for $1100 by paying $100 when collecting the car and $100 a month for ten months. The car-buyer thus purchased the car ten months sooner than he might otherwise have done. The retailer/finance company made an extra $100 profit. 'Buy now, pay later' proved so irresistible that soon Americans were using it to purchase all kinds of things. Instalment-buying filled American homes with products and its roads with cars. It also meant that many families were in debt, gambling on prosperity continuing into the future. If this did not happen, Americans would find themselves with cars, radios and furniture on which they could not pay the remaining instalments.

Speculation on the stock market

KEY TERM

Securities Stocks and shares.

In the 1920s increasing numbers of Americans speculated on the stock market. Prior to 1917 only very rich people invested in the limited number of public and private **securities** offered for sale by government bodies, railroads, public utilities and industrial corporations. Then between 1917 and 1919 the US government created a new market of middle-class investors by selling $27 billion in Liberty Bonds and Victory Bonds to finance the war against Germany. Over 22 million Americans, responding to the patriotic calls of the US Treasury, bought war bonds.

The spectacular success of the government's wartime bonds encouraged corporations to seek public financing. By selling their own securities, corporations gained greater autonomy from commercial banks. Thus, by 1929, nearly 2 million Americans held stock in corporations. On Wall Street, one of 29 exchanges where the buying and selling of securities took place, shoppers could choose from over 1200 issues. New investment firms appeared, willing to help buyers and sellers. Stocks and bonds were sold like cars and toothpaste. It seemed sensible to buy securities in the mid-1920s because their values were rising. There were sound reasons for this rise: the steady growth of GNP, rising productivity, and higher corporate profits. The problem, of course, was that at some stage the value of stocks and shares was likely to fall.

Buying on the margin

Americans who wished to speculate on stocks and shares could do so by margin trading – buying securities on credit with a loan from a broker. This device promised a high return with a minimum cash investment. The rapid expansion of instalment-buying for many consumer goods encouraged many to think of brokers' loans as just another way to buy today and pay later. Moreover, the benefits could be much greater. With a cash downpayment of $100, it was possible to buy on instalments a new car that in a year's time would be worth far less than the original purchase price. The same $100 down, combined with a broker's loan of $900 secured by the stocks and shares, allowed an investor to purchase 100 shares, selling, say at $10 a share. Assuming the stock rose to $20 a share in six months, the lucky buyer stood to make a 100 per cent profit. Given the rise of the market, the lure of brokers' loans became irresistible.

The stock market boom 1927–29

By cutting both personal and corporate income taxes, Treasury Secretary Andrew Mellon and Congress stoked the stock market's rise. Wealthy individuals and corporations had more money to spend and invest. Paying less in taxes, corporations also reported higher profits, which made their securities more attractive to investors. Thus, between 1927 and 1929 money poured into New York to purchase securities and to sustain the demand for brokers' loans. The Federal Reserve Board – the central bank – did raise its discount rate in an effort to discourage banks from making speculative loans to brokers. But this did not dampen margin trading. Non-banking lenders, mainly corporations, pumped even more money into brokers' loans. Corporations preferred speculating on the stock market to investing in new plant and equipment.

Unfortunately, the magnitude of the increases that took place in 1928–29 were out of all proportion to the securities' real worth. There were some prophets of gloom.

- Paul Warburg, head of Kuhn, Loeb and Co, a major investment bank, warned in early 1929 that brokers' loans had reached 'a saturation point' and unless 'the orgy of unrestrained speculation' stopped it would plunge the USA into a depression.
- Federal Reserve Board governor Roy Young condemned market speculation in February 1929 and threatened sanctions against member banks that continued to finance brokers' loans.

But a wave of optimistic forecasts swamped these alarms. Thus, by mid-1929 hundreds of thousands of investors had purchased shares on credit, borrowing from brokers and using the stocks and shares as security for the loan. Just as a rise in share prices might bring fortunes to their owners, so a drop might bring ruin.

ACTIVITY

Write a brief explanation of the following terms:

- buying on the margins
- stock market boom
- oversupply.

Mass production and oversupply

America was renowned for its mass production techniques, particularly in the automobile industry. (Mass production was sometimes called 'Fordism' in honour of its most famous pioneer.) Mass production made mass consumption a necessity. If there were insufficient buyers, American companies would be in serious difficulty.

Mass production benefits

Increased productivity was the result of increased mechanization. Machine power continued to offer employment to large numbers of workers. By 1920 the number of workers in manufacturing and mechanical industries eclipsed the number in farming. For most workers, industrial growth brought substantial gains. Hours of work declined (a 48-hour week was the norm) and real wages increased by a third. Many employers, in an effort to prevent labour unrest, improved working conditions, extended recreational facilities, and introduced profit-sharing, life insurance and pension plans.

Oversupply

Rising wages disguised the fact that the income of most industrial workers did not keep pace with their soaring productivity. The gap between what they produced and what they could buy therefore widened over the course of the 1920s. In the countryside, most farmers were unable to afford – or use due to the lack of electricity – many of the new products. Too large a share of the profits from industry went into too few pockets. The 27,000 families with the highest annual incomes in 1929 earned as much money as the 11 million at the bottom of the scale. There was a limit to the amount of goods that the top 0.3 per cent of Americans could buy. Their money was often invested in further industrial expansion, which simply aggravated the problem of oversupply, or it went into stock market speculation.

If the domestic market was unable to absorb the huge quantities of items pouring from the factories, the best hope was to sell the goods abroad. Unfortunately, the rest of the world could not afford them. This was partly the result of high US tariffs. The Fordney–McCumber Tariff Act (1922) restored to industry the protection that had prevailed before the Underwood–Simmons Tariff (see page 175). Since the USA erected a tariff barrier against goods coming from abroad, many countries retaliated by erecting tariff barriers against US goods. This meant it was difficult for American firms to sell their goods abroad. 'Without new foreign outlets or a significant redistribution of domestic purchasing power – especially in the impoverished rural half of the country – the boundaries of consumer demand were apparently being approached', writes the historian David Kennedy (1999).

The impact of government policies

By 1920 progressive reform (see pages 154–80) was running out of steam. Weakened by a stroke, President Wilson proposed no further reform measures during his last two years in office. As the presidential election approached, the political tide was running in favour of the Republicans.

The 1920 presidential election

Confident of victory in 1920, Republican bosses chose Warren Harding, a conservative, as their presidential candidate. The Democrats nominated James Cox. Voters, concerned about rising prices, industrial strife, and the post-war recession, blamed the Democrats – the party in power. In the campaign, Harding, in a typical bland speech, declared that 'America's present need is not heroics but healing, not nostrums but normalcy'. Whatever 'normalcy' was supposed to mean, it was apparently what Americans wanted. Harding won by a greater margin (61 per cent) than any previous presidential candidate.

President Warren Harding

Harding, an amiable, outgoing man, often found complex issues beyond him. He enjoyed the company of his cronies – his 'Ohio Gang' – who shared his taste for whiskey, poker and women. Fortunately, he appointed a number of able men to key posts.

- Ex-governor of New York, Charles Hughes became secretary of state.
- Herbert Hoover became secretary of commerce (see page 207).
- Millionaire banker Andrew Mellon became secretary of the treasury.

Sympathetic to big business, Harding believed that government intervention in the economy should be kept to a minimum. He declared, 'We want less government in business and more business in government'. His administration repealed the high wartime taxes, returned to the traditional Republican policy of high tariffs, did not enforce the anti-trust laws, and supported employers in industrial disputes. His administration also passed laws restricting immigration.

In 1923 it emerged that there was extensive corruption within Harding's administration. The most sensational scandal involved Secretary of the Interior, Albert Fall. Fall had secured the transfer of government lands earlier set aside for naval use to his own department. He had then secretly leased those at Elk Hills, California, and Teapot Dome, Wyoming, to two oil magnates, receiving in return large 'loans'. Fall, convicted of receiving a bribe, was sentenced to a year in prison – the first cabinet member in American history to go to jail for crimes committed in office. Harding, who was not personally implicated in the corruption, unexpectedly died in 1923.

President Calvin Coolidge

Vice-President Calvin Coolidge then became president. He was honest and incorruptible. Liberal intellectuals criticized Coolidge for sleeping a lot and saying little. (He was nicknamed 'Silent Cal': when he died in 1933, writer Dorothy Parker quipped: 'How can they tell?') But to most Americans, Coolidge's presence in the White House was reassuring: he became a symbol of traditional values threatened by the forces of change. He believed that private enterprise was the backbone of society. The role of government should be kept small. This belief in laissez-faire seemed to make sense at a time when most Americans enjoyed prosperity. The notion that governments should not intervene too much in economic matters, however, would be a problem in the event of a recession or depression.

The 1924 presidential election

In 1924 the Democrats, deeply divided, South against North, rural against urban, and 'dry' against 'wet', eventually chose John Davis, a corporation lawyer, as their candidate. Since the Republicans re-nominated Coolidge, there were two conservative candidates with similar platforms. A genuine alternative appeared when a coalition of western farmers, trade union leaders, and ex-progressives nominated Robert La Follette (see page 178) as candidate of a new Progressive Party. Its platform condemned monopoly, called for railway nationalization, and proposed tariff reduction and aid to farmers. The voters 'kept cool with Coolidge'. He won 15.7 million votes to Davis's 8.4 million. La Follette won a respectable 4.8 million votes. He died in 1925, the Progressive Party with him.

ACTIVITY

'American prosperity in the 1920s was built on insecure foundations and was a major cause of the Depression.' In pairs, examine the previous and following sections and find four points that might support this view. Discuss which point is the most important, then try and put the points in order of importance. If you disagree, try and work out why.

Prosperity 1925–28

Coolidge's victory in 1924 led to an extension of Republican pro-business policies – low taxation, low interest rates, balanced budgets and frugal government expenditure.

- The Tariff Commission continued to raise the duties on foreign goods, pricing them out of the American market.

- The Coolidge administration commenced over 70 anti-trust suits but the results did not pose a threat to economic concentration. The largest fine ($2000) was levied against an official of the National Cash Register Company for price-fixing. (An appeals court reduced the fine to $50.)
- The Federal Trade Commission (see page 166), charged with rooting out 'unfair methods of competition', was packed with big business supporters. It promoted trade association conferences where business groups adopted their own rules of competition.
- Congress approved additional tax reductions in 1924, 1926 and 1928. Those who benefited were people on incomes that exceeded $100,000. Some paid no federal income tax at all between 1924 and 1929.
- Despite tax cuts, federal receipts exceeded expenditure in each of the Coolidge years.

Progressivism in the 1920s

Progressivism did not disappear in the 1920s. Progressives were powerful in Congress, even while the White House was in conservative hands. The progressive desire for 'good government' and public services remained strong at state and local levels. Here, movements for education, public health and social welfare all gained momentum.

The presidential election of 1928

Coolidge refused to stand in 1928. In his place the Republicans selected Herbert Hoover (see page 207). The Republican platform called for continued high tariffs, tax cuts, help for farmers, and upheld Prohibition. Republicans promised 'a chicken in every pot and two cars in every garage'. 'We shall soon with the help of God', Hoover said, 'be in sight of the day when poverty will be banished from this nation'. The Democrat candidate was New York governor Al Smith, a Catholic, who, like Hoover, was sympathetic to big business (but, unlike Hoover, opposed Prohibition). Not surprisingly, given the prevailing prosperity, Hoover won 58 per cent of the popular vote – 444 electoral college votes to Smith's 87. The Republicans also won large majorities in Congress. The Democrats' only solace was that Smith carried the nation's 12 largest cities – cities which the Republicans had won in 1924.

SOURCE A

From a Republican election leaflet of 1928

During eight years of rule we have built more homes, erected more skyscrapers, passed more laws to regulate and purify immigration, done more to increase production, expand export markets and reduce industrial and human junk piles than any previous quarter century.

Prosperity is written on fuller wage packets, written in factory chimney smoke, written on walls of new constructions, written on bank books, written in business profit sheets, and written in the record value of shares.

Wages, dividends, progress and prosperity say 'Vote for Hoover'.

What is the message of Source A? What additional knowledge could you use to determine whether the views expressed in the source are justified?

Summary

The American economy appeared strong for most of the 1920s. However, there were serious underlying problems that were ultimately to lead to the Great Crash of October 1929. These problems included structural weaknesses in the US economy, not least the disparity between agriculture and industry, and between traditional and new industries. The growth of consumerism, which fuelled the popularity of hire purchase and buying on the margins, was a potential nightmare if the US economy went into recession. This was possible because mass production by the late 1920s had led to oversupply in many areas, as a result of which corporations and companies were unable to sell all their goods. Government policies, which were pro-business and pro-laissez-faire, had done little to deal with the underlying problems.

SUMMARY DIAGRAM

What were the causes of the Great Crash?

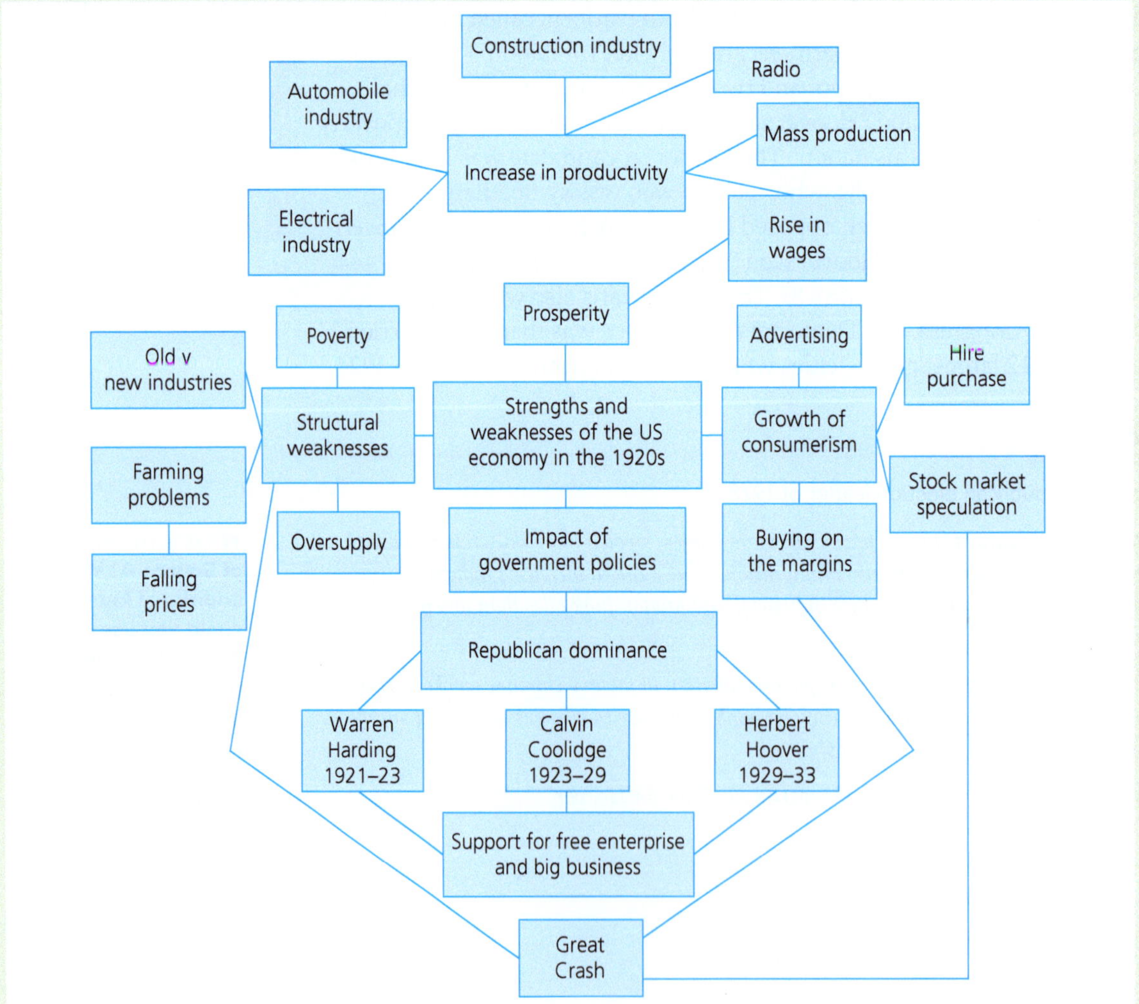

2 What were the causes and impacts of the Depression?

In October 1929 prices on the Wall Street stock exchange crashed. The Great Crash was soon followed by the Great Depression. Economists and historians continue to debate to what extent the Crash and Depression were linked.

The main features of the Great Crash

'I have no fears for the future of our country', said Hoover in March 1929. 'It is bright with hope'. However, there were signs by early 1929 that all was not well with the American economy.

Economic and financial problems in 1929

These included:

- The continuing suffering of farmers.
- The slowing down of the rate of automobile manufacturing.
- The decline of house building after 1925.
- The decline in US exports.

In addition, while business activity steadily fell, stock prices rose wildly (see pages 197–98). From mid-1927 to mid-1929, the average price of stocks increased by nearly 300 per cent. The rise in share prices did not reflect the performance of the companies concerned.

The events of the Great Crash

By September 1929 the stock market had clearly lost touch with reality and some speculators began selling their holdings. On 24 October (Black Thursday) 13 million shares were sold and prices plummeted. Only a buying effort by a syndicate of prominent bankers prevented an even bigger sell-off. But on 29 October (Black Tuesday) 16.5 million shares were sold. The gains of months vanished in a few hours, ruining hundreds of investors. The trading floor of the stock exchange degenerated into anarchy as **brokers** literally fought one another to place selling orders. Shirts and suits were ripped. Men lost shoes, spectacles, false teeth and even a wooden leg in the melee. Reports of ruined investors taking their own lives were greatly exaggerated. Nevertheless, Black Tuesday was, according to economist John Kenneth Galbraith, 'the most devastating day in the history of the New York stock market, and it may have been the most devastating day in the history of markets'.

KEY TERM

Broker A person who buys and sells stocks and shares.

By November 1929 the value of stocks and shares had fallen by a third. Relatively few people suffered a direct loss of money but those who had invested in stocks and shares lost billions in the space of a few weeks. Banks and corporations, having made large commitments to brokers' loans, now held depreciated paper assets that could not be turned into ready cash. Faced with frightened depositors, the banks called in other loans and refused to make new ones, thereby cutting off the flow of credit. Corporations deferred new spending and began to lay off workers. Within a year, employees' salaries were reduced by more than $4 billion and unemployment rose from 1.5 million to 4.3 million. The slide into economic chaos had begun.

SOURCE B

Look closely at Source B. Are there any indications of actual panic? Explain your answer carefully.

The original 1929 caption reads: 'Photograph shows the street scene on Black Thursday, the day the New York stock market crashed, and the day that led to the Great Depression'

SOURCE C

Extract from *Only Yesterday* by Frederick Lewis Allen, published in 1931. This is a classic account of the 1920s in the USA by a leading journalist of the period and has been republished many times

How useful is Source C in explaining what happened in October 1929?

As the price structure crumbled, there was a sudden stampede to get out from under. By eleven o'clock traders on the floor of the Stock Exchange were in a wild scramble to 'sell at the market'. Long before the lagging ticker could tell what was happening, word had gone out by telephone and telegraph that the bottom was dropping out of things and the selling orders redoubled in volume … Down, down, down … Where were the bargain hunters who were supposed to come to their rescue at times like this? … There seemed to be no support whatsoever. Down, down, down. The roar of voices which rose from the floor of the Exchange had become a roar of panic.

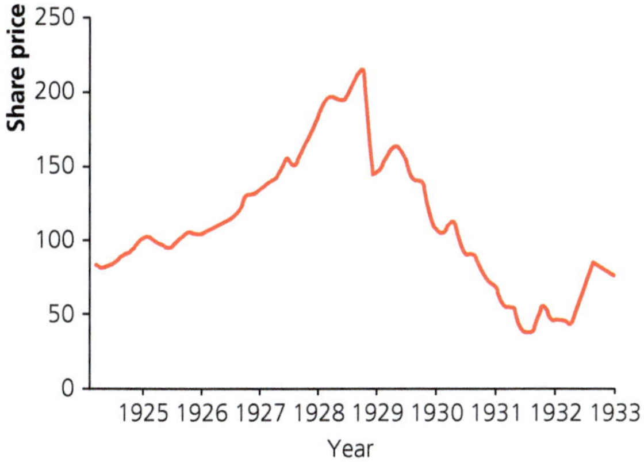

Figure 4.1 A graph showing the changes in the price of shares in the USA in the years 1925–33

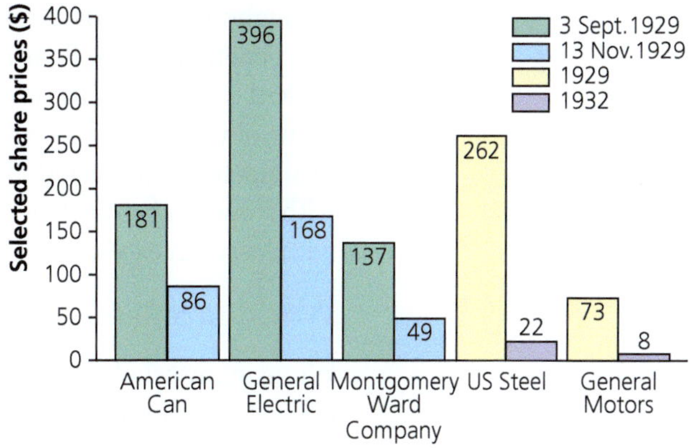

Figure 4.2 A graph showing the decline in share values in the years 1929–32

What caused the Great Depression?

Scholars today, like politicians at the time, disagree about the Depression's causes. Most would agree that there were a number of inter-related factors. Different historians stress different factors.

The Wall Street Crash

The Wall Street Crash and the Great Depression are often seen as the same thing. The Crash took money out of the system and led, by a vicious circle, to Depression. However, the USA actually weathered the Crash.
By April 1930 share prices had regained a fifth of the losses of the previous autumn. Business activity did not begin to decline significantly until mid-1930. Arguably the Crash was more a symptom than a cause of the Depression.

Normal business cycle

At the time, many economists thought that the Depression was just part of the normal business cycle. They believed there would be an inevitable natural recovery.

Economic flaws

Some think the US economy was fundamentally unsound. The main charge is that income was not fairly distributed. By 1929 the richest 5 per cent owned a third of the income, while 71 per cent had incomes of less than $2,500 a year, the minimum thought necessary for decent comfort. Unable to afford to buy their share of consumer goods, ordinary Americans could not sustain the level of mass production.

The banking system

Arguably the banking system was the weakest link in the US economic system. Historian David Kennedy (1999) claims that 'American banks were rotten even in good times'. The Federal Reserve System's low-interest money policy encouraged wild lending, not least for stock-market speculation, throughout the 1920s. Another major problem was the lack of regulation. The Federal Reserve Board, which supervised the banking system, had only limited control over the larger banks and less control over the smaller banks, many of which were far too small. Short of resources and often incompetently managed, the small banks were vulnerable if depositors withdrew funds – as they did after 1929. By 1933 over 5500 banks had failed with losses in excess of $3 billion.

World problems

While many scholars believe the Depression arose from problems within the US economy, others point out that there was a world depression. World factors, over which the USA had little control, might have been the major cause of the American Depression (rather than the Wall Street Crash being the cause of world slump). Different historians have stressed different aspects of the world economy which possibly led to a depression becoming the Great Depression.

- Some emphasize the world overproduction of food which led to a fall in prices for farmers.
- Some stress the chaotic financial situation after 1918. In the 1920s the USA provided Germany with massive amounts of short-term loans. Germany used these to pay **reparations** to Britain and France. They, in turn, used the money to pay the interest on US war debts. This money was then returned to Germany in loans. Once US bankers stopped investing in Germany and called in their short-term loans, the German economy found itself in difficulty. This had a knock-on effect across Europe.
- Some think a serious banking collapse, first in Austria and then in Germany in early 1931, at a time when it seemed that the USA was pulling out of depression, was an important factor. This produced a world financial crisis which had a devastating effect on the US banking system.
- Some point the finger of blame at Britain which went off the gold standard in September 1931. This caused disturbances in the world's money markets and to world trade.

KEY TERM

Reparations Under the settlements after the First World War Germany was required to pay compensation of $33 billion or 132 billion marks to the victorious countries.

The responses of the Hoover administration and industry to the Great Crash

Hoover was ridiculed at the time and has been criticized by historians since for his response to the economic catastrophe. His lack of action after 1929 is often seen as making a terrible situation even worse. However, unlike Harding or Coolidge, Hoover's reputation has grown with the passing of time. Although his sombre manner conveyed an impression of indifference, most scholars now accept that he very much cared about people's suffering. Compared with other presidents who faced financial panics (for example, Grover Cleveland in 1893), Hoover was a dynamo of energy, a president who mobilized as never before the powers of the federal government to combat the Depression.

Herbert Hoover

1874	Born in Iowa: his parents were Quakers
1883	Orphaned: brought up by relatives in Oregon
1895	Graduated from Stanford University: became an engineer
1899	Married Lou Henry
1908	Set up his own engineering business: soon became a millionaire
1914	Helped feed starving Belgians in the First World War
1917	Appointed food administrator in Wilson's administration
1921	Became secretary of commerce
1928	Elected Republican president
1932	Defeated by Roosevelt in presidential election
1964	Died

Hoover was a man of immense energy who was committed to public service. His organizational and administrative skills served his nation well as a famine relief director, wartime food administrator and secretary of commerce. A self-made businessman, he seemed an ideal president in troubled economic times but he lacked the political skills and charisma needed to lead a nation caught in the throes of the Great Depression. Many historians now reject the view that he was a 'do-nothing' president: they see his presidency as activist and reformist, and in some ways anticipatory of the New Deal. However, Hoover was opposed to government's intervention in economic and social affairs. His attempts to promote voluntary co-operative recovery and relief efforts did not work. The man who had 'never known failure' ultimately failed.

Hoover's ideological outlook

Hoover rejected direct government intervention, putting his faith instead in voluntary co-operation. He hoped that the actions of others – farmers, big businessmen and charity workers – with government help and encouragement, could put matters right. He believed that too much government interference in economic and social matters would destroy individuals' character, self-reliance and initiative and ultimately the nation. Hoover's ideology might seem flawed but in his defence, it should be said that:

- In the early 1930s there was little in the way of a federal bureaucracy. This limited the scope of the federal government's action, whatever the president's political beliefs.
- Few politicians at the time advocated more radical measures than those Hoover supported.

Hoover's initial actions

Determined to take some action, Hoover called the USA's leading businessmen and elected officials to the White House for a series of meetings at which he urged them to continue as if the panic had not occurred. Since corporations combined with state and local governments contributed the lion's share of investment in the economy, this action made sense. From the businessmen, Hoover secured pledges that they would not reduce wages, lay off employees, engage in price cutting or lower production. The nation's mayors and governors similarly pledged that they would not reduce expenditures for public works such as roads and schools. For his own part, Hoover promised to maintain and expand major federal construction projects. He supported the Federal Reserve Board's decision to lower interest rates. He also proposed an immediate reduction in federal personal and corporate income taxes in order to stimulate investment and consumer spending. Trying to maintain confidence, he proclaimed that 'the fundamental business of the country is sound'.

Unfortunately, Hoover was let down by business. Facing a slowdown of sales, business leaders soon cut production, reduced wages and laid off workers. Promises by mayors and governors to maintain expenditures were broken as tax revenues shrank and budgets became tight. Overwhelmed by demands for unemployment relief, local governments shelved building plans and began to lay off public employees. Hoover and Congress fulfilled federal spending plans but the tax cut, which Hoover hoped would be a powerful anti-depression measure, did not work. By 1931 GNP had fallen almost 30 per cent in two years and unemployment stood at 16 per cent of the work force. Growing unemployment meant less consumer spending.

The agricultural situation

Prior to the Great Crash, Congress had passed the Agricultural Marketing Act (1929). This established the Federal Farm Board. Although having greater powers than any other agricultural agency in US history, its mandate depended mainly on the voluntary co-operation of farmers. Congress gave the board a budget of $500 million and authorized it to help farmers help themselves in several ways.

- It could make loans to existing agricultural co-operatives and finance the organization of new ones. Farmers could use the co-operatives to reduce the profits of middlemen and prevent sharp price declines that resulted when crops came on the market all at once.
- The Farm Board could loan money to crop stabilization corporations organized by co-operatives as part of their effort to promote 'orderly marketing'. The stabilizing corporations could buy, sell, store and process crops such as wheat and cotton.

What seemed to Hoover a bold expansion of federal aid to agriculture in 1929 proved to be woefully inadequate. In 1930 mountains of grain from the USA, Argentina, Canada and the USSR swamped the international market and wheat prices continued to fall. Across the West farmers and country banks that had made mortgage and crop loans faced **bankruptcy**. The stabilization corporations seemed the only institutions with any hope of salvaging the situation. Drawing on federal funds, the Grain Stabilization

KEY TERM

Bankruptcy When firms or individuals have insufficient money to pay their debts.

Corporation began buying surplus wheat from co-operatives but the grain-buying scheme failed. By mid-1931, when it ceased making more purchasers, the Corporation owned 300 million bushels of wheat for which it had paid on average 82 cents per bushel. The world price was then under 40 cents and heading downwards. While the Farm Board had aided US farmers, it was basically throwing money away.

The Hawley–Smoot tariff

In mid-1930 Congress passed the Hawley–Smoot tariff. This measure raised manufacturing import duties to sky-high levels. This simply encouraged other nations to retaliate with their own protectionist measures. The Hawley–Smoot tariff thus had a negative effect on world trade. Hoover could have vetoed the tariff act. He did not do so.

The National Credit Corporation

In October 1931, under pressure from Hoover, the nation's great bankers organized the National Credit Corporation (NCC). With a capital fund of $500 million contributed by some of the USA's major financial institutions, Hoover hoped that bankers would help other bankers weather the storm. His hopes were quickly dashed. NCC managers, reluctant to take over dubious assets offered to them by other bankers, spent only $10 million of the NCC's funds. Meanwhile the banking crisis continued to deteriorate. In 1931 total bank failures hit 2293. Hoover in his memoirs was critical of the NCC. It became, he said, 'ultra-conservative, then fearful, and finally died'.

Unemployment relief

With little or no savings to fall back on and no government assistance, millions of unemployed Americans and their families faced destitution. From Hoover's perspective, the nation's private charities and disaster relief organizations, such as the Red Cross and Salvation Army, offered the first line of defence. He therefore created the President's Emergency Committee for Employment to assist private and state relief efforts. However, he opposed a larger role for the federal government, believing this would discourage private charity, undermine voluntarism, and destroy self-reliance by creating a class of dependent citizens.

Moratorium on war debts

In mid-1931 Hoover tried to boost American exports and ease the worsening economic situation in Europe by declaring a **moratorium** on war debts for eighteen months. His action simply recognized the fact that European countries, similarly suffering from Depression, could not pay their debts. It did little to stop the collapse of the world economy

KEY TERM

Moratorium An emergency measure allowing the suspension of payment of debts.

The collapse of the financial system

Hoover continued to issue reassuring statements, predicting that prosperity would soon return. In the spring of 1931, it seemed briefly as though he might be right. Production and employment began to creep upwards. But then a fresh collapse, triggered by the failure of a great Austrian bank, the Kreditanstalt, arrived. This produced a world financial crisis which had further devastating effects on the enfeebled US economy.

By early 1932:

- The farming situation was desperate. More farmers went broke, as did rural banks and local merchants. Fear, frustration and anger among farmers increased as prices of wheat, corn and cotton continued to fall.
- Unemployment rose.
- It seemed that the USA's financial system was on the point of collapse.

The Reconstruction Finance Corporation

In January 1932 Hoover's administration established the Reconstruction Finance Corporation (RFC). Approved by Congress, it was authorized to lend up to $2 billion to rescue ailing banks, railroads and insurance companies and other institutions. Hoover's critics complained that his administration's first dose of direct federal aid targeted big financial institutions and corporations instead of unemployed people. Hoover declared that the RFC was 'not created for the aid of big industries or big banks'. He later claimed that 90 per cent of the RFC's loans went to small and medium-sized banks but Hoover's critics pointed out that 7 per cent of the borrowers, usually the largest banks, received over half the money lent by the RFC. Loans to railroads and public utilities presented a similar picture, most money going to the biggest companies. By saving the largest firms from insolvency, Hoover's administration could claim they saved more jobs and prevented further economic chaos.

Other government actions

Hoover's administration took other measures to try to prevent collapse.

- The Glass-Steagall Banking Act released gold to support the dollar and expanded credit facilities.
- The Federal Home Loan Bank Act established a system of loans to building societies.
- The Emergency Relief and Construction Act empowered the RFC to lend state and municipal governments $1.5 billion for public works and a further $300 million for relief.

As a result of the Emergency Relief and Construction Act, Hoover's administration took some responsibility for relief, albeit indirectly. But the creation of the RFC and the Emergency Relief and Construction Act were as far as the president was willing to go to utilize directly the fiscal resources of the federal government to tackle the Depression. Both measures proved totally inadequate.

Balancing the budget

Hoover remained committed to balancing the federal budget: he regarded this as 'the most essential factor to economic recovery'. The government had less money because it obtained less in taxation as a result of falling personal and corporate income. Accordingly, Hoover reduced government spending in 1931. Nevertheless, by early 1932 the federal government spent $2 billion more than it received from taxes. Most Congressmen criticized the growing deficit. In June 1932 Hoover thus signed into law the largest peacetime tax increase in American history. There were new levies on income and new taxes on luxuries such as yachts and jewellery.

ACTIVITY

Make a copy of the table below then fill it in to show the arguments for and against the view that Hoover was a 'do-nothing' president.

Evidence that Hoover was a 'do-nothing' president	Evidence that Hoover was not a 'do-nothing' president

Conclusion

By 1932 it seemed to many Americans that Hoover preferred building confidence with bankers and businessmen by budget-balancing to providing jobs by building public works and providing relief payments. In fairness to Hoover, it should be said that he had nearly doubled federal public works expenditure in three years. This was, in part, why the 1932 federal budget ended up over $2 billion in the red – the largest peacetime deficit in US history. (No New Deal deficit would be proportionately larger.) Moreover, Congress, Democrat-controlled after 1930, advocated a balanced budget. It had no real programme except to obstruct Hoover and ensure Democrat victory in the 1932 election.

Mass unemployment and its social impact

The Great Depression, the most devastating economic collapse in US history, had enormous social consequences.

Mass unemployment

After 1929 business confidence evaporated as bankruptcies multiplied. US trade fell from $10 billion in 1929 to $3 billion in 1932. By mid-1932 industrial output had dropped to half the 1929 level. In early 1929 some 1.5 million were unemployed – 3 per cent of the workforce. By December 1932 it was over 12 million – 25 per cent of the workforce. There was no unemployment benefit. Thus, unemployment brought fear and despair. Private charity was unable to cope with the scale of the emergency. People roamed the countryside, stealing rides on freight trains, searching for work.

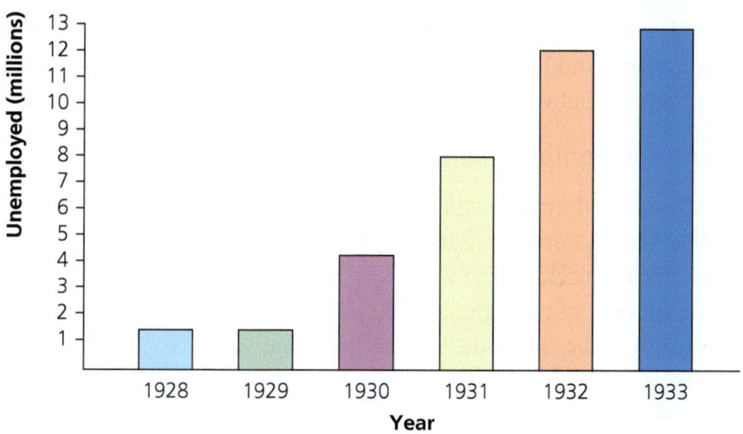

Figure 4.3 A graph showing the growth of unemployment, 1929–32

ACTIVITY

In groups decide what were the most serious problems facing urban dwellers and farmers in the period 1929–32 and explain your choice. Were the consequences of the Depression greater for those living in the towns and cities or those living in the countryside?

It was not just unemployed people who suffered.

- Those in full-time work saw their earnings fall by a third.
- Many Americans were only employed part-time.
- Farmers, badly off to begin with, suffered more than anyone as farm prices collapsed. In 1929 wheat was $1.05 a bushel: by 1932 it was 39 cents a bushel. Cotton fell from 17 cents a pound in 1929 to 6 cents a pound in 1932. Farmers' income plummeted from $6 billion in 1929 to $2 billion in 1932.

The Great Depression affected virtually every industrialized country but the US collapse was more complete than elsewhere (except Germany) and more damaging psychologically, if only because it was in such contrast to the prosperity of the 1920s.

How useful is Source D as evidence for understanding US social problems in 1932?

SOURCE D

A report, undertaken by social workers in 1932, on the inadequacy of local relief in 44 American cities

In the cities and counties specifically covered in this report, there has been a tremendous increase in the number of families and individuals receiving relief during the past year. This increase in the number of families aided has been greater than the increase in the amount of relief expended, indicating a continuation of the conditions reported to this committee in May 1932, when a tendency to stretch meagre relief funds over an increasingly large number of applicants was already generally prevalent ... There is a general expectancy that the number of families in need of relief will continue to increase during the winter months, although a few cities are anticipating a corresponding increase in relief funds to cover this expansion in relief responsibility ... Homes are lost, insurance policies cancelled, aid from relatives and friends has been terminated, families are forced to exhaust and destroy indefinitely their credit before relief is granted to them. This statement on the degree of destitution reached before relief is granted is applicable in practically all communities.

Malnutrition

Grim though American sufferings were, they were not comparable to those of, say, the USSR in 1920–21 when famine claimed millions of lives. The total reported number of American deaths from starvation was 110. Even so, there was a dramatic rise in cases of malnutrition. As late as 1935, it was estimated that 20 million people were not getting enough to eat.

The situation in 1932

By the summer of 1932, despair and bitterness were almost universal. Hoover was condemned for his supposed cold-heartedness. Destitute people found it hard to understand how it could be right to use federal funds to save banks and corporations but wrong to do so to feed people who were hungry.

Black Americans and employment discrimination

The group which suffered most from the Depression were black Americans. In northern cities, black people were usually the first to be fired. Unemployment among black people was twice that among white. In the South, where 75 per cent of black people Americans still lived, most were dependent on cotton, the crop hardest hit by the Depression.

SOURCE E

A Hooverville in New York City. Note the squalor in which people lived

What is the value of Source E in showing how American people lived during the Depression?

Hoovervilles

Shanty towns, lacking water and sanitation, began to develop on wasteland around the edges of American cities. Shacks, usually made of cardboard or corrugated iron, were inhabited by men without jobs looking for work. These places were called Hoovervilles. Hoover's name generally became synonymous with misery and hardship.

The bonus marchers

Astonishingly, in view of the suffering, there was little violent protest. In some places people looted food shops; in others demonstrations by people without jobs led to clashes with the police. But the only large-scale organized protest movement was the march of 22,000 unemployed former servicemen on Washington in June 1932. The marchers threatened to stay there until Congress passed a bill authorizing immediate payment of a bonus due to First World War veterans in 1945. Hoover had no sympathy with the bonus marchers. Aware that communists had helped organize the march and believing it a threat to democracy, he ordered General Douglas MacArthur to evict the veterans from the government buildings they had occupied. Troops armed with machine-guns, tanks and tear gas drove the marchers out of Washington and burned down their shanties. Many Americans believed the government had over-reacted. The episode seemed further proof of Hoover's insensitivity to the plight of unemployed people.

SOURCE F

Gerald W Johnson, a historian, writing an article in February 1932 about the impact of the Depression

Assess the value of Source F to a historian studying the effects of the Depression on the USA.

... we are by no means in despair ... We do not believe for a moment that the hard times are going to continue for the next six years. 1931 was a hard year, but it saw no bayonets, heard no firing in the streets, afforded no hint of the dissolution of our institutions ... The revolutionists have gained no following worth mentioning in this country. There has been a great outcry against the Reds, and some persons confess to be very much frightened by them; but the sober truth is that their American campaign has fallen flatter than their campaign in any other country. To date the capitalist system seems to be as firmly entrenched in America as the Republic itself.

The 1932 presidential election

The Republicans re-nominated Hoover as their presidential candidate in 1932. The Democrats chose Franklin D Roosevelt. As governor of New York, Roosevelt had won a reputation as a moderate reformer who tried to help those in need but there had been little in his career to suggest his future greatness; indeed, some contemporaries thought him a lightweight. Nevertheless, Roosevelt stood for change. In his acceptance speech in July 1932, he pledged himself to a 'New Deal for the American people' and promised 'bold, persistent experimentation'. But neither then nor during the rest of the campaign did he spell out exactly what he intended to do. The Democrat platform differed little from the Republican, except that it called for an end to Prohibition.

Roosevelt's campaign was upbeat: his theme tune was 'Happy Days Are Here Again'. He vowed to bring about 'a wiser, more equitable distribution of the national income'. Republicans cast doubts about his health and stamina but he travelled 13,000 miles (21,000 km) on the campaign trail, attacking Hoover's record. His zest contrasted strongly with Hoover's gloom. On election day Roosevelt obtained 22.8 million popular and 472 electoral college votes to Hoover's 15.8 million popular and 59 electoral votes. The Democrats also won large majorities in both houses of Congress. The Socialist candidate won 882,000 votes, the Communist 103,000 votes. The election seemed to confirm the faith of Americans in capitalism and democracy. It also confirmed the fact that the voters wanted change. How much, no one, not even Roosevelt and his advisers could foretell.

SOURCE G

Hoover speaking in October 1932

(From CP Hill, *Franklin Roosevelt and the New Deal*, The Archive Series, Edward Arnold, 1975, p. 14.)

Summarise in your own words the message in Source G.

This campaign is more than a contest between two men. It is more than a contest between two parties. It is a contest between two philosophies of government. [Our opponents] are proposing changes and so-called new deals which would destroy the very foundations of our American system ... You cannot extend the mastery of government over the daily life of a people without somewhere making it the master of people's souls and thoughts. Expansion of government in business means that the government is driven irresistibly ... to greater and greater control of the nation's press and platform. Free speech does not live many hours after free industry and free commerce die ... The proposals of our opponents represent a radical departure from the foundations of 150 years which have made this the greatest nation in the world.

Summary

Historians and economists continue to debate whether the Wall Street Crash in October 1929 was merely a symptom or the main cause of the Great Depression which followed. The financial collapse did not affect most ordinary Americans until 1931. Thereafter, there was mass unemployment and awful social consequences. Hoover, who opposed direct government intervention in economic matters, worked hard to remedy matters, trusting in banks, big business and local government to improve the situation. Hoover's hopes were not realized. By the winter of 1932–33 there were at least 12 million unemployed people and many of those in work saw their wages or hours of work cut. The desperate situation was summed up by the Hoovervilles which grew up around many cities. Farmers suffered as much, if not more, than industrial workers as food prices collapsed. Black Americans suffered most of all.

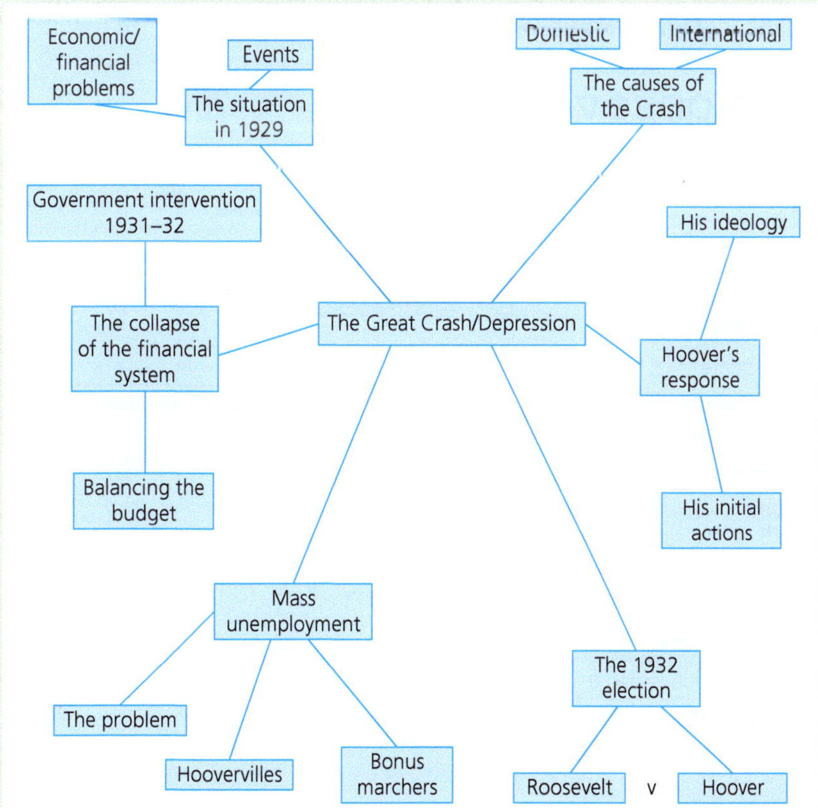

SUMMARY DIAGRAM

What were the causes and impacts of the Depression?

3 How effective were Roosevelt's strategies to deal with the domestic problems facing the USA in the 1930s?

KEY TERM

Interregnum The time between the end of one government and the establishment of the next.

Hoover remained as a 'lame duck president' until March 1933. Over the winter of 1932–33, the economic situation got worse. Many blamed the length of the **interregnum**, a view which led to the adoption in 1933 of the Twentieth Amendment, which reduced the interval between election and inauguration to two and a half months.

Roosevelt's first Hundred Days

In his inaugural address in March 1933, Roosevelt proclaimed: 'the only thing we have to fear is fear itself'. He said that he would ask Congress for 'broad executive power to wage a war against the emergency, as great as the power that would be given to me if we were invaded by a foreign foe'. Historian William Leuchtenburg (1963) believed that his inaugural address 'had made his greatest single contribution to the politics of the 1930s: the installation of hope and courage in the people'.

Franklin Delano Roosevelt

1882	Born to wealthy parents in New York
1900	Went to Harvard University
1905	Married Eleanor Roosevelt, niece of Theodore Roosevelt
1910	Elected to the New York state assembly as a Democrat
1913	Became under-secretary of the navy
1920	Democrat vice-presidential candidate
1921	Stricken with polio: despite years of physical therapy, he never regained the use of his legs. He could stand, only with the use of heavy steel braces and when he could lean on something or someone. Remaining cheerful and optimistic, he refused to let his disability end his political career (but took care to hide the extent of it)
1928	Became governor of New York
1930	Re-elected as governor
1932	Won presidential election
1936	Won presidential election for the second time
1940	Won presidential election for an unprecedented third time
1941	The USA entered the Second World War
1944	Won fourth presidential election
1945	Died

Inaugurated in 1933, Roosevelt remained president for the rest of his life. Virtually everything he did sparked controversy. He was both the most loved and the most hated president in modern times. His political career is a paradox. Conservative in disposition, he favoured experimentation. Committed to certain moral principles, he could be deviously pragmatic. While projecting extraordinary charm and warmth, he also possessed a remote quality. Raised in affluence, he was loved by ordinary people and seen as a traitor to his class by rich Americans. The complexities of his character baffled contemporaries and still baffle historians today. Roosevelt once told his close friend Henry Morgenthau, 'You know I am a juggler, and I never let my right hand know what my left hand does'. 'He was the kind of man to whom those who wanted him convinced of something could talk and argue and insist, and come away believing they had succeeded, when all that happened was that he had been pleasantly present', said Roosevelt's adviser Rexford Tugwell.

Who made the New Deal?

Roosevelt took the credit – and blame – for the New Deal but a great number of people were involved in its making.

- Roosevelt took advice from an unofficial group of academics, lawyers and journalists. Key members of this 'Brain Trust' were Samuel Rosenman, Rexford Tugwell and Raymond Moley. While the Brain Trust attracted a lot of media attention, it had less influence than many thought.
- Roosevelt's cabinet played a crucial role, not least Frances Perkins, secretary of labour (the USA's first female cabinet member) and Harold Ickes, secretary of the interior.
- Democrat leaders in Congress influenced Roosevelt's thinking and played a pivotal role in shaping New Deal legislation.
- Some of the 1933 measures were similar to those Hoover's administration had been planning or had already adopted.

Roosevelt's role

Although Roosevelt was not a great legislator, he led and shaped the recovery package – more so than Congress in 1933. He was responsible for choosing his advisers and officials. He chose well. The historian Michael Heale (2015) has written: 'It may be doubted whether any other US administration of the twentieth century has been staffed at all levels with such a wealth of ability and skill'. Another of Roosevelt's strengths was the fact that he was receptive to new ideas. 'It is common sense to take a method and try it. If it fails, admit it frankly and try another. But above all try something', he said in 1932. He had the skill to convey his intentions to the American people. In his radio 'fireside chats', he projected a sense of utter self-confidence and emanated optimism: 'He knew how to make half a loaf sound like a feast', wrote historian Ted Morgan (1985). He was also on good terms with journalists. Most liked him and the light banter of his frequent press conferences was translated in newspapers into a president who was in command of his job.

He had faults. He was loath to admit mistakes. He was a poor administrator. He often avoided stating the truth. But he was a masterly politician. His main function – by no means an easy one – was to reconcile the sharply conflicting views of his reform-minded supporters.

What were Roosevelt's aims?

Roosevelt's main concern in 1933 was to get the USA out of Depression. If Roosevelt's specific policies were ill-defined, his general intentions were clear. He meant to preside over an administration which was more interventionist and directive than Hoover's. Ordinary Americans, he believed, should have some measure of economic security. His programme soon involved an unprecedented amount of national economic planning. However, contemporary allegations that he sought to introduce socialism are absurd. He intended to save, not destroy, US capitalism. He hoped, eventually, to balance the budget and believed that the dole was demoralizing – 'a narcotic: a subtle destroyer of the human spirit'.

SOURCE H

Roosevelt addressing Congress in 1938

Government has a responsibility for the well-being of its citizenship. If private co-operative endeavour fails to provide work for willing hands and relief for the unfortunate, those suffering hard-ship from no fault of their own have a right to call upon the government for aid: and a government worthy of its name must make a fitting response.

To what extent did Roosevelt's views, as expressed in Source H, differ from those of Hoover?

The Hundred Days' measures

In his first Hundred Days Roosevelt peppered Congress with proposals and draft bills. Congressmen, glad to be given a lead, responded by passing 15 major bills. This legislation, as unparalleled in scope and volume as in the speed with which it was enacted, was full of contradiction and overlap. There were some well-considered moves but much was knee-jerk reaction and experimentation. As the historian Michael Parrish (1992) says, 'it bore the stamp of many authors, arose from no master plan, and did not fit neatly into a single ideological box'.

The banking crisis

Over the winter of 1932–33 an epidemic of bank failures prompted panic-stricken withdrawals. By March 1933, three-quarters of banks had stopped trading and 38 states had proclaimed indefinite 'bank holidays'. The entire banking structure seemed in danger of collapse. On his first full day in office, Roosevelt moved swiftly to deal with the crisis, proclaiming a nationwide bank holiday and calling Congress into special session to deal with the crisis. His Emergency Banking Relief Bill was essentially a product of Hoover's administration. It placed all banks under federal control and arranged for the reopening under licence of those found to be **solvent**. Between 11 and 15 March, auditors and accountants from the RFC, the Treasury and the Federal Reserve fanned out across America to implement the legislation. They quickly separated the solvent banks from the insolvent. Those with sufficient capital or assets received a licence to reopen: nearly 70 per cent did so. The rest were placed under government control to be refinanced and reorganized before doing business again.

KEY TERM

Solvent Able to pay all debts.

On 14 March, Roosevelt delivered the first of his radio 'fireside chats'. He told Americans it was safe to bank their savings. They believed him. Deposits flowed back into the banks and the crisis was over. By speedy, dramatic action, Roosevelt had restored confidence in America's banks. 'Capitalism was saved in eight days', said Raymond Moley, one of Roosevelt's advisers. Roosevelt's right-wing critics argued that if he had co-operated with Hoover over the winter, he could have saved many of the banks which never reopened. Critics on the left were critical of his failure to introduce more radical banking changes. They claimed that the Emergency Law (and the later Glass–Steagall Act, see page 220) was written largely by bankers for big bankers and they reaped the greatest benefits, including lavish government subsidies.

The Agricultural Adjustment Act (AAA)

Roosevelt gave farming problems his top priority. The AAA tried to raise farm prices by cutting output. In return for reducing production, farmers received government subsidies. The AAA programme required the partnership of farmers to help set quotas and administer production controls.

The National Industrial Recovery Act (NIRA)

The NIRA created the National Recovery Administration (NRA). The act, often seen as the centrepiece of the Hundred Days, was an attempt at joint economic planning by government and industry. It aimed to regulate prices and wages with the goal of keeping both high enough to ensure fair profits and decent wages. Manufacturers were virtually invited to set prices that might give them a reasonable return, thus avoiding overproduction and bankruptcies. They were also encouraged to draw up codes of fair competition that would become legally binding to all in a given industry. Codes forbade or restricted a broad range of practices, for example, the use of child labour. Section 7a of the law guaranteed employees the right to form unions and bargain collectively.

The Federal Emergency Relief Act (FERA)

Unlike Hoover, Roosevelt accepted that unemployment relief was a federal responsibility. In 1933 $500 million was given to FERA to provide direct relief.

Administration of the programme was entrusted to Harry Hopkins, who believed that the self-respect of people without jobs required that the government should provide them with paid jobs instead of putting them on the dole. With a skeletal Washington staff, FERA necessarily relied on state and local governments to propose and oversee public projects, sometimes on a matching funds basis (which meant that relief payments varied enormously from state to state). By the time it closed in 1935, FERA had spent $4 billion on all kinds of work-relief projects: road repairs, improvements in schools, parks and playgrounds.

The Civilian Conservation Corps (CCC)

The CCC recruited unemployed young men (aged 17–24) for work on conservation projects including planting trees, fighting forest fires, reseeding grazing lands and constructing roads and bridges. By the summer of 1933 300,000 men had been enlisted.

The Tennessee Valley Authority (TVA)

The TVA became the most widely admired New Deal achievement. Ever since 1916, when the federal government had built a dam and two munition plants at Muscle Shoals on the Tennessee River, progressives had urged the government to use the facilities to develop power resources. Progressive proposals now became the basis of a much broader plan to develop the Tennessee River basin, a region covering 40,000 square miles (105,000 km^2) and reaching into seven states. The whole area was placed under the control of the TVA which built dams and hydro-electric plants to provide cheap electricity. It also embarked on a programme of flood control, afforestation, and re-housing. Though cheap electricity did not attract industry on the scale that had been hoped, the TVA dramatically raised living standards throughout the region.

Monetary experiments

- In April 1933 the USA officially went off the gold standard. This lowered the exchange rate of the dollar by about 40 per cent. It made American goods more competitive abroad.
- To strengthen the banking structure, the Glass–Steagall Banking Act extended the Federal Reserve System. It prohibited commercial banks from engaging in investment banking, a practice that had encouraged speculation in the 1920s. It also created the Federal Deposit Insurance Corporation to guarantee individual deposits under $2500.
- The Home Owners' Loan Corporation aimed to help those with mortgages in towns.
- The Farm Credit Act helped farmers who were having difficulty repaying their mortgages.
- The Federal Securities Act brought some regulation to the stock market. In 1934 a Securities and Exchange Commission was set up to curb speculation of the pre-1929 variety.

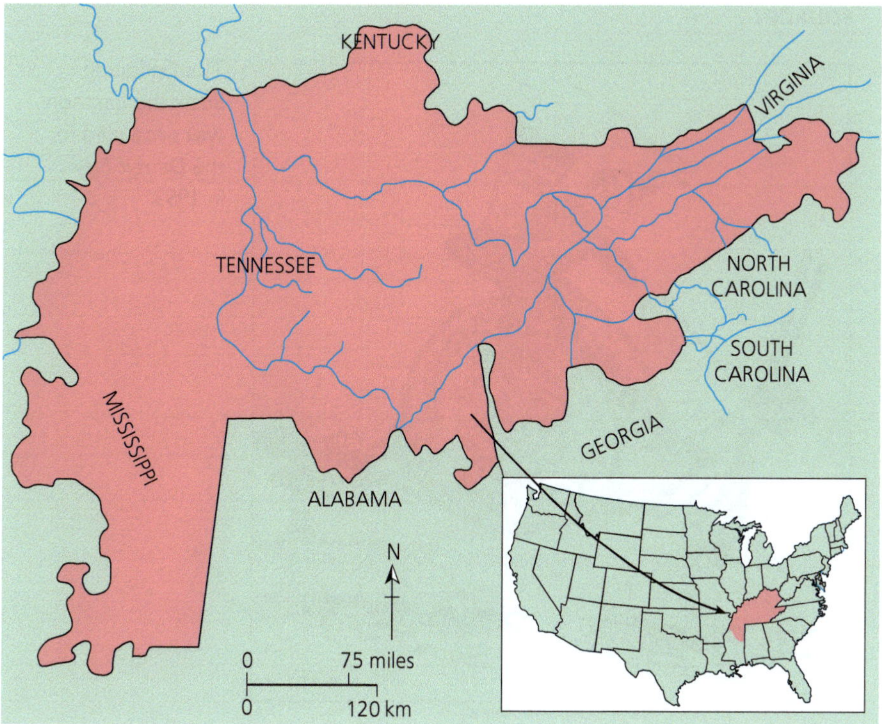

Figure 4.4 The area affected by the TVA

The end of Prohibition

In 1933 Congress passed the Twenty-first Amendment, repealing the Eighteenth. By December 1933, the repeal amendment had been ratified and control over drinking reverted to the individual states. Only seven of them voted to retain Prohibition.

Conclusion

Rex Tugwell, one of Roosevelt's advisers, called the Hundred Days 'a time of rebirth after a dark age'. Never before had the federal government become so deeply involved in the day-to-day economic and social arrangements of the American people. Historian David Kennedy (1999) says that 'Taken together the accomplishments of the Hundred Days constituted a masterpiece of presidential leadership unexampled then and unmatched since (unless in the second Hundred Days)'. Roosevelt had halted the banking panic, created new institutions to reconstruct industry and farming, authorized the largest public works programme in US history, set up the TVA and set aside millions of dollars for relief to unemployed people. Inevitably there were critics of Roosevelt's measures. The right saw them as unprecedented forms of government intervention that threatened tyranny. The left complained that Roosevelt was simply shoring up a dying economic system.

ACTIVITY

Discussion point: What exactly was achieved in Roosevelt's first Hundred Days?

SOURCE I

The Galloping Snail: this cartoon was produced for the *Detroit News* in 1993

What point is the cartoonist trying to make in Source I?

Development of the New Deal policies and the need for a Second New Deal

The development of New Deal policies in 1933–34 soon indicated that there was a need for further measures.

The farming situation

The results of AAA activity were decidedly mixed. By the spring of 1934 farmers had formed over 4000 local committees with more than 100,000 farmer members to carry out the AAA's production-control efforts. By then over three million farmers had agreed to participate. In the South, this translated into the writing of over one million individual contracts through which cotton farmers agreed to take 10 million acres out of production and produce 4.4 million fewer bales. Money from the federal government began to reach the cotton producers by the end of 1934. By then the AAA's basic programme had been expanded to include the production of barley, cattle, peanuts, rye, flax and other crops. Under the AAA programme, farmers slaughtered six million pigs.

Despite the enthusiasm of participating farmers, there were problems. Only the worst drought in 70 years had kept wheat and corn production down in 1934–35. Elsewhere surpluses continued to mount as local committees miscalculated or fudged on quotas and as other farmers cheated on their contracts or refused to participate. The situation became so unstable in cotton and tobacco that in 1934 Congress imposed a heavy tax on those who violated their quotas.

The Commodity Credit Corporation

In an allied effort to raise prices, the Commodity Credit Corporation, set up in late 1933, helped farmers keep their surpluses off the market by making loans somewhat below parity prices and taking the crops as security. Only if prices rose above a given level would the loans have to be repaid. This was the start of a price-support system which would provide stability for farmers for the next half century. It was good news for farmers. The downside was that it set the federal government on the path of storing huge surpluses. The Commodity Credit Corporation became the world's largest holder of scores of farm commodities ranging from cowhides to dates.

The impact on farming and farmers

The AAA pumped $4.5 billion into the pockets of farmers through direct benefit payments between 1934 and 1940. The Commodity Credit Corporation extended $1.5 billion in crop loans. By 1936 gross farm income was up by 50 per cent and farm prices had risen by 66 per cent. However, the rise in prices was in part accounted for by drought and dust storms and the devaluation of the dollar rather than as a result of production controls. Moreover, by 1940 per capita farm income remained less than 40 per cent of that received by non-farmers. The New Deal ended agriculture's downward slide but failed to reverse the imbalance between country and town.

Who benefited?

The AAA demonstrated the federal government's capacity to carry out a complex nationwide programme. AAA leaders claimed that their organization represented the finest tradition of 'grassroots democracy' because farmers did most of the planning through local committees. However, the system favoured the interests of larger, commercial farmers:

- Wealthy farmers dominated the county committees that fixed quotas.
- AAA payments only benefited farmers who owned their own land.
- Given that AAA programmes reduced the acreage farmed, there was less need for farm labourers, who often lost their jobs. Many tenant farmers were also evicted.

In the South, racism compounded class oppression. White landlords ran the county committees. When the landlords signed their acreage reduction contracts, they did not renew long-standing agreements with tens of thousands of (mainly black) tenants and sharecroppers on lands taken out of production. Landless black Americans thus swelled the ranks of unemployed migrants. In Arkansas and Alabama, tenants, sharecroppers and farm labourers organized the Alabama Sharecroppers Union and the Southern

Tenant Farmers Union in 1934 in an attempt to stem the tide of evictions. But southern landlords, backed by local law enforcement officials and vigilantes, struck back. Tenants and croppers who joined the Southern Tenant Farmers Union had their credit cut off by local merchants and their houses burned down. Union organizers were beaten and threatened with death.

The Dust Bowl

In the mid-1930s drought, over-planting and over-grazing combined to create a huge dust bowl in Oklahoma, Arkansas and neighbouring states. The acreage reductions prescribed by the AAA and the increasing use of tractors also forced large numbers of farm workers off the land. Tens of thousands of families piled their belongings into ramshackle cars and headed for California to become migrant labourers. The plight of such people was highlighted in John Steinbeck's novel *The Grapes of Wrath* (1939).

The impact of the NRA

The NRA probably helped to prop up US industry at a time when it needed support. However, it soon suffered from both personal and institutional problems.

Hugh Johnson

Roosevelt appointed businessman Hugh Johnson to supervise the NRA. Thanks to Johnson's flair for publicity, the NRA initially generated great enthusiasm. By the autumn of 1933 most major companies had signed codes endorsing wages and hours agreements and enabling them to display the NRA's Blue Eagle symbol. But Johnson faced a huge task in attempting to develop a nationwide programme within a very short time. Nor could he call upon a corps of skilled bureaucrats to help him. Johnson drove himself to near collapse. Then, as criticism of the NRA began to mount, he took refuge in drink. He was eventually eased out of the agency.

Problems

The NRA experiment soon turned sour.

- Small firms resented the fact that big business dominated the code-writing process, often taking the opportunity to strengthen monopolistic practices.
- Consumers complained that the codes restricted output and encouraged higher prices.
- Some big companies looked with suspicion on the Blue Eagle and hated the encouragement given to trade unions by Section 7a. Some companies responded by firing employees who joined unions, hired thugs to bust union meetings, and brought in strike-breakers as necessary.

- Labour leaders were dissatisfied by the NRA's failure to create new jobs. They also criticized the agency for failing to enforce the wages and hours provisions in the codes adequately.

The Public Works Administration (PWA)

The PWA was set up (as part of the NRA) with a fund of $3.3 billion. Under the prudent direction of Secretary Ickes, the PWA built schools, hospitals, dams and roads. Ickes, determined to give taxpayers value for money, insisted on rigorous appraisals before approving projects. Thus the money was invested too slowly to give immediate relief. However, the PWA was ultimately responsible for some 34,000 projects, including the Golden Gate Bridge and the Grand Coulee Dam.

Conclusion

By 1935 the NRA had become a source of disillusionment, denounced by businessmen and labour leaders alike. Roosevelt's adviser Moley described NIRA as 'a thorough hodge-podge of provision ... a mistake'. Historians have been no kinder. Most think the NRA created a muddled bureaucracy which did little to promote industrial recovery. But it was not a total failure. It brought about some improvements in labour standards. The cotton textile code, for example, ended child labour in southern mills.

The situation in 1934

The main economic indicators ceased to turn down and looked stronger by 1934. Average earnings for workers were moving up. Farm-mortgage debts were declining: so was the number of business failures. However, real economic recovery proved elusive. As the winter of 1933–34 loomed, Roosevelt secured another emergency measure, the Civil Works Administration (CWA), to provide work relief for people in need. Better-funded during its short life (it lasted only until March 1934) than FERA, it found work for four million people. By 1934 the various relief agencies – FERA, CCC and CWA – were helping over a fifth of the population.

The Second New Deal

In 1935 Roosevelt demanded that Congress enact several major measures – measures usually called the Second New Deal. Over a three-month period, he used all his political skills to ensure his proposals passed through Congress. The result, in the opinion of journalist Walter Lippman, was 'The most comprehensive programme of reform ever achieved in this country in any administration'. 'The Hundred Days may have saved capitalism but 88 days in 1935 literally changed the face of America for the next half century', says historian Michael Parrish (1992).

The need for the Second New Deal

Roosevelt's motives for introducing the Second New Deal have been much debated.

- The 1936 election was in the offing and Roosevelt needed to impress the electorate.
- To counter criticism from men like Long and Townsend (see page 235–36), he may have incorporated aspects of their programmes into his own agenda.
- In 1935 the Supreme Court struck down some key New Deal measures (see page 238).
- Big business seemed opposed to the New Deal.
- The economy was still struggling with millions unemployed.

The Emergency Relief Appropriation Act

In April 1935 Congress approved the Emergency Relief Appropriation Act which authorized the single largest expenditure up to that time in the USA's history – $4.8 billion. The act breathed new life into existing agencies like the CCC and PWA. It also helped fund new bodies, most importantly the Works Progress Administration (WPA) which was allocated $1.4 billion.

The Works Progress Administration (WPA)

During its eight-year history the WPA employed a total of 8.5 million people and spent $11 billion on work relief. At its peak in 1936–37, it employed more than 3 million workers a month. Under Harry Hopkin's energetic direction, the WPA was responsible for over 250,000 projects: in 7 years it built 570,000 miles (920,000 km) of rural roads, 2500 hospitals, 5900 schools, 350 airports and 8000 parks. Its associated projects were also successful.

- The National Youth Administration gave part-time employment to millions of college and high school students, thus enabling them to continue their education.
- The Federal Writers' Project helped unemployed writers. It prepared a series of regional guidebooks and published local histories.
- The Federal Arts Project gave out-of-work artists the chance to adorn schools, libraries and other public buildings with murals.
- Under the Federal Music Project, WPA orchestras gave concerts to over 100 million people: free music classes attracted 500,000 pupils a month.
- The Federal Theatre Projects' travelling companies brought drama, ballet and puppet shows to rural communities.

The WPA had its critics. The left were disappointed that it aided only about a third of people without jobs at any one time, that it paid less than the average wage, and that it discriminated against black people, Mexican-Americans and women. The right thought that many of its projects created work for the sake of creating work: writer John Steinbeck, for example, was tasked with taking a census of dogs. There was also much waste and political favouritism. But in accepting government responsibility for providing public work and relief, the WPA went far beyond anything imagined by Hoover. Its building work also left a useful legacy for future generations of Americans.

The Social Security Act

The USA was virtually alone among modern industrial countries in having no national system in place to help unemployed and older people. In 1935 only 27 of the 48 states had introduced (limited) old-age pensions. Only Wisconsin had an unemployment scheme. The Social Security Act created a compulsory national system of old-age pensions and a joint federal–state system of unemployment insurance. Although falling far short of Roosevelt's hopes, Labour Secretary Perkins (who played a major role in its passing) claimed that the final bill was 'the only plan that could have been put through Congress'. Conservative Republicans and many southern Democrats denounced the measure, claiming it would encourage people who were workshy.

The Act undoubtedly had major defects.

- The system it introduced was to be financed out of current contributions rather than out of general tax revenues; hence no pension payments could be made until 1942.
- Benefits were low and were proportionate to previous income rather than being based on minimum subsistence needs.
- Many millions of people were exempt, including some groups most in need of protection, like farm labourers and domestic servants.
- The extent of the coverage, the levels of benefit and the structure of administrative control varied from state to state, creating a welfare system of bewildering complexity and inequality. In 1939, for example, a poor child in Massachusetts received $61 a month: Mississippi granted a similar child only $8. Both states received the same amount per child from the federal government.

Despite its limitations, the act provided a foundation on which all subsequent administrations have built. Roosevelt regarded it as 'the cornerstone of his administration'.

SOURCE J

Roosevelt hailing the 1935 Social Security Act when he signed it into law

Today a hope of many years' standing is in large part fulfilled. The civilisation of the past hundred years, with its startling industrial changes, has tended more and more to make life insecure. Young people have come to wonder what would be their lot when they came to old age. The man with a job has wondered how long the job would last.

This social security measure gives at least some protection to 30 million of our citizens who will reap direct benefits through unemployment compensation, through old-age pensions and through increased services for the protection of children and the prevention of ill health.

Read Source J. How does Roosevelt defend his Social Security Act? Is his argument convincing?

The Wealth Tax

Roosevelt asked Congress to impose high taxes on inherited wealth, corporate profits and 'very great individual incomes'. In its final form, the Wealth Tax did not set rates at the level Roosevelt proposed. Nevertheless, the act identified him with the 'have-nots' and provoked an outcry from conservatives who termed it a 'soak the successful' tax. In truth, the measure was probably designed more to gain votes from poorer people than to gain revenue from richer citizens.

The National Labor Relations (or Wagner) Act

The National Labor Relations Act was the brainchild of Senator Wagner. Roosevelt, who remained uneasy about organized labour, supported it only after the Supreme Court had invalidated the NIRA (see page 219), whose Section 7a had tried to guarantee collective bargaining. Wagner's Act threw the government's influence behind the right of workers to join trade unions. It created a National Labor Relations Board empowered to bargain on behalf of workers and also to restrain management from using 'unfair labour practices' such as blacklists and company unions. The act opened the way to a growth of union membership and power. Wagner's hope was that this would raise wage rates so that there was more consumer purchasing power in the economy.

Other 1935 measures

- The Banking Act gave the USA something akin to a central banking system. The revamped board of governors was given enhanced power over the regional Federal Reserve banks.
- The Public Utilities Holding Company Act helped provide cheap power. It gave the Federal Power Commission extensive regulatory powers over public utility companies.
- The Resettlement Administration provided aid to displaced tenant farmers.
- The Rural Electrification Administration was established. At this point less than a fifth of American farms had electricity. By 1945 electrification of farms had risen to 90 per cent.

Were there two New Deals?

Some historians have argued that there were two distinct New Deals with different goals. They claim that the first New Deal had been concerned primarily with relief and recovery while the second was concerned with social reform. They see Roosevelt giving up the attempt to work with big business and instead seeking allies in the labour movement and among the 'have-nots'. There was some change of emphasis along these lines but it is probably a mistake to exaggerate the sharpness of the break. Most of the measures of the first Hundred Days were necessarily emergency measures. Many of the 1935 reforms had been long in preparation and some owed less to Roosevelt than to Congress. They do not necessarily represent a change of heart on his part. Reform elements were built into the early recovery policies

ACTIVITY

Summarise the work of the agencies during the First and Second New Deals. Decide whether the agency succeeded or failed and explain your reasons why.

and recovery policies remained integral to the 1935 reform phase. Thus, the New Deal is probably best seen as a whole.

SOURCE K

Year	Unemployed (in millions)	Unemployed (% of workforce)
1929	1.5	3.2
1930	4.3	8.7
1931	8.0	15.9
1932	12.1	23.6
1933	12.8	24.9
1934	11.3	21.7
1935	10.6	20.1
1936	9.0	16.9
1937	7.7	14.3
1938	10.4	19.0
1939	9.5	17.2
1940	8.1	14.6

Unemployment figures 1929–40

Do the statistics in Source K suggest that the New Deal was failing or succeeding? Explain your answer.

Roosevelt's political strategies

Although Roosevelt had not succeeded in leading the USA out of depression, most Americans were better off in 1936 than in 1932. This strengthened Roosevelt politically.

The 1936 presidential election

At the Democratic convention in 1936 Roosevelt was re-nominated on a platform praising the achievements of the New Deal and promising more reform. The Republicans chose Kansas Governor Alfred Landon – a progressive. Landon promised more aid to farmers, denounced the New Deal's centralizing tendencies and emphasized the Republican commitment to reduce federal spending and to balance the budget. He had the support of big business and most of the main newspapers.

Roosevelt's advantages

- A third party threat did not seriously materialize. The National Union Party, created by the supporters of Coughlin, Townsend and Long, had relatively little support after Long's murder (see page 236).
- The Republican Party was in a bad shape. Divided between its conservative and progressive wings, it was still associated with the onset of the Depression.
- Millions of Americans had benefited from New Deal programmes. Although eight million Americans were still unemployed, the economy was doing better than at any time since 1930.
- Roosevelt was seen as a champion of labour. Trade unions gave support and generous funds to the Democrats.

The result

The campaign was bitterly fought. Roosevelt, the perceived leader of the 'have-nots', seemed to go out of his way to stir up class hatred, something that was almost unprecedented for a major party candidate. His strategy worked. He won 27,750,000 votes – 60.8 per cent of the total – and carried every state in the Union except 2, winning 523 and losing only 8 electoral college votes. The Democrats won three-quarters of the seats in the Senate and almost four-fifths of those in the House. Landon won 16,679,000 votes. The National Union, Socialist and Communist candidates won 888,000, 180,000 and 80,000 votes respectively.

The Democrat coalition

Roosevelt and the New Deal ensured a realignment of the USA's major political parties. His political success began a Democratic reign that lasted until 1952. Moreover, if the Democrats did not always control the presidency, they usually controlled Congress until the end of the twentieth century. Roosevelt succeeded in retaining traditional Democrat supporters – white southerners and Catholics and Jewish people in the northern cities. But he added to these, winning support from middle-class liberals, black Americans, small farmers in the West, and most working men in the cities. Moreover, people who voted for the first time cast their vote overwhelmingly for Roosevelt.

To a remarkable extent, Roosevelt forged a coalition of economic, ethnic and cultural minorities – men and women driven to some extent by their common experience of alienation from the old establishment. Roosevelt gave status and power as never before to Irish Catholics (like Charles Fahy and Joseph Kennedy) and Jewish people (like Felix Frankfurter and Samuel Rosenman).

Black Americans and the New Deal

In 1932 nearly 75 per cent of black people had voted Republican – the party of Abraham Lincoln. In 1936 over 75 per cent voted Democrat. Why?

In some respects, black Americans do not seem to have gained much from the New Deal.

- The AAA displaced many black farmers.
- The NRA excluded black people from most skilled jobs and adopted discriminatory wage rates.
- The CCC operated segregated camps.
- Roosevelt, unwilling to antagonize white southern Democrats, did nothing to attack segregation and disenfranchisement. He even refused to support legislation which aimed to prevent lynching.

However, most black people were positive about both Roosevelt and the New Deal.

- By 1935 nearly 30 per cent of black families were on relief – three times the proportion of white families. Thus, Roosevelt's measures helped them proportionately far more than they helped white people.

- Hopkins and Ickes fought to guarantee black people a fair share under WPA and PWA.
- Roosevelt made some gestures which pleased civil rights activists. Black leaders, for example, were given posts in the administration.
- Roosevelt's wife Eleanor had a well-deserved reputation as a champion of racial equality.

The Roosevelt Depression 1937–38

After his 1936 election triumph, Roosevelt seemed to have all the authority he needed for more reform. In his second inaugural address in January 1937 he seemed to promise as much for he drew attention to 'one third of a nation ill-housed, ill-clad, ill-nourished'. But Roosevelt's second term was to prove something of an anticlimax and he was soon to face another economic downturn.

SOURCE L

Part of Roosevelt's second inauguration address

In this nation I see tens of millions of citizens who at this very moment are denied the greater part of what the very lowest standards of today call the necessities of life. I see millions of families trying to live on incomes so meagre that the pall of family disaster hangs over them day by day ... I see millions denied education, recreation, and the opportunity to better their lot, and the lot of their children. I see millions lacking the means to buy the products of farm and factory and by their poverty denying work and productivity to many other millions.

Read Source L. Why do you think Roosevelt spoke as he did in 1937?

Reasons for the Roosevelt Depression/Recession

In mid-1937 the USA's output finally surpassed that of 1929. Worried about the mounting national debt, Roosevelt tried to balance the budget by cutting government spending. This promptly sent the economy into reverse. In October 1937 stock prices collapsed suddenly: investors dumped 17 million shares. The rate of economic decline in 1937–38 was sharper than it had been in 1929. Over a ten-month period, industrial production fell by a third and national income by a tenth. By 1938 some 11.5 million people were unemployed – a fifth of the workforce.

Dealing with the Depression/Recession

The historian Alan Brinkley (2009) believes there was now an ideological struggle within FDR's administration: 'a struggle to define the soul of the New Deal'. Conservatives who wanted to cut government spending were at odds with progressives who wanted to spend more. Only in April 1938, when it was apparent that the recession could spell disaster for the Democrats in the mid-term elections, did Roosevelt accept the advice of those who favoured additional spending even if this meant creating a larger budget deficit. Accordingly, he asked Congress for $3.75 billion for relief and public works. Congress obliged and by the summer the economy had begun a slow upward climb. A few other progressive measures were enacted.

- The Farm Security Administration was created with the authority to lend money to help small farmers and migratory labourers.
- The Wagner–Steagall Act created a Housing Authority to provide aid for slum clearance.
- A new Agricultural Adjustment Act tried to stabilize farm prices by fixing marketing quotas and acreage allotment.
- A Fair Labor Standards Act set a minimum wage of 25 cents an hour rising to 40 cents within 2 years, and a maximum working week of 44 hours, to be reduced in the same period to 40 hours. Southern Democrats had opposed the act, fearing that any measure that raised wages across the board would deprive their region of its competitive advantage as a cheap labour market. It also threatened to overturn the prevailing system under which black people earned less than white. The bill was finally passed in 1938 but only after it had been amended to exclude domestic workers and farm labourers.

Although the economy strengthened after 1938, unemployment remained high until 1941, when the threat of war, not enlightened New Deal policies, led to an increase in government expenditure at levels previously unimagined.

SOURCE M

What point is the cartoonist in Source M intending to make?

A cartoon commenting on FDR's spending

Was the New Deal new?

In historian Richard Hofstadter's view (1955) the New Deal was a 'drastic new departure ... in the history of American reformism ... different from anything that had yet happened'. David Kennedy (1999) agrees: 'the country was, in measurable degree, remade'. Those historians who think the New Deal might claim to be 'the third American Revolution' argue as follows:

- Roosevelt founded the modern American welfare state based on the concept that the federal government has a responsibility to guarantee a minimum standard of living and to intervene in a variety of economic and social matters.
- The federal government's assertion of power reduced the autonomy of individual states. Americans now looked to Washington, not their state capitals, for solutions to problems.
- In expanding the federal government's authority, Roosevelt transformed the institution of the presidency, becoming in William Leuchtenburg's view, 'the first modern president'. He expanded the president's law-making functions, introduced and skilfully stage-managed presidential press conferences and mastered the technique of communicating directly with Americans by means of radio. Future presidents found it hard to escape from his legacy. They took centre-stage politically, becoming the focus of people's hopes and expectations.

However, it is possible to claim that the New Deal was at best a halfway revolution.

- Roosevelt's aims were not revolutionary. He wanted to save, not destroy, capitalism.
- With very few exceptions (for example, the TVA), the New Deal did not challenge the basic tenets of capitalism. In contrast with the pattern in most other industrial societies, no significant state-owned enterprise emerged in New Deal America.
- Much of Roosevelt's policy echoed that of Herbert Hoover, Woodrow Wilson and Theodore Roosevelt.
- The New Deal failed to redistribute national income.
- Roosevelt was reluctant to engage in massive deficit spending, as the economist Keynes proposed. The president hankered after balancing the budget. 'He was no big spender until driven there by absolute necessity', says Michael Parrish (1992).

Summary

Roosevelt dealt energetically with the USA's economic and social problems after 1933. The legislation of his first Hundred Days, although something of a mixed assortment, was particularly impressive. His New Deal policies gave Americans some hope and led to a slight decrease in unemployment. However, by 1935, with the 1936 presidential election approaching, it was clear to Roosevelt that he needed to do more. The result was the Second New Deal which in many ways was more comprehensive and better thought out than the first. In 1936 Roosevelt portrayed himself as the enemy of big business. This helped win him the support of most of the poor Americans, younger people and many liberals, as well as traditional Democrat voters. This so-called New Deal coalition ensured he won a huge victory in 1936. Unfortunately, Roosevelt's second term was less successful than his first and his attempt to balance the budget helped bring about a new recession.

SUMMARY DIAGRAM

How effective were Roosevelt's strategies to deal with the domestic problems facing the USA in the 1930s?

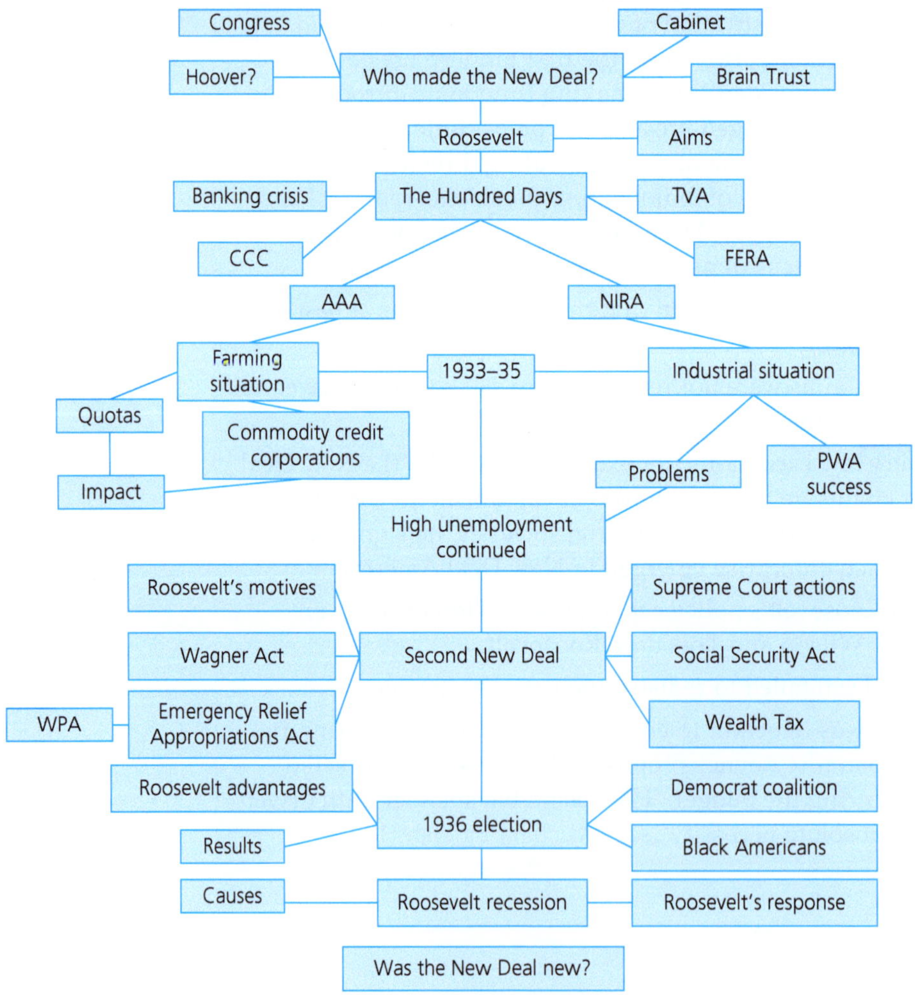

4 Why was there opposition to New Deal laws and policies and what impact did it have?

In 1933–34 Roosevelt enjoyed huge support. The 1934 mid-term elections were a triumph for the Democrats, with the Republicans winning only a quarter of the seats in the House and only a third in the Senate. The Democrats' success seemed a ringing endorsement of the New Deal. However, by 1935 Roosevelt found himself under attack from left-wing critics, who demanded more sweeping reform, and from right-wingers, who believed the administration had moved too far to the left.

Opposition from the liberal left

'The thunder on the left' is the term historians have used to describe the clamour of visionaries and **demagogues** who claimed to speak for less well-off people. It was not surprising that a radical outcry should have developed. Eleven million people were still without jobs in mid-1934. The New Deal had often benefited big business and big agriculture rather than disadvantaged people. 'Have-nots', though they were little attracted to socialism or communism, were ready to turn to leaders whose ideas seemed to offer an end to the prevailing misery.

KEY TERM

Demagogue A popular orator who appeals to the baser emotions of his or her audience.

Independent parties

While the 1934 mid-term elections were a triumph for the Democrats, independent candidates who sounded more radical than Roosevelt made a strong showing.

- Floyd Olson became governor of Minnesota for the third time on a platform that called for state ownership of mines, transport and public utilities.
- In Wisconsin, Philip La Follette and Robert La Follette Jr recaptured the state's governorship and the state's US Senate seat on a Progressive Party ticket that called for unemployment insurance and old-age pensions.

Neither Olson nor the La Follettes had any intention of mounting a nationwide crusade against the inadequacies of the New Deal. But others were prepared to do so.

Dr Francis Townsend

Many elderly Americans had seen their savings vanish in the Crash. Others could no longer count on help from hard-pressed families. Many found a potential saviour in Dr Francis Townsend. Townsend, a retired Californian medical practitioner, proposed that everyone over 60 should be granted a federal monthly pension of $200 on condition that they spent it within

30 days. The pensions were to be financed by a two per cent tax on business transactions. He claimed that older people's spending would lift the economy out of depression. At a time when only 28 states had any kind of old-age pensions, ranging from $8 to $30 a month, Townsend's plan (which was economic madness) was attractive to the eight million Americans over 60 who flocked to join Townsend Clubs. By 1935 the movement claimed one million members.

Father Charles Coughlin

Coughlin, a Catholic priest, was a radio star whose weekly broadcasts reached an audience of some 30 million. He had supported Roosevelt in 1932 and praised him for much of 1933. But by late 1934 his enthusiasm had cooled. The New Deal, he declared, was both a communist conspiracy and a Wall Street plot intended to keep the people enslaved. Roosevelt, according to Coughlin, presided over a 'government of bankers, by the bankers, and for the bankers'. In 1934 Coughlin created the National Union for Social Justice, advocating such measures as the nationalization of the banks, redistribution of the nation's wealth, and inflation of the money supply. His hatred of international (especially British) bankers won him support from working-class Irish Catholics while his cheap money was popular with debt-ridden farmers.

Huey Long

The most formidable of FDR's opponents was Huey Long of Louisiana. A shrewd, ambitious, ruthless politician and an effective orator, Long became Governor of Louisiana in 1928 by stirring up poor-white resentment toward the strong business interests which had long dominated the state. He brought some reform, building roads, improving education and introducing a fairer tax system. In the process he set up a near-dictatorship, disregarding legal processes when it suited him. He entered the Senate in 1931. After initially supporting Roosevelt, Long became a fierce critic. He denounced big business and attacked the New Deal for encouraging big government. In 1934 Long proposed a reform plan under the slogan 'Share Our Wealth'. Essentially, he proposed a guaranteed minimum wage ($2,500 a year) to be achieved through taxing wealthy people. No personal fortune would exceed $5 million and no individual could keep as earnings more than $1.8 million in a year. Long's sums did not add up but that did not worry his supporters. By 1935 Long claimed a membership of eight million in Share Our Wealth clubs. He planned to run against Roosevelt in 1936 as a third-party candidate. Fortunately for Roosevelt, Long was murdered in 1935.

Opposition from the conservative right

While those on the left believed that the New Deal had not gone far enough, many on the right believed that Roosevelt had gone too far. Conservatives opposed the New Deal's intervention in the economy, the huge costs of its relief measures and the consequent budget deficits. This opposition came mainly from wealthy people who feared that Roosevelt was set on establishing socialism. Fortunately for Roosevelt, the views of rich people did not attract mass support.

The American Liberty League

Conservative hostility found open expression in the American Liberty League, established in 1934 with the financial backing of wealthy businessmen and the support of two former Democrat presidential candidates, Al Smith and John Davis. The League attacked the New Deal for trying to 'regimentalize' and 'Sovietize' America. It pledged 'to defend and uphold the Constitution ... to foster the right to work, earn, save and acquire property and to preserve the ownership and lawful use of property'.

SOURCE N

A cartoon from September 1935

What point is the cartoon in Source N making about Roosevelt's policies?

Judicial problems

As conservatives intensified their attacks on Roosevelt in 1935, they were supported by federal judges who were called upon to decide whether the legislative and executive actions of the New Deal were in the spirit of the Constitution. Suspicious of legislation that touched the rights of property and

ACTIVITY

Draw a spider diagram to show the groups or individuals who opposed the New Deal and the reasons why they opposed it.

contract or that seemed to upset the traditional balance between federal and state jurisdiction, judges issued hundreds of injunctions staying the enforcement on constitutional grounds of virtually every New Deal measure.

The Supreme Court

Roosevelt knew that the real test would come in the Supreme Court. All but one of the nine justices owed their appointment to Republican presidents. In May 1935, in *Schechter versus United States*, the Supreme Court declared that the NIRA was unconstitutional because it delegated legislative power to the executive. In *United States versus Butler* (1936) the Court invalidated the AAA on the grounds that it represented an unconstitutional misuse of taxing power.

Roosevelt's response to opposition

Roosevelt responded to the opposition in different ways. His actions in 1935–36 were successful. But his moves against the Supreme Court in 1937 proved to be the biggest blunder of his political career.

Roosevelt's response in 1935–36

Long, Coughlin and Townsend tapped different sources of discontent with the New Deal and offered clashing solutions to their followers. But the message they sent to Roosevelt was clear. Unless he did something to counter their rising influence, he risked losing substantial support. Roosevelt's response was the Second New Deal (see page 225), which was, in part, an effort to satisfy his left-wing critics. It should be said that he was not necessarily forced leftwards: he probably moved in a direction he wanted to go.

The attack from big business angered Roosevelt. He believed he had rescued the bankers from insolvency and saved capitalism. Big business seemed ungrateful for his favours. His turn to the left in 1935 meant he could hit back. He depicted the Republicans as a party controlled by, and operating in the interests of, big business. This helped him win the 1936 election.

The Supreme Court plan

Roosevelt thought it wrong that the Supreme Court majority, appointed by his Republican predecessors and reflecting a laissez-faire attitude which public opinion no longer shared, should render the federal government powerless to deal with pressing problems. Immediately after his 1936 victory, he determined to do battle with the Court's 'nine old men' (their average age was 71), presenting to Congress a Supreme Court reorganization plan. The plan proposed that the president be authorized to appoint one additional judge for every member of the Court who passed the age of 70 without retiring. Since six of the existing justices were above that age, Roosevelt would be able to increase the Court's membership to 15. He claimed that the Court's efficiency would be improved by an influx of younger members but his real motive was to secure a more sympathetic bench.

The storm of protest that Roosevelt's plan provoked showed that he had miscalculated. He was accused by his Republican opponents of seeking to increase his executive powers. Some Democrat Congressmen shared this fear. They accepted that expanding or reducing the size of the Supreme Court was constitutional and not unprecedented. In 1789 Congress had fixed the number at six, reduced it to five in 1801, expanded it to ten in the Civil War and settled on nine in 1869. But Democratic Congressmen were angry that Roosevelt had made no effort to consult them on the matter. Nor had it been mentioned in the 1936 election. Even some of those who wished to curb the Court disliked Roosevelt's devious approach.

In Congress a long and bitter debate on the Court bill seriously divided the Democrats, especially northerners from southerners. Moreover, Roosevelt was fighting an unnecessary battle. He should have been patient. Given the age of the judges, he would soon be able to make appointments, ensuring that a majority of Court members supported his actions. Indeed had Roosevelt allowed the Court judges to retire on full salary, several may well have done so.

Roosevelt still appearing cheerful despite political setbacks in 1937

A succession of events in 1937 made reform seem less necessary. One conservative judge retired while others decided to support the administration. In a number of decisions between March and May the Court upheld such key measures as the Social Security Act and the National Labor Relations Act. Aware that the Senate was likely to oppose his Court plan, Roosevelt abandoned the measure in July 1937. During the next four years, deaths and retirements enabled him to fill seven Court vacancies, thus giving it a strong liberal character. The New Deal measures enacted in 1935 were thus constitutionally safe but Roosevelt's Court plan had shattered Democrat unity.

SOURCE O

Cartoon of Roosevelt's Supreme Court plan

What point is the cartoonist in Source O making about Roosevelt's Supreme Court plan?

Opposition from southern Democrats

Some conservative southern Democrats had long been uneasy about the direction of the New Deal. Many disliked the fact that Roosevelt seemed more responsive to the urban North than the rural South. Some suspected that he had dictatorial tendencies and feared he intended to revolutionize race relations. Others supported states' rights and revered a balanced budget. Thus in 1937–38 conservative Democrats united with Republicans to oppose a number of reform measures. Nothing of major importance was passed in 1937.

Administrative reform

The New Deal had resulted in the presidency having increased power. However, a lack of staff made it difficult for Roosevelt to exercise those powers effectively. In 1937 he asked Congress for more White House staff and the creation of new departments. His proposals, which aroused further fears of presidential dictatorship, were rejected. A modified bill, passed in 1939, watered down the provisions of the original measure.

Industrial strife

As well as discord in Congress, Roosevelt also faced serious industrial unrest. The collective bargaining guarantees of the NIRA and the Wagner Act helped union membership rise from just over two million in 1933 to almost nine million in 1938. This resulted in bitter conflicts both within the ranks of labour and with employers. Though the American Federation of Labor (AFL) shared in the expansion, most of its leaders, wedded to the principle of craft unionism, were not greatly interested in organizing unskilled workers. In 1935 a frustrated minority of union leaders formed what became the Congress on Industrial Organization (CIO) with the aim of organizing all workers in given industries into single unions. Over the winter of 1936–37 the USA was hit by a wave of strikes as CIO unions demanded recognition. The Union of Automobile Workers forced General Motors to capitulate. A few weeks later US Steel gave in to union pressure. In previous eras troops would have been sent in to break the strikes. This did not happen. Conservatives were appalled: here it seemed was further evidence of Roosevelt's socialist leanings.

Employers fought back, using lock-outs, strike-breakers and private armies. They could also often count on help from the local police. In the Memorial Day Massacre (30 May 1937) Chicago police clashed with strikers picketing a steel plant, killing 10 and injuring 75. Strikers responded by intimidating non-unionists and adopting a new, effective 'sit-down' technique in order to seize control of factories. By the end of 1937 'sit-down' strikes had enabled the United Automobile Workers to win union recognition from every car manufacturer except Ford.

Middle-class opinion, initially pro-labour, was suspicious of union power, particularly as evidence suggested that many unions were run by racketeers or communists. Thus, much public support ebbed away from the unions and from Roosevelt who was blamed for the union activity. Ironically, Roosevelt did not have much sympathy with the strikers but he realized that to condemn their action might lose him support from workers.

The end of the New Deal

Roosevelt had to fight hard for the 1938 measures (see pages 231–32). Other presidential recommendations were either ignored or rejected. Smarting from these reverses, he set out to purge his party of anti-New Dealers. He thus intervened in Democratic primaries, especially in the South, appealing to voters to replace conservatives with liberals. His strategy failed. Almost all the candidates he campaigned against were re-elected and now had even less reason to support him.

The 1938 mid-term elections were a setback for Roosevelt. Although the Democrats retained control of both houses of Congress, the Republicans made striking gains, almost doubling their numbers in the House. The new Congress was more conservative than any Roosevelt had so far faced. It was clear that the New Deal had run out of steam. Roosevelt acknowledged the fact in his annual message in 1939. For the first time since coming to office, he proposed no new reforms. Increasingly pre-occupied with world affairs, he was reluctant to press for measures which might alienate Congressmen whose support he needed for foreign policy initiatives.

The 1940 presidential election

Roosevelt stood for an unprecedented third time in 1940. There was no obvious Democrat successor and the international situation (arising from the Second World War) meant there was need for an experienced pair of hands to steer the USA. Roosevelt's opponent was Wendel Wilkie – a Democrat until 1938. Faced with the prospect of war, most Americans decided this was not the time to replace Roosevelt. Helped by the start of a war boom, he won almost 55 per cent of the popular vote – 449 electoral college votes to Wilkie's 82. The fact that Roosevelt won was an indication that, despite all the problems of his second term, he remained popular and had managed to ward off the attacks of his opponents.

ACTIVITY

Discussion point: How valid were the criticisms of the New Deal?

Extension: How effective was the New Deal?

It is possible to claim that the New Deal was not very successful.

- At best it brought about only partial recovery. The USA was less successful in reducing employment than Germany or Britain. In no year after 1933 did the unemployment rate in the USA fall below 14 per cent. Some 10 million Americans were still out of work in 1939. Not until 1941 would full employment and prosperity return, and only then because of the war and rearmament.
- The work programmes were inefficient, doing little to enhance skills. WPA, for example, became known as 'We Piddle Around'.

- The New Deal did little for women. Its agencies were riddled with gender discrimination. Many NRA codes allowed employers to pay women less than men, even when they did the same job. Married women were not considered a priority. The Social Security Act made no provision for housewives.
- There was limited social reform. Welfare payments were limited. Many groups were excluded from pensions and from unemployment insurance. Poorer people remained poor.
- Right-wing critics claim that Roosevelt had gone too far in terms of government intervention. Too much government regulation undermined the incentive of businessmen to invest, thereby prolonging the USA's economic misery. By setting up too many overlapping and inefficient agencies, Roosevelt created something close to administrative anarchy. The agencies simply got in the way of recovery. Arguably whatever economic success there was occurred despite New Deal policies, not because of them.
- Left-wing critics claim that the New Deal did not eradicate poverty or economic inequality. They stress that many measures benefited privileged groups (like large-scale farmers), not weaker workers (like sharecroppers). There was little redistribution of wealth. The New Deal left big business intact. According to one estimate, the wealthiest one per cent of the population saw its share of personal income increase over the course of the decade.

However, most historians stress the New Deal's achievements.

- It brought jobs, electricity and hope to some of the USA's most depressed areas.
- It introduced much-needed controls on banks and stock exchanges.
- Federal government guarantees ensured that Americans' mortgages and bank savings were secure.
- It gave the USA new roads, dams, hospitals, sports facilities and public buildings.
- It laid the foundation of the American welfare state, giving all Americans a measure of security. While it did not eradicate poverty or economic inequalities, it did begin to deploy the federal government's resources on behalf of those who had received little help in the past.
- It guaranteed millions of workers the liberty to join a union.
- It helped restore national morale and prevent the risk of revolution.
- It was a successful political slogan. The fact that Roosevelt won four presidential elections suggests that most Americans perceived the New Deal to be successful.
- In legitimizing and strengthening trade unions, Roosevelt helped them to secure for their members the generous wages and benefits that they were to enjoy for a generation after 1945.

Summary

By 1934 Roosevelt faced opposition from the liberal (and sometimes not-so-liberal) left who felt his measures had not gone far enough. He also faced opposition from the Conservative right who felt he had gone too far and was threatening to overthrow the Constitution. Roosevelt was able to see off the 'thunder on the left' in 1935–36. But conservative opposition in the Supreme Court led the president to attempt to change the composition of the court. This had serious political repercussions. By 1937–38 he had lost the support of many Southern Democrats who joined forces with the Republicans and claimed that Roosevelt had dictatorial ambitions. Despite his political difficulties, and helped by the coming of war in Europe, Roosevelt won the 1940 presidential election for an unprecedented third time.

SUMMARY DIAGRAM

Why was there opposition to the New Deal policies and what impact did it have?

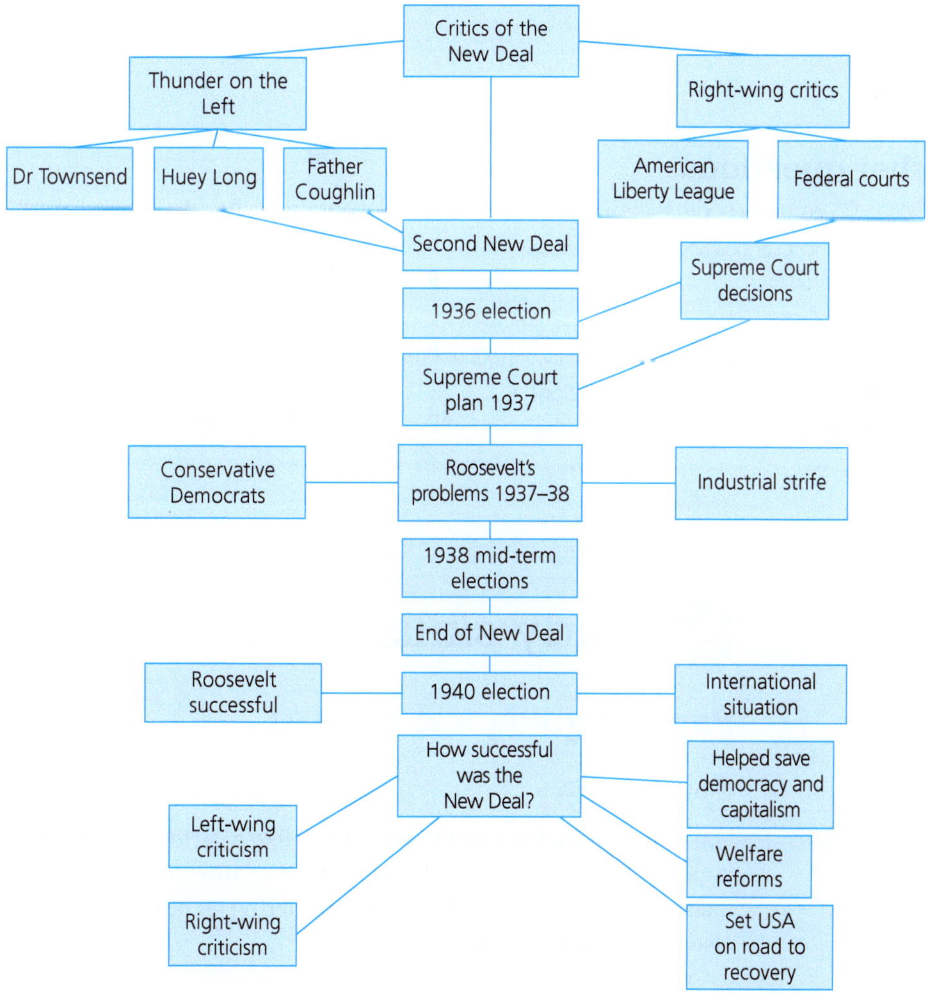

Chapter summary

In the 1920s the USA prospered. American industry churned out manufactured goods and American consumers, using instalment-buying, purchased them. The Republicans, supporting big business, benefited politically, winning presidential elections in 1920 (Harding), 1924 (Coolidge) and 1928 (Hoover). However, there were economic problems. Not all Americans prospered and farmers, in particular, suffered. By 1929 manufacturers were overproducing goods. Meanwhile Americans speculated in stocks and shares. In October 1929 the Wall Street Crash saw share values plummet. The Great Depression followed. By 1932–33 there were over 12 million unemployed people. Hoover, although more active than previous presidents, was blamed for the distress. In 1932 Franklin Roosevelt was elected president, promising Americans a New Deal. In his first Hundred Days, he passed 15 major bills, affecting most aspects of the US economy. In 1935 Roosevelt introduced a Second New Deal which saw the passing of more radical measures, including a Social Security Act. He won a landslide victory in the 1936 election, despite opposition from right and left. His second term was marred by the Supreme Court battle and by the Roosevelt Recession. Unemployment remained high until 1940–41. Nevertheless, Roosevelt won the 1940 election for an unprecedented third time.

Refresher questions

1. Why did the US economy boom in the 1920s?
2. What were the most serious underlying economic problems in the 1920s?
3. What caused the Great Crash?
4. What caused the Great Depression?
5. How well did Hoover deal with the Depression?
6. How successful were Roosevelt's first Hundred Days?
7. Why were some Americans critical of the New Deal?
8. Why did Roosevelt introduce the Second New Deal?
9. To what extent was Roosevelt responsible for the problems of his second term?
10. Was the New Deal successful?

Study skills

Paper 1 guidance: sources

Visual sources

You may be asked to use a visual source like a cartoon or a poster. It is important to be able to see its meaning in relation to the issue in the question and to test its validity by considering its purpose and origin and also to use contextual knowledge.

Take the following example.

SOURCE C

A cartoon from 1935 which shows a happy Roosevelt surrounded by dancing children

How would you assess Source C as evidence that the New Deal measures were successful?

To begin, think about the cartoon itself.

It shows a smiling Roosevelt surrounded by happy children. Roosevelt is standing unassisted. In reality, as a result of polio, he could not easily do so. Three of the children have the initials of New Deal agencies on the backs of their shirts – the WPA (Works Progress Administration), PWA (Public Works Administration) and AAA (Agricultural Adjustment Act). The assumption is that the other three children would have similar New Deal initials – possibly the CCC (Civil Conservation Corps), TVA (Tennessee Valley Authority) and FERA (The Federal Emergency Relief Act). Given the expression on the faces of the children, the impression given by the cartoonist is that Roosevelt's measures are working successfully.

While the cartoon suggests that all was going well for Roosevelt and the New Deal, the reality was less clear cut. The AAA programme, for example, was hated by many farmers while the PWA invested money too slowly to give America immediate relief in 1933. The WPA also had its critics. Many of its projects were of doubtful value and there was much waste and political favouritism.

SOURCE D

THE ILLEGAL ACT.

PRESIDENT ROOSEVELT. "I'M SORRY, BUT THE SUPREME COURT SAYS I MUST CHUCK YOU BACK AGAIN."

A cartoon from *Punch*, a British, Republican-supporting magazine, in June 1935

Activity

Look at Source D. Assess how far it supports the view that Roosevelt's New Deal measures were not working. Think about the following:

The message of the cartoon

The provenance of the cartoon

Knowledge to apply to the cartoon

Paper 2 guidance: essay questions

Writing a conclusion

What is the purpose of a conclusion? A conclusion should come to a judgement that is based on what you have already written and should be briefly supported. It should not introduce new ideas – if they were important they should have been discussed in the main body of the essay. You must also take care to avoid offering a contrary argument to the one you have pursued throughout the rest of the essay as that will suggest to the reader that you have not thought through your ideas and are unclear as to what you think.

It might be that you are largely re-stating the view you offered in the vital opening paragraph, or in stronger answers there might be a subtle variation to the judgement – you confirm your original view, but suggest, with an example, that there were occasions when this was not always correct.

If the question has named a factor then you should give a judgement about that factor's relative importance, either explaining why it is or is not the most important and the role it played in the events you have discussed. If the question asks you to assess a range of factors, the conclusion should explain which you think is the most important and should support the claim. At first sight a claim might appear to be judgement, but without supporting material it is no more than an assertion and will not gain credit.

Consider the following essay question.

> **'President Hoover failed to deal with the problems created by the Great Depression.'**
> **How far do you agree with this view?**

In order to answer this question you may consider:

- The growing economic and social problems in 1930–31.
- Hoover's response to the crisis in 1930–31.
- The deteriorating situation in 1932.
- What measures did Hoover adopt in 1932?
- Should he have done more?

Now consider this sample conclusion.

This is an excellent final paragraph because it focuses immediately on the issue in the question; provides a clear judgement on that issue; that judgement is supported with good argument and evidence and it provides a balanced view on Hoover's success/failure.

In conclusion, it may be that Hoover was unfairly blamed at the time and has been too much maligned since. Although his sombre manner conveyed an impression of indifference, he did very much care about people's suffering and worked tirelessly to try to improve the situation. Despite his belief in laissez-faire, he assumed government responsibility and intervened in the economy more energetically than any of his predecessors. Few politicians advocated more radical measures than those Hoover supported. Congress, Democrat controlled after 1930, had no real programme except to obstruct Hoover. Thus, he deserves some credit for his actions. Nevertheless, by the autumn of 1932 some 12 million Americans – a quarter of the workforce – were unemployed and there was no dole. Even those Americans who were in work saw their hours and wages reduced. Despair and bitterness were almost universal. Given this situation, it cannot be denied that Hoover had failed to deal with the social and economic problems arising from the Depression. The president had done his best. Unfortunately, his best was not good enough.

QUESTION PRACTICE

In light of these comments and the sample conclusion, write conclusions to the following questions.

1 'The Great Crash in 1929 was caused by mass production and oversupply.' How far do you agree?

2 How successful were Roosevelt's New Deal measures in the years 1933–36?

3 To what extent did Roosevelt face serious opposition in the years 1933–40?

You have now covered all the main skills you need to write a good essay. It is worth looking back at these skills before you write each essay you are set. This will help you to build up and reinforce the skills you need for the examination and ensure that you are familiar with the skills needed to do well.

EXPLAIN QUESTIONS

Answer one of the sample explain questions below and highlight where you have explained and where you have described.

1 Explain why the farming situation contributed to the Great Crash.

2 Explain why President Roosevelt felt there was need for a second New Deal in 1935.

3 Explain why Roosevelt was blamed for the economic depression/recession in 1937–38.

4 Explain why Roosevelt's Supreme Court proposals were so unpopular.

Glossary

Abolitionist Someone who wanted to end slavery.

Agrarian Relating to land and farming.

Amnesty Act A measure granting a general pardon for past crimes.

Anarchist A person whose ideal of society is one without a government of any kind. Late-nineteenth-century anarchists often sought to bring this about by violent means.

Arsenal A place where military supplies are stored or made.

Article of faith A main belief.

Bankruptcy When firms or individuals have insufficient money to pay their debts.

Belligerent status Recognized legally as waging war.

Black Republicans A term used by southerners to describe Republicans who were seen as being sympathetic to enslaved people.

Border states The slave states between the North and the Confederacy – Virginia, Kentucky, Maryland, Delaware, Tennessee, Arkansas and Missouri.

Broker A person who buys and sells stocks and shares.

Call to Arms A presidential order calling up troops and putting the USA on a war-footing.

Carpetbaggers Northern white people who settled in – and were accused of exploiting – the South. (A carpetbag was the suitcase of the time.)

Civil liberties The rights of individuals.

Commerce raiders Confederate warships that attacked Union merchant ships.

Contraband of war Goods which can be confiscated from the enemy.

Craft unions Organizations which were set up by workers to try to improve pay and conditions in particular (often skilled) occupations.

Demagogue A popular orator who appeals to the baser emotions of his or her audience.

Despot Someone who has absolute power and rules like a dictator.

Disfranchise Deprive someone of the right to vote.

Egalitarian A society in which people are equal.

Emancipation The act of setting free from bondage.

Evangelical A passionate belief in Christianity and a desire to share that belief with others.

Federal A government in which several states, while largely independent in home affairs, combine for national purposes.

Fire-eaters People who look for quarrels.

Free homesteads The Republicans hoped to provide 160 acres of land to farmers who settled in the West.

Freeport Doctrine A view that voters in a territory could exclude slavery by refusing to enact laws that gave legal protection to owning enslaved people.

GNP (Gross National Product) The total value of all goods and services produced within a country.

Gold reserves Most currencies are based on a country's gold holding.

Gold standard A monetary system according to which the unit of currency has a precise value in gold.

Guerrilla war Warfare by which small units harass conventional forces.

Impeachment The process by which a president who has been found guilty of grave offences by Congress can be removed from office.

Impressment law A law allowing the government to confiscate goods – in this case enslaved people.

Impressment of supplies Confiscation of goods by the government.

Inaugural address A president's speech, made immediately after he has been sworn in as president.

Inflationary pressure An undue increase in the quantity of money in circulation. The result is that the value of money goes down.

Injunction A court order.

Interregnum The time between the end of one government and the establishment of the next.

Jim Crow laws Segregation laws, passed in most southern states in the 1890s.

King Cotton Cotton was so important to the US economy that many Americans claimed that 'cotton was king'.

Laird rams These vessels had an iron ram projecting from the bow, enabling them to sink an enemy by smashing its hull.

Laissez-faire The view that governments should not intervene in economic and social matters.

Lame duck president A president who has little power because he does not control Congress or because he will soon be out of power.

Louisiana Purchase Territory The huge area bought from France in 1803.

Lower South This area comprised Alabama, Louisiana, Georgia, Texas, Florida, South Carolina and Mississippi.

Lynching Putting to death without the usual forms of law.

Manifest destiny The USA's god-given right to take over North America.

Martial law The suspension of ordinary administration and policing and, in its place, the exercise of military power.

Mid-term elections The whole of the House of Representatives and a third of the Senate are re-elected every two years. This means that there are major elections half way through a president's term of office.

Militia draft Conscription of men in the state militias.

Mobilization Preparing for war, especially by raising troops.

Monopoly A situation where someone or some company has sole command or possession of something.

Moratorium An emergency measure allowing the suspension of payment of debts.

Mormons Members of a religious sect, founded in the 1820s by Joseph Smith, a visionary who claimed that an angel had appeared to him.

Muckraking Focusing attention on unpleasant matters rather than noticing what is good.

Muzzle-loading Loaded down the barrel.

Nationalism Loyalty and commitment to a country.

Native-born Americans People born in the USA.

Nativism Suspicion of immigrants.

Oligopoly A situation in which a small number of competitive firms control the market.

Ordnance Bureau The government agency responsible for acquiring war materials.

Paramilitary groups Organized along military lines, these groups often engage in rebellion against the government.

Patronage The giving of jobs or privileges to supporters.

Peculiar institution Southerners referred to slavery as their 'peculiar institution'.

Pinkerton Detective Agency Allan Pinkerton, a Scotsman who had emigrated to the USA, set up his Detective Agency in 1850. He organized an intelligence service for the Union in the Civil War. After 1865 his force was often used by business leaders who wished to take action against trade unions.

Plantation agriculture Sugar, rice, tobacco and cotton were grown on southern plantations.

Planters Men who owned plantations with 20 or more enslaved workers.

Platform The publicly declared principles and intentions of a political party.

Polygamy The practice of having more than one wife.

Popular sovereignty The notion that colonists, not Congress, should decide whether a territory should or should not allow slavery.

Posse A group of men called out by a sheriff or marshal to aid in enforcing the law.

Producers' co-operatives Organizations in which workers or small-scale manufacturers work together to try to help each other in a variety of ways.

Proviso A provision or condition.

Radicalism The principles of those who want to bring about massive change in society, usually by overthrowing those in control.

Recession A period when the economy goes into decline.

Redeem To restore to white rule.

Referendum A vote on a specific issue.

Reparations Under the settlements after the First World War Germany was required to pay compensation of $33 billion or 132 billion marks to the victorious countries.

Rifle-musket The barrel of this type of firearm was grooved. The lead bullet expanded into the grooves when fired and the spin made the weapon far more accurate than the smoothbore musket.

Robber barons Great industrialists who dominated particular industries and who were seen as exploiting their power – at the public's expense. The first robber barons were railway magnates.

Scalawags Southern white people who supported the Republican Party.

Second party system The period from the mid-1830s to the mid-1850s when the Democrats and Whigs were the two main parties.

Securities Stocks and shares.

Segregation The system whereby black and white people are separated from each other on grounds of race.

Self-determination The right of a population to decide its own government.

Slave patrol Armed men who rode round slave areas, especially at night, to ensure that there was no disorder.

Slave Power conspiracy A northern notion that southerners were plotting to expand slavery.

Smoothbore musket These firearms had been in use from the seventeenth century. The barrels of the guns had no grooves. This reduced the accuracy of fire.

Solvent Able to pay all debts.

Sovereignty Ultimate power.

State militia All able-bodied men of military age (in most states) could be called up to fight in an emergency.

Strike-breakers People who are prepared to work during a strike or who are brought in because they are willing to work during a strike.

Suffragettes This was the name given to militant women campaigners for the right to vote in Britain. From 1906 to 1914 they used radical tactics including arson and damage to property as well as marches and demonstrations.

Tariff Customs duty on imported goods.

Territories Areas in the USA that had not yet become states and which were still under federal government control.

War of attrition Relentless wearing down of an enemy's morale and strength using continual attacks.

War Democrats Those Democrats who were determined to see the war fought to a successful conclusion.

Writ of *habeas corpus* The right to know why one has been arrested.

Yankees Americans who live in the Northern, as opposed to the Southern, states.

Internet resources

- This site contains a host of useful material: **www.gutenberg.org/files/11255-h/11255-h.htm**
- A massive Civil War portal with thousands of links: **www.civil-war.net**
- A decent site for primary sources: **www.civilwar.org/education/history/primary**
- The Library of Congress has many online sources. A good starting point for research would be: **www.loc.gov/topics/content.php?subcat=8**
- It's also worth searching the archives of the *New York Times* for contemporary accounts of the entire period. See: **www.nytimes.com**

Further reading

General texts on the USA: 1820–1941

M.A. Jones, *The Limits of Liberty 1607–1992*, Oxford University Press, 1995.

My favourite one-volume book of US history: clear, well-organized and containing a vast amount of information.

G.B. Tindall, *America: A Narrative History*, W.W. Norton & Company, 2013.

Another splendid book, still in print after four decades.

Carnes and J.A. Garraty, *The American Nation: A History of the United States*, Pearson, 2007.

A huge book – in every sense.

The Causes of the American Civil War

J.M. McPherson, *Battle Cry of Freedom*, Penguin, 1988.

The best one-volume survey of the causes and course of the Civil War.

D.M. Potter, with D. Fehrenbacher, *The Impending Crisis 1846–61*, Harper and Row, 1976.

This is still an essential text on the causes of the war.

R.M. Sewell, *A House Divided: Sectionalism and Civil War, 1848–1865*, John Hopkins University Press, 1988.

A short and succinct account of both the causes and course of the war.

A. Farmer, *The Origins of the American Civil War*, Hodder & Stoughton, 2002.

A more detailed version of Chapter 1!

P.J. Parish, *Slavery: History and Historians*, Icon Editions, 1989.

This provides a splendid overview of the main debates about slavery.

W.E. Gienapp, *The Origins of the Republican Party*, Oxford University Press, 1987.

The most detailed account of the rise of the Republican Party.

M. Holt, *The Fate of Their Country: Politicians, Slavery Extension, and the Coming of Civil War*, Hill & Wang, 2005.

This book distils the wisdom of several of Holt's vast books about the politics of the 1840s and 1850s into an incisive, short overview.

The Civil War

J.M. McPherson, *Ordeal by Fire: The Civil War and Reconstruction*, McGraw-Hill, 1992.

Another excellent work by McPherson. (Everything he writes is excellent!)

A. Farmer, *The American Civil War 1861–1865*, Hodder & Stoughton, 1996.

A more detailed version of Chapter 2!

P.S. Paludan, *The Presidency of Abraham Lincoln*, University of Kansas, 1994.

A succinct analysis of all aspects of Lincoln's work as president.

G.W. Gallagher, *The Confederate War*, Harvard University Press, 1997.

This book has eminently sensible things to say about Confederate morale.

G.W. Gallagher, S.D. Engle, R.K. Krick and J.T. Glatthaar, *The American Civil War: This Mighty Scourge of War*, Osprey Publishing, 2003.

A lucid and concise narrative of the main campaigns, as well as penetrating analyses of strategies and leadership.

J.M. McPherson, *For Cause and Comrades: Why Men Fought in the Civil War*, Oxford University Press, 1997.

An important book examining why northerners and southerners fought and died for their respective causes.

G.C. Ward (with R. Burns and K. Burns), *The Civil War: An Illustrated History*, Alfred A. Knopf, 1990.

This book accompanied Burns' splendid television documentary. It is magnificently illustrated.

P.S. Paludan, *A People's Contest: The Union and Civil War 1861–1865*, Harper and Row, 1988.

A good survey of the impact of the war on northern society.

Reconstruction

E.F. Foner, *Reconstruction: America's Unfinished Revolution 1863–1877*, Harper and Row, 1988.

This remains the best book on Reconstruction.

E.F. Foner, *Forever Free: The Story of Emancipation and Reconstruction*, Knopf Doubleday, 2013.

A short and very satisfactory survey.

A. Farmer, *Reconstruction and the Results of the American Civil War 1865–77*, Hodder & Stoughton, 1996.

Another longer version of Chapter 2.

I. Berlin (et al), *Slaves No More*, Cambridge University Press, 1992.

A concise summary of a two-volume work on emancipation.

The Gilded Age and the Progressive Era 1870–1920

F. Russell, *American Heritage History of the Confident Years: 1866–1914*, New World City, 2016.

This book covers most of the period.

C.M Nichols, N.C. Unger, *A Companion to the Gilded Age and Progressive Era*, John Wiley and Sons, 2017.

A collection of essays covering the years 1877 to 1920.

J.M. Cooper, Jr., *Pivotal Decades: The United States 1900–1920*, W.W. Norton & Company 1990.

This remains the best book on the Progressive Era.

D.McCullough, *Mornings on Horseback*, Simon and Shuster, 2004.

A marvellously readable book about a remarkable man.

E. Morris, *Theodore Rex*, Random House, 2002.

Another excellent biography about Teddy Roosevelt.

D.K. Goodwin, *The Bully Pulpit: Theodore Roosevelt, William Howard Taft and the Golden Age of Journalism*, Viking, 2013.

A tremendous book by a tremendous writer.

J.M. Cooper Jr., *Woodrow Wilson: A Biography*, Knopf Publishing Group, 2009.

Perhaps the best biography of Wilson.

The Great Crash, Depression and New Deal policies 1920–41

M.E. Parrish, *Anxious Decades, America in Prosperity and Depression, 1920–1941*, W.W. Norton and Company, 1992.

Impressively detailed and illustrated and a really good read.

D.M. Kennedy, *Freedom From Fear: The American People in Depression and War 1929–1945*, Oxford University Press, 1999.

Provides both brilliant narrative and analysis.

W.E. Leuchtenburg, *The Perils of Prosperity 1914–32*, University of Chicago Press, 1993.

This is still one of the best books on the Roaring Twenties and the Great Depression.

D.J. Goldberg, *Discontented America: The United States in the 1920s*, Johns Hopkins University Press, 1999.

Proof that not all was well with 1920s America.

G. Jeansonne, *Herbert Hoover: A Life*, Berkley Books, 2016.

A sympathetic biography of Hoover.

A.J. Badger, *The New Deal: Depression Years 1933–40*, Palgrave, 1989.

A good introduction to the New Deal.

E. Rauchway, *The Great Depression and New Deal: A Very Short Introduction*, Oxford University Press, 2008.

Short but sweet.

W.E. Leuchtenburg, *Franklin D. Roosevelt and the New Deal 1932–1940*, Harper Perennial, 2009.

Concise and competent.

Index